Celebrating Divine Mystery

Celebrating Divine Mystery

A Primer in Liturgical Theology

Catherine Vincie, RSHM

A Michael Glazier Book

LITURGICAL PRESS
Collegeville, Minnesota

www.litpress.org

A Michael Glazier Book published by Liturgical Press

Cover design by David Manahan, OSB. Cover illustration courtesy of © Surpasspro and Dreamstime.com.

1   2   3   4   5   6   7   8   9

Library of Congress Cataloging-in-Publication Data

Vincie, Catherine, 1951–
    Celebrating divine mystery : a primer in liturgical theology / Catherine Vincie.
        p. cm.
    Includes bibliographical references and index.
    ISBN 978-0-8146-5375-3 (pbk.)
        1. Catholic Church—Liturgy.   I. Title.

BX1970.V54 2009
264'.02—dc22

2008017641

Contents

Abbreviations   vii

Introduction   ix

Chapter One: Vatican II and the Liturgical Reform   1
  Antecedents to the Vatican II Reform of the Liturgy   3
  The Liturgical Reforms of Vatican II   12
  Conclusions   17

Chapter Two: The Liturgical Assembly   19
  The Pre–Vatican II Scholars and Their Agenda   20
  The Assembly in Conciliar and Postconciliar Writings   33
  Conclusions   49

Chapter Three: Liturgy as Divine Human Dialogue   51
  The Dialogical Nature of the Liturgy   52
  Liturgy and Sacrament as God's Gift   58
  Conclusions   62

Chapter Four: The Paschal Mystery and Liturgical Anamnesis   64
  The Paschal Mystery   64
  Liturgical Anamnesis/Keeping Memorial   69
  Conclusions   79

Chapter Five: Naming Toward God   81
  The Problem   81
  Theological Issues of Naming Toward God   84
  Conclusions   99

Chapter Six: Liturgy and Time   101

 The Daily Cycle of Prayer   103
 The Weekly Cycle of Prayer   107
 The Yearly Cycle of Prayer   111
 Conclusions   118

Chapter Seven: Symbolic Nature of Liturgy and Sacrament   120

 Philosophical and Theological Approaches   121
 Anthropological Approaches to Symbol and Ritual   135
 Conclusions   142

Chapter Eight: Symbol and Liturgical Celebration   144

 Liturgy and the Body   145
 The Various Symbolic Vehicles   150
 Conclusions   164

Chapter Nine: Liturgy and Culture   166

 Culture and the Social Sciences   166
 Christianity and Culture   168
 Liturgy: Adaptation and Inculturation   173
 Conclusions   179

Epilogue   181

Notes   186

Recommended Readings   199

Index   203

Abbreviations

AG	*Ad Gentes*, Decree on the Missionary Activity of the Church
BCL	Bishops' Committee on the Liturgy, USCCB
BLS	*Built of Living Stones: Art, Architecture and Worship*
CSL	*Sacrosanctum Concilium*, Constitution on the Sacred Liturgy
DD	*Dies Domine*, On Keeping the Lord's Day Holy
DOL	*Documents on the Liturgy*
EI	*Ecclesiae Imago*, Directory on the Pastoral Ministry of Bishops
E&A	*Environment and Art*
EM	*Eucharisticum Mysterium*, On worship of the Eucharist
FC	*Fidei Custos*, On special ministers to administer communion
GIRM	*General Instruction of the Roman Missal*
GNLYC	*General Norms for the Liturgical Year and the Calendar*
GS	*Gadium et Spes*, Pastoral Constitution on the Church
IC	*Immensae Caritatis*, On facilitating reception of communion in certain circumstances
LG	*Lumen Gentium*, Dogmatic Constitution on the Church
LI	*Liturgicae Instaurationes*, Third Instruction on the orderly carrying out of the Constitution on the Liturgy
LMD	*La Maison Dieu*
LMT	*Liturgical Music Today*
MCW	*Music in Catholic Worship*
MD	*Mediator Dei*, Encyclical on the Liturgical Movement
MF	*Mysterium Fidei*, On the doctrine and worship of the Eucharist
MQ	*Ministeria Quaedam*, On first tonsure, minor orders, and the subdiaconate
MR	*The Milwaukee Symposia for Church Composers: A Ten-Year Report*
MS	*Musicam Sacram*, Instruction on Sacred Music
NCCB/USCC	National Conference of Catholic Bishops/United States Catholic Conference (now USCCB)
TLS	*Tra le sollecitudini*, The Restoration of Church Music
VL	*Varietates Legitimae*, The Roman Liturgy and Inculturation

Introduction

Ministry students and other students at the beginning of their liturgical formation need an entry-level book that exposes them to key ideas and concepts in contemporary liturgical theology and to certain neuralgic issues. Topics such as the twentieth-century liturgical reform movement; the liturgical assembly; liturgical anamnesis, naming God, time and symbols, among others, all need careful consideration for those entering ministerial careers as well as those going on for further work in liturgical studies. This text is meant to be used as an overview of the field, a digested view if you will, with the expectation that other articles and texts by major theologians will be used as well. There is no substitute for in-depth reading of the key liturgical theologians working today and in past decades, but for the student overwhelmed by the demands of an M.Div. or a MAPS degree, such broad exposure is usually not possible. It is sometimes enough to touch on the broad outlines, attain a certain level of literacy in the field, and become aware of key texts and authors so that the students may continue their learning beyond degree requirements.

While Christians of any denomination could fruitfully use this text, attention to Roman Catholic documents of the liturgical reform in certain chapters will make it particularly suitable to Roman Catholic students. The reader is invited to dialogue with the text, whether or not agreeing with the author on specific points. The hope is that the reader might develop an informed and critical eye toward the field in general and toward liturgical practice in particular. The goal of the text is to provide tools for understanding contemporary liturgical practice and the broader tradition.

I have not attempted to remain neutral in a number of areas of concern. I am deeply invested in the success of the Vatican II reform agenda and think that we are on the right track, even if there have been some unfortunate practices along the way. My particular bias is toward the full subjectivity of the liturgical assembly and their full and active participation in the liturgical rites. I am equally passionate about the dialogical nature of the liturgy, that it is both a divine and a human work. Perhaps our emphasis on the work of the assembly in recent years has taken the light off the liturgy as a work of God, but I believe that it is only by keeping the two sides of the dialogue visible that we have a true understanding of Christian worship. I have been informed by the social sciences in my own work and think that they can play a helpful role in the theological endeavor. They need not substitute for theology's proper task any more than philosophy took the place of theology in ages past. Rather, I am convinced that religious behavior (e.g., Christian liturgy) is deeply human behavior and anything that can give us insight into that behavior serves the theological task. Finally, I am interested in questions of gender in society in general and in Christian liturgical praxis in particular. I do not come at this study from a neutral standpoint but as one committed to the full humanity and dignity of women in church and society. It is sometimes painful to trace the gender bias of our tradition, as it is to trace the racial bias of our practice, but in an age of reform and renewal, knowing our failures gives us direction and focus for the future. I encourage the reader to find your own place in the dialogue and stand with equal amounts of courage and humility as we seek to worship together, confident that the Holy Spirit is with us as we struggle forward.

CHAPTER ONE

Vatican II and the Liturgical Reform

An ecumenical council often functions as a pivotal moment in the life of the church. It develops out of the experiences of the church in the preceding decades. It addresses the questions, concerns, even crises that afflict the church at a specific historical moment. The council itself may resolve certain issues or concerns, but it may also choose to allow differences of opinion to proceed toward their own natural evolution. The moment of the council is often one of ecclesial excitement, anticipation, and sometimes fear of what will unfold in the council's decisions and documents. For those waiting for the resolution of pressing concerns, it is a time of high hopes; for those content with the status quo, the council may seem threatening or unnecessary. Nonetheless, a council is a significant marker in the church's history; it cannot be ignored.

While the council itself may be the highpoint of the process, the conciliar experience does not end with the closing of the last session and the printing of the last document. There is a natural extension of the conciliar process in the ensuing years as local churches begin to absorb the implications of the council's work and apply them to their specific life experience. This process of listening, sifting, and applying or not applying, as the case may be, is known technically as "reception." While the council itself may be the explicit work of the bishops, it is in fact an ecclesial event. Indeed, whether or not the council has significance in the life of the church is dependent upon the reception or nonreception of its goals, values, teachings, and hopes. It is the church at large, laity and clergy alike, who in the end determine how important the council will be in the life of the church.

Those of us alive today are living in a privileged moment, in that we have either witnessed the road leading to the council, the council itself, or now some forty years after the council, its unfolding in the life of the church. It is impossible to take a neutral stand toward it, in that this council's challenges press upon us in every dimension of our lives. The renewed understanding of the church in the modern (or now postmodern) world affects everyone. The renewed understanding of the church in relation to other Christian churches and other religions affects our attitude as we open the newspaper and try to interpret the events of the day. The renewed understanding of the laity as full members of the Body of Christ and equally called to holiness affects all, clergy and laity alike. And in regard to our particular interests, the renewed liturgies of the council affect us from our baptism, through our ongoing eucharistic life, through our death and burial. The changes the Second Vatican Council wrought infringe upon us and call us to accountability. It is important that we continue to explore its teachings and attend to its as yet unrealized agenda. Even if we were born after the close of the council in 1965, we remain Vatican II Catholics and need to take our part in living out its challenges.

Some of the changes inaugurated by the council, such as the newly configured relationship of Catholicism to other religions, have taken significant time to develop. New scholarship was required, new structures were created to initiate dialogue, new efforts by the popes and curial officials all slowly took shape over the last four decades. Needless to say, their work is not in any way finished. Indeed, both ecumenical and interreligious dialogue remain important agenda items in this complex global village in which we live. Liturgical changes, on the other hand, while they too required a great deal of study and the creation of new structures to implement the changes, had their effect on the Catholic community relatively quickly after the end of the council in 1965.

For good or ill, we began with changes in the Mass, the eucharistic celebration that is at the heart of our faith. As early as 1969 we felt the impact of the call for the vernacular, for greater participation, for changed orientation of the priest at Mass. For many in most areas of the United States church these changes came as a shock, seemingly out of nowhere. In some circles they were welcomed as much-needed changes, while in others they were greeted with anger, consternation, and even rejection. Misunderstanding was rife. In hindsight, we must acknowledge that we would have benefited greatly from better catechesis about the need for the changes and perhaps with a more gradual implementation of them.

Not able to go back on that history, we must make up for that lack and move forward with new efforts to inform and consult the newly empowered laity of the church. It is partly to respond to this need that I have written this book.

Antecedents to the Vatican II Reform of the Liturgy

Although this may come as a surprise to many U.S. Catholics, the liturgical reform movement began over one hundred years prior to Vatican II. Efforts toward change were made in light of several perceived problems with the liturgy as celebrated according to the Tridentine books. While the sixteenth-century Council of Trent was itself a reform council and the changes it made to the liturgy directly treated abuses that had crept into the Mass and the sacraments, the continued use of the Tridentine books without modification for some three hundred years left many issues unaddressed. The list is familiar to students of the liturgy: in the nineteenth century there was no vocal participation by the assembly—not even the simple response to the priest's *Dominus vobis cum. Et cum Spirito tuo* (The Lord be with you. And with your Spirit.). Because they were completely in Latin, the texts of the prayers were unintelligible except to an infinitesimally small minority. It is interesting to note that even in the nineteenth century there were efforts to translate the missal into the vernacular because of the desire of the people to understand, but these translations were banned. In fact, vernacular missals were on the Index of Forbidden Books until 1877. Because of use of the Latin language, the fact that the priest faced away from the people most of the time, and that certain parts of the Mass were said very quietly, the laity necessarily occupied themselves with popular devotions. Some of these devotions were prayers that united the worshiper with the general intention of the Mass, while others, such as the rosary or the stations of the cross, focused in a quite different direction.

The reception of Communion was limited in several ways. First, because of the Jansenist influence on Catholic spirituality, most Catholics received very infrequently, perhaps only twice a year, under the false notion that they were not worthy. In the actual celebration of the Mass there were other problems; for one, the laity did not receive Communion at the actual time of Communion but throughout the Mass or even before or after Mass. The distribution of ministries within the Mass was also a problem. Because of factors going back even to the ninth century and the creation of the full Missal, the priest had all the parts of the Mass in his own book—thus it is called the full Missal. When, for instance, in a Solemn High Mass there were sufficient ministers to take their own parts, the priest nonetheless spoke all parts himself—whether the choir was singing their parts or the deacon was reading the epistle or gospel. Perhaps the most serious problem was that the lay faithful had become alienated from the liturgical life of the church. Rather than being the fount and center of the Christian life, liturgy was either not attended to, at best, or not understood, at worst. In addition, the assembly had lost a sense of itself as the actual subject of the liturgy, and it looked to other areas of ecclesial life for its spirituality and nurturance. There were other problems as well, but those that I have reviewed here were some of the most obvious and egregious.

These problems began to be addressed during the nineteenth century in scholarly circles, in monasteries, in parishes, and at liturgical conferences. A liturgical movement was emerging. We owe an enormous debt of gratitude to those liturgical scholars who indexed and edited countless liturgical manuscripts and made them available for wider study. Scholars such as Adalbert Ebner (1861–98), André Wilmart (1876–1941), and Victor Leroquais (1875–1946) are particularly noteworthy in this regard. A second generation of historical liturgiologists followed these individuals, giving us critical editions and commentaries on liturgical books from throughout the church's history. We must make mention of Jean Deshusses, Antoine Chavasse, Klaus Gamber (1919–89), Michel Andrieu (1886–1956), Josef Jungmann (1899–1975) and Theodor Klauser (1894–1984), among many others. It was through this historical work that we gained a clearer picture of the history of the liturgy from the first centuries of the church to the present. This rise in "historical consciousness" opened our imaginations to conceive of different ways of worshiping than the medieval or Tridentine models.

The liturgical movement is unthinkable without the work of the monasteries of both the nineteenth and twentieth centuries. Among the leaders of the Benedictine renewal, we must credit Prosper Guéranger (1805–75). In 1833 he and several associates joined together under the rule of Benedict to live the monastic life with an emphasis on the celebration of the liturgy. Guéranger's monastery, St. Peter's Abbey at Solesmes, served as a model for the proper celebration of the Mass and the Divine Office. His revival of Gregorian chant and its use in Mass and Office was an effort to foster participation of the assembly. Previously there was singing "at the Mass"; he wanted singing "of the Mass." Guéranger was the first to use the term "liturgical movement" and spoke of it in the following terms:

> Let us hope . . . that the liturgical movement which is expanding
> and spreading will awaken also among the faithful the meaning
> of the Divine Office, that their attendance at it in church will
> become more intelligent, and that the time will come when, once
> more imbued with the spirit of the liturgy, they will feel the need
> to participate in the sacred chants.[1]

Toward that end, Guéranger was one of the first to write a history of the
liturgy from ancient Israel to his own time (the three-volume work *Institutions liturgiques* 1840, 1841, 1851). He was convinced that the renewal
of the liturgy could happen only if all the church, laity and clergy alike,
grew in knowledge and love of the liturgy. Related to this, he insisted
on using the liturgical year, rather than thematic preaching, as the source
for the sermon. He was also deeply concerned that the church recover a
sense of itself as the Body of Christ instead of merely the hierarchy, a
movement also encouraged by the ecclesiologists of his day. Guéranger
was also the first to use the term the "paschal mystery," a term referring
to the salvific work of God accomplished in Christ—a topic we will return
to in later chapters.

His historical contributions, his meditations on the Mass and the
Divine Office (*L'Année liturgique, The Liturgical Year*—some 5,000 pages!),
his work in copying and reviving the use of Gregorian chant, all be-
queathed to future generations a solid foundation upon which to build.
Pius X would not have been able to promote the use of Gregorian chant
throughout the world at the turn of the century had Guéranger and his
monastery not revived the Gregorian chant tradition and its use in liturgical celebrations. Other scholars likewise built on his conviction that
the liturgy was the source of the true Christian spirit and that participation in the actual liturgy was the goal to be sought. It is interesting to
note that the first official vernacular translation of the Missal was that
published by Dom Gerard van Caloen of the Maredsous monastery in
Belgium in 1882. This Latin-French model would be duplicated in many
languages in the ensuing decades.

Other monasteries like that of Beuron (founded in 1863) and Maria-
Laach (a daughter house of Beuron founded in 1892) in Germany, and
Mont César in Belgium (founded in 1899) also contributed to the growth
of the liturgical movement. They contributed scholarship and pastoral
leadership, promoted liturgical conferences, and created journals specifically dedicated to the study and practice of the liturgy. In spite of the work
of Prosper Guéranger and others during the nineteenth century, the birth
of the modern liturgical movement is often marked by the speech of the

Benedictine monk Lambert Beauduin (1873–1960) given at the Malines Catholic Congress in 1909. In that presentation he set forth what was to become the ongoing agenda of the liturgical movement: the active participation of the faithful in the liturgy and the promotion of greater understanding of liturgical texts and rites, all aimed at the transformation of Christian life. Liturgical theologian Louis Bouyer speaking on Beauduin and the Belgian liturgical movement, stated:

> The liturgical movement was not the work of a party or of specialists, nor was it a kind of separate activity in the church. From the first everyone understood it to be a general renewal of Christian teaching and life, both individual and collective, a renewal of the church itself through the renewal of its parochial life.[2]

Within this broad agenda, however, influential individuals took on specific tasks.

Abbot Ildefons Herwegen, abbot of Maria-Laach, led the first "Liturgical Week" in Germany during Holy Week 1914, the first of many conferences that were to follow. He created the series *Ecclesia Orans* in 1918, a journal that was geared to a popular audience. Other more technical journals, such as *Liturgiegeschichtliche Quellen und Forschungen*, superseded by *Archiv für Liturgiewissenschaft* (in 1950), were dedicated to intellectuals and priests. Also of importance was the magazine *Questions liturgique et paroissiales* and its Flemish equivalent *Liturgisch Tijdschrift*.

The monastery at Maria-Laach was also a leader in bringing concerns for art and architecture into the liturgical movement. So-called liturgical experiments were undertaken at some of these monasteries. As early as 1921 the prior of Maria-Laach, Albert Hammenstede, began celebrating Mass facing the people. Further, the community pioneered the "dialogue Mass" where the assembly recited the *Gloria* and *Credo* and made responses to the priest celebrant. They also had members of the community bring up the gifts during the preparation of the altar.

It would be an oversight if we did not mention that much of the historical work of this period was a retrieval of past liturgical practice, particularly of the patristic period. Along with the revival of patristic studies and biblical studies, this movement helped to contextualize contemporary practice within the whole sweep of Christian history. It was not done with the intention of reviving the past, although some have accused the movement of a kind of "archeologism," but of moving toward the future with a more sound foundation.

The creation of liturgical centers of study was also important in the training of new scholars and the dissemination of the work being done. The *Centre de Pastorale Liturgique de Paris* was founded in 1943, while other centers were founded in Germany (Liturgisches Institut in Trier Germany, 1947) and in Italy (Centro di Arione Liturgical, 1947).

It is important to recognize that Europe was not the only venue where the liturgical movement was taking root. Through the influence of another Benedictine, Dom Virgil Michel of the monastery at Saint John's, Collegeville, Minnesota, the fruits of the research and experiments were brought to the United States church. During the years 1924 and 1925 Michel studied at Maria-Laach, Beuron, Solesmes, Maredsous, and Mont-César and brought what he was learning back to Collegeville. He too used the publishing media to promote the concerns of the liturgical movement. He was especially interested in moving the movement out of monastic circles and into parishes. Toward that end, with the help of Martin Hellriegel and Gerald Ellard, he founded the journal *Orate Fratres* in 1926 (renamed *Worship* in 1951) as well as The Liturgical Press, which translated many of the European publications for an English audience and served as a vehicle for ongoing liturgical scholarship.

Perhaps Virgil Michel's greatest contribution was his conviction that the liturgy was the source of the Christian spirit and that active participation and understanding of the liturgy would lead to social transformation. Writing in the decades between the two World Wars, he was critical both of the fascism and communism of the East and the individualistic capitalism of the West. It was, he thought, through participation in the corporate work of the liturgy that the social nature of the human person would be fostered and the creation of a more just society would be achieved. We would do well to revisit his work in this area.

There were many others in the United States church that helped to bring the liturgical movement alive, but we must admit that its influence was felt only in select areas. Mention must be made of the popularization of the liturgical movement by scholars like Gerald Ellard and parish priests like Martin Hellriegal of St. Louis, Missouri. Hellriegal began to implement the liturgical reforms in the community of the Sisters of the Most Precious Blood in O'Fallon, Missouri, where he was chaplain for twenty-two years. He then was transferred to Holy Cross parish in St. Louis where he was able to successfully implement those same changes in a parish setting. Father Reynold Hillenbrand of the Chicago archdiocese was extremely important in bringing the liturgical movement to the Chicago area. He cochaired the first National Liturgical Week held at Holy Name Cathedral in 1940. The theme of the Week was "The Living Parish: Active and Intelligent Participation of the Laity in the Liturgy of the Catholic Church." The participants numbered 1,260, and this was the first of many Liturgical Weeks to follow. He also followed in Virgil Michel's footsteps by stressing the connection between liturgical life and social action.

Among the leaders of the liturgical movement was the laywoman Justine Ward, who, responding to the challenge of Pius X's *motu proprio* on sacred music, was responsible for creating a method for teaching Gregorian chant, especially to children. Unlike much of the work of the liturgical movement that moved from Europe to the United States, Ward's method moved from the United States to Europe with enormous success. In 1916 she founded with Mother Georgia Stevens, RSCJ, the Pius X Institute of Liturgical Music at Manhattanville College of the Sacred Heart. It was through her work (in collaboration with that of Solesmes) that participation in the liturgy by singing the Gregorian chants became a reality.

Finally, we need to mention other scholars who were influential in moving us from the twentieth-century liturgical movement through the Vatican II changes. Two of distinction are Godfrey Diekmann and Frederick McManus. Diekmann (1908–2002) was a monk of Saint John's in Collegeville and worked as an editor for *Orate Fratres* (*Worship*) and in organizing and speaking at the national and international Liturgical Weeks in the 1940s and 1950s. It was at these international Weeks that scholars, pastors, and members of the Sacred Congregation of Rites engaged with one another on matters of liturgical change. They were to presage the working of the council. Diekmann himself was a participant in the preparatory work for the Liturgy Constitution of the council, a *peritus* or expert at the council, and a member of the postconciliar commission mandated to implement the changes of *Sacrosanctum Concilium*, the Constitution on the Sacred Liturgy (*CSL*) of the council.

Frederick McManus (1923–2005) is another pioneer of exceptional importance to the liturgical movement, both immediately before and after the council. Active in the United States liturgical movement, McManus moved to international prominence through his participation in the very important Liturgical Conference held in Assisi, Italy, in 1956. This conference brought together scholars, pastors, editors, and members of the Sacred Congregation of Rites to speak of liturgical concerns and changes that were necessary to the vitality of the church. There he initiated relationships with the European scholarly community with whom he would work in preparation for the council, at the council as a *peritus*, and after the council on the committee to implement the council's decrees. As a canonist and liturgical specialist he was particularly important in assisting the U.S. bishops at the council and in serving on the panel that made daily press briefings. He played a role in the creation of the International Commission on the Liturgy, founded during the council to prepare vernacular translations of the liturgy. He worked with other Christian denominations in the creation of common texts, and he was the first executive director of the newly formed U.S. Bishops' Committee on the Liturgy. McManus' influence in both the academic and pastoral area has been enormous, and we are indebted to him for the amazing volume and quality of his work in the liturgical reform at the local, national, and international levels.

The work of the liturgical reformers of both the nineteenth and twentieth centuries had its influence on papal legislation. Pius X, himself a teacher of sacred music and a pastor, was deeply influenced by Guéranger and the work done by the monastery at Solesmes. In his early pastoral practice he introduced the singing of Gregorian chant by the congregation and the creation of a *schola cantorum*. Later, as pope, he brought these same interests and concerns to the attention of the wider church in his *moto proprio Tra le sollecitudini* (Instruction on Sacred Music) that was chiefly on the revival of Gregorian chant.[3] This document would serve as a model for future legislation on sacred music in the decades that followed. It was important on a number of counts. First, as I have already stated, it fostered the singing of the assembly and the ministry of the choir. Regarding the choir, however, it did have its limits. He stated that the choir exercised a genuine liturgical service, but this service was possible only for men. "Women," he said, "as being incapable of exercising such an office, cannot be admitted to form part of the choir or of the musical chapel" (13). This requirement was only modified in the 1958 Instruction on Sacred Music, *Musica Sacra*, which stated that women may participate in the choir, but that it must move outside the sanctuary area.

A second important aspect of *Tra le sollecitudini* is that it was the first piece of papal legislation to include a call for "active participation." Pius X states in that introduction that the "foremost and indispensable fount" of the true Christian spirit is "the active participation in the holy mysteries and in the public and solemn prayer of the Church." This teaching is exceedingly important because it has so many ramifications. First, it roots Christian life in the liturgy; second, it makes it imperative that the laity understand the liturgy; and finally, it leads to questions concerning the vernacular and participation of laity in the ministries of the liturgy. This call for active participation remained the byword for the twentieth-century liturgical movement and in Vatican Council II's document on the Sacred Liturgy.

Another important issue in the liturgical reform was Pius X's teaching on frequent Communion. As I indicated above, many Catholics refrained from daily or even weekly Communion because of a misguided sense of unworthiness. In 1905 Pius X issued a decree, *Sacra Tridentina Synodus*, on the daily reception of Holy Communion.[4] He stated that frequent and daily Communion is a practice that "should be open to all the faithful, of whatever rank and condition of life; so that no one who is in the state of grace, and who approaches the holy table with a right and devout intention . . . can be prohibited therefrom" (1). Pius X also mitigated the eucharistic fast for those ill for a month or more and lowered the age for Communion to seven.

Pius XI, pope from 1922–39, also called for greater participation by the faithful during his pontificate. Issuing an apostolic constitution, *Divini cultus*, twenty-five years after *Tra le sollecitudini*, Pius XI too joined his concern for more active participation with his concern for Gregorian chant. His statement is so important on this idea of participation that it is necessary to quote it at length.

> In order that the faithful may more actively participate in divine worship, let them be made once more to sing the Gregorian chant, so far as it belongs to them to take part in it. It is most important that when the faithful assist at the sacred ceremonies . . . they should not be merely detached and silent spectators, but, filled with a deep sense of the beauty of the liturgy, should sing alternately with the clergy or the choir, as it is prescribed. If this is done, then it will no longer happen that the people either make no answer at all to the public prayers—whether in the language of the liturgy or in the vernacular—or at best utter responses in a low and subdued manner. (9)[5]

Had such documents been well known by the Catholic community at large, it is doubtful that the Vatican II changes would have been seen as so dramatic and unprepared for.

Pius XII is remembered as providing endorsement of the liturgical movement of the nineteenth and early twentieth centuries. His encyclical of 1947, *Mediator Dei*, is a landmark document in the history of papal legislation on the liturgy. In the document, Pius XII praised the fruits of the liturgical movement and *Mediator Dei* served as its Magna Carta. The movement, he said, made the Eucharist better known, understood, and appreciated, and by fostering more frequent sacramental reception,

> the worship of the Eucharist came to be regarded for what it really is: the fountainhead of genuine Christian devotion. Bolder relief was given likewise to the fact that all the faithful make up a single and very compact body with Christ for its Head, and that the Christian community is in duty bound to participate in the liturgical rites according to their station. (5)[6]

Pius XII was likewise open to the use of the vernacular, if not in the Mass at least in the rites of the Roman Ritual, stating that "the use of the mother tongue in connection with several of the rites may be of much advantage to the people" (60). However, experiments and translations were not to be tried willy-nilly; they were to be done in consultation with the Apostolic See. Taking that admonition seriously, the United States church obtained permission from the Congregation of Sacred Rites for its publication of a bilingual Roman Ritual in 1954.

Perhaps Pius XII's special commission, the Pontifical Commission for the General Liturgical Restoration (sometimes known as the Piana Commission), which was established in 1948 and worked until the very eve of the council, did perhaps the most important work that led most directly to the reforms of Vatican II. Responding to requests that came from various parts of the world, the pope, through this commission, ordered the nocturnal celebration of the Easter Vigil in 1951. Since the Middle Ages it was celebrated in the early morning, and reports stated that very few of the faithful participated. This change and the reform of all the rites for Holy Week in 1955 inaugurated a new day in restoring to the laity the participation that was theirs by right of baptism. In his commentary on the reform of Holy Week, liturgical scholar and canonist Frederick McManus writes:

> Perhaps the feature of the new *Ordo* of Holy Week which is most striking concerns the participation of the faithful in the solemn rites. . . . The Roman Missal speaks rarely of the part to be taken by the *laici*: the new *Ordo* is insistent that the faithful should express openly, by word and song and deed, the interior worship which they offer to Christ and through Him to the Father.[7]

There were also changes in the participation of the faithful in the Mass. First, the faithful were encouraged to pay attention to the words of the priests and servers; the bilingual Missal aided in this task. Songs in the vernacular or prayers that were parallel to the liturgical text (though not exact translations) also enhanced their participation. The best form of participation, however, was the dialogue Mass in which the people responded to the priest in Latin. Pius XII also published another important document on sacred music in 1958, *De musica sacra et sacra liturgia* (Instruction on Sacred Music and Sacred Liturgy), which further enhanced the participation of the laity.[8] Moving slightly beyond the position of Pius X on the issue of participation in the choir, this document stated that women could be part of the *schola*. In that case, however, the choir would not perform a proper ministerial service but was only a "choir of the faithful" and had to sing from a place outside the sanctuary area (93). This gender distinction in liturgical roles and ordering also held in other rites, such as baptism where the ritual action with men always preceded that of the women.

In addition to its concerns for liturgical music, this document also addressed the use of the vernacular. At Low Masses it permitted the commentator to read a translation of the texts while the priest read it softly in Latin; at solemn Masses, however, the Scriptures were to be chanted in Latin without benefit of translation. Thus the importance of the laity's comprehension of the liturgical rites was being stressed on a number of levels: first by the use of bilingual Missals, then with the use of the vernacular directly within the liturgies of Eucharist, and in the other rites of the Roman Ritual.

More liturgical changes were being introduced during the early years of Pope John XXIII's pontificate through the work of the Piana Commission. The rubrics for Mass and the Office were simplified in 1960. It was decided that Communion could be given only during the Rite of Communion. Fuller participation of the assembly was encouraged and their understanding was to be facilitated. In 1962 the first move to introduce an adult catechumenate was made.

This brief survey of the liturgical movement brings us to the eve of the council. Pius XII's special liturgical commission worked until John XXIII called the Second Vatican Council to gather in 1962. It was then superseded by the council itself and by the postconciliar commission charged with the implementation of the council's work.

The Liturgical Reforms of Vatican II

In preparation for the Second Vatican Council, Cardinal Tardini, president of the Antepreparatory Commission, requested suggestions on matters of concern for the upcoming council. Fully 25 percent of those suggestions regarded the liturgy. It was clear that the structure and celebration of the liturgy was becoming an urgent concern of the world church. Rather than interpreting this primarily as a problem, I think it can be viewed very positively. Because of the work of the liturgical movement of the previous century, bishops, scholars, and pastors were becoming more conscious of the important place of the liturgy in ecclesial life. Changes that fostered more participation and intelligibility by the assembly whet the church's appetite for even more participation and understanding. The bishops made the liturgy an issue at the council because it had become a pressing pastoral concern in the best sense of the term.

Accordingly, the preparation of a preliminary schema (draft) was facilitated both by the work that had been done during the previous century and by the relationships formed at International Conferences and Liturgical Weeks. Simply put, the members of the preparatory commission knew both the issues and the significant players among the bishops and the scholars. All in all, the liturgy schema presented to the world's bishops for consideration at the council was in the best shape of any of the other preliminary drafts. This was fortunate on two counts. First, the liturgy document became the first document discussed, and second, in spite of some strong disagreements, the schema was so well crafted it made the process of discussion and revision relatively easy. The good experience the bishops had in dealing with this document in the first and second sessions gave them confidence to take on the more daunting task of the document on the church and divine revelation, among others. Without going into the intricacies of how the document was revised (it certainly was not a problem-free process), it must be said that after the discussions and amendments the document received extraordinary support from the council fathers. No other document received this kind of approbation. In the final, formal vote the Constitution passed with a vote of 2,151 in favor and 4 opposed. It was only with the decades of preparatory work on liturgical matters that such a consensus could have been reached.

Because it is now more than forty years since the council closed, and since such a large number of Catholics were born after the council, it will be helpful to review some of the main contours of the Liturgy Constitution. I would like to suggest that the Constitution could be best understood by addressing the underlying questions posed by the authors of the document. Namely, what is the fit between our understanding of Christ's work and the mission of the church? What is the fit between our understanding of the church and the liturgy? What is the fit between the liturgy and the work of Christ? It is in answering these questions that we arrive at an understanding of the document's theology of the liturgy, and from there we can address the Constitution's principles of reform.

After four introductory paragraphs, the Constitution begins with its first doctrinal statement: God "'wills that all be saved and come to the knowledge of the truth' (1 Tm 2:4)" (*CSL* 5).[9] This is the foundation upon which all else stands: God desires the salvation of all persons. The Constitution is quick to follow this primary statement with a litany of convictions about Jesus the Christ. He was sent by the Father, is the Word made flesh, was anointed by the Holy Spirit—to preach the Gospel, to heal and forgive. As the incarnate Word he is the instrument of our salvation. "Therefore in Christ 'the perfect achievement of our reconciliation came forth and the fullness of divine worship was given to us'" (*CSL* 5). This twofold purpose of giving perfect glory to God and redeeming humanity is repeated several times throughout the document. It will be key to understanding the ministry of the church and the purpose of the liturgy.

The work of God in Christ is not finished, however, with his cross, death, and resurrection. As the Father sent him, so he sends the church to complete his mission. The sacrament of church was born of "the side of Christ as he slept the sleep of death upon the cross" (*CSL* 5). It too was sent to preach the Gospel, but now embodied in Christ Jesus. The church was sent to usher in the reign of God by its preaching but also "through the sacrifice and the sacraments" (*CSL* 6). In this mission Christ is one with his Body, and Christ "always truly associates the Church with himself in this great work wherein God is perfectly glorified and the recipients made holy" (*CSL* 7). The church is filled with the Holy Spirit to accomplish its mission, and Christ continues to act in the church in all its ministries. The church is both "human and divine, visible yet endowed with invisible resources" (*CSL* 2). The church is the Body of Christ, "'a chosen race, a royal priesthood, a holy nation, God's own people' (1 Pt 2:9)" (*CSL* 14). The church is a community of persons and a sacrament of unity (*CSL* 26).

At times the church comes together in sacred assembly to hear the Word and celebrate the sacraments. The Constitution never uses the term "assembly" as such, but it is implied in many of its statements. The church gathered is an assembly of God's people. It is a community and hierarchically ordered around the bishop (*CSL* 26). The assembly must be imbued with the spirit of the liturgy, and when gathered together it is the place of Christ's presence (*CSL* 7). Most important, the church assembled under the bishop is the subject of the liturgy. The liturgy is the work of Christ and his Body the church. "Therefore liturgical services involve the whole Body of the Church; they manifest it and have effects upon it" (*CSL* 26).

The liturgy must be understood in light of these two entities—Christ and the church/assembly. The liturgy, first of all, manifests the saving work of Christ: "the liturgy is the source for achieving in the most effective way possible human sanctification and God's glorification" (*CSL* 10). The liturgy expresses the mystery of Christ and the mystery of the church (*CSL* 35.2). The liturgy celebrates the paschal mystery, that is, the mystery of salvation revealed in the Scriptures, fulfilled in Christ, and now continued by the church in the power of the Spirit (*CSL* 6, 7). In the liturgy the church encounters the mystery of Christ. The Liturgy Constitution is quite specific in referring to five forms of presencing. Christ is present in a most excellent way in the Eucharist and he is present in the person of the priest. These were traditional and familiar ways of speaking of Christ's presence. However, the council added two more modes of presencing that are of great significance, that of Christ present in the assembly and present when the Word is proclaimed. Finally, Christ is present in all the sacraments "so that when a man baptizes it is really Christ himself who baptizes" (*CSL* 7).

The liturgy manifests not only the mystery of Christ; it manifests the mystery of the church (*CSL* 26). Liturgy is the source of the church's strength and it builds up the Body of the church (*CSL* 59). Most important, the liturgy is an action of Christ and the church: "in the liturgy the whole public worship is performed by the Mystical Body of Jesus Christ, that is, by the Head and his members" (*CSL* 7). Through the liturgy, as through Christ and the church, God is glorified and human sanctification achieved.

Thus we have come full circle. God's desire for human salvation is made known most fully in Christ Jesus who incorporates the church into his mission of praise and sanctification. The church in its turn, empowered by the Spirit, celebrates the liturgy that is a manifestation of the Christ mystery and the church mystery, and it accomplishes the work of glorification and sanctification, first intended by God.

It is within this context of a theology of Christ, church, and liturgy that the council fathers spoke of the particular characteristics of the liturgy and enunciated norms for its renewal. By its nature, the liturgy is a communal action (*CSL* 26). It is accomplished by Christ and by the Mystical Body of which he is head (*CSL* 7). Because it is a communal action, it demands full participation by the members of the assembly. As the document says so clearly, "the Church earnestly desires that all the faithful be led to that full, conscious, and active participation in liturgical celebrations called for by the very nature of the liturgy" (*CSL* 14). The council mandated that the liturgy be revised so as to take participation of the whole assembly into account.

If the church is manifested in the liturgy, then the liturgy ought to reflect the nature and diversity of the church community. It follows too that the liturgy ought to involve a diversity of ministries according to the church's different orders, offices, and actual participation (*CSL* 26, 28). If the liturgy by its nature is communal, then a reform of the liturgies of the church is necessary so that it might better display this communal character. So too the liturgy is to be revised so that each minister does only her or his own responsibility, including the presiding celebrant (*CSL* 28). No longer will the presider duplicate whatever the other ministers are doing.

The liturgy is by its nature a symbolic activity and achieves its purposes by means of signs (*CSL* 7). These signs should not be so obtuse that the Christian people cannot understand them, nor so obscure that they fail to express those holy things they signify (*CSL* 21). Because the liturgy is for the benefit of the Christian faithful, then the rites "should be within the people's powers of comprehension and as a rule not require much explanation" (*CSL* 34). However, the Constitution acknowledges, "a more explicitly liturgical catechesis should also be given in a variety of ways" (*CSL* 35.3) to enlighten the community. And priests "are to be helped by every suitable means to understand ever more fully what it is they are doing in their liturgical functions" (*CSL* 18). By being shaped in the spirit of the liturgy, pastors may in their turn provide for the liturgical instruction of the faithful so that they may take part in it externally and internally (*CSL* 19).

If the liturgy is the work of the church, then its liturgical celebrations can and do develop over time and are determined by culture and context. Thus "careful investigation is always to be made into each part of the liturgy to be revised" (*CSL* 23). Once that investigation has been done, "provision shall also be made . . . for legitimate variations and adaptations to different groups, regions, and peoples . . ." (*CSL* 38). In other words, the council is officially allowing for the first time in many hundreds of years the possibility of diverse practices by local churches. This was an extraordinary opening for change, one that we are only tasting the firstfruits of some forty years later. Not unrelated to this, the Constitution gave to episcopal conferences the right within certain defined limits to regulate the liturgy (*CSL* 22.2). Once again, this was a huge step forward in allowing a local church a sharing in the responsibility of liturgical regulation with the Congregation of Sacred Rites (later renamed the Congregation of Worship and the Sacraments). How this actually works in practice is something being worked out even as we speak.

Conclusions

Generally the method for revision of texts and rites was suppression of useless repetitions, additions where appropriate, restoration where necessary, adaptation, and development.[9] The Constitution is a mix of general principles and some very specific recommendations, particularly regarding the other sacraments and the Divine Office. It was left to the postconciliar liturgical commission to produce revised liturgical books that were faithful to both the letter and the spirit of the Constitution.

The Constitution on the Sacred Liturgy is not without its faults. In some ways it is a compromise document in order to please both the more conservative and more progressive members of the council. The use of the vernacular was quite limited at first, but this changed quickly in the ensuing years. The reception of the cup was allowed in very limited circumstances, although this too would be extended. Adaptations of the liturgy to culture were intended primarily in mission lands. Sadly, the document made no connection between the liturgy and social transformation, as had been such a passion of the members of the liturgical movement.

Because it was the first document discussed by the council fathers, it did not benefit from the advances in ecclesiology achieved in the Constitution on the Church (*Lumen Gentium*) or by a more open relationship to the world reflected in the Constitution on the Church in the Modern World (*Gaudium et Spes*). Nonetheless, it gathered the momentum of the European and United States liturgical movements and extended it to the world church. The Constitution left many questions unanswered and opened up new areas that were yet to be explored. It would be left to the postconciliar liturgical commission to translate the principles of the reform into actual liturgical rites. Clarifications of the Constitution were also forthcoming. To date we have received five Instructions on the proper implementation of the Liturgy Constitution and can expect more to follow.

In the meantime, it is up to parish liturgical assemblies to bring the newly revised books to life in actual celebration. Many of our assemblies have yet to be imbued with the "Spirit of the Liturgy" and to become knowledgeable about the church's liturgies. It remains for pastors and lay ecclesial ministers of the church to delve more deeply into the liturgy themselves and then imbue their communities with its spirit and potential.

CHAPTER TWO

The Liturgical Assembly

In the first chapter we dealt with the preconciliar liturgical reform movement and with the council itself. We suggested that because of the enormous work of the preceding century, the liturgy schema was quite mature when it came to the floor of the council. Although there was much debate and many emendations to improve the text, in the end it was affirmed overwhelmingly by the conciliar bishops. We also considered the triad of concerns within the Liturgy Constitution—Christ, church, liturgy—that served as the foundation of the reform agenda. It was noted that the document spoke often of the church, but not specifically of the gathered assembly. This suggests that the identity and theology of the liturgical assembly was not clear to the council fathers at the time. We are led to ask if nothing had been done regarding the liturgical assembly in the preceding period, or if it simply had not reached a critical state of importance and so had not been incorporated. We can ask further if there was more interest in the liturgical assembly in the postconciliar period, and if so, was it incorporated into magisterial documents on the liturgy. The identity and theology of the liturgical assembly is indeed an important topic and one that deserves serious review and assessment.

Accordingly, we will first explore preconciliar work on the topic because the decade immediately preceding the council saw a preponderance of literature on the liturgical assembly generated primarily by Belgian and French liturgical scholars. My purpose here is to outline the achievement of these scholars in this area and then to review the impact of their work on conciliar and postconciliar texts. While the council did not pick up on their work directly, the topic certainly has come to the fore since that time, and tracing its development in ecclesial documents is an interesting and informative exercise.

The Pre–Vatican II Scholars and Their Agenda

Henri Chirat set the process in motion with his 1949 study of the liturgical assembly in the apostolic church,[1] but it is Aimé-George Martimort who must be credited with the most sustained interest in the liturgical assembly from 1949 until the council.[2] Robert Gantoy, Pierre Jounel, Thierry Maertens, Anselme Robeyns, Philippe Rouillard, and A. M. Roguet also made significant contributions.

Martimort claimed that the most urgent task of the early phase of the nineteenth-century liturgical movement was to convince Christians of the value of liturgical prayer. By the mid-twentieth century, however, he saw the task as a recovery of the communal nature of liturgical prayer. Accordingly, Martimort argued that the most characteristic element of this phase of the movement was the rediscovery of the liturgical assembly and of its significance.

Liturgical scholars of this period focused on three issues regarding the liturgical assembly in the history of the church: the fact of liturgical assembling, patterns of participation in the assembly, and the concept or the theology of the assembly. These scholars understood the liturgical assembly as the actual gathering of a local Christian community for worship, and they were interested in uncovering the fate of the assembly throughout Christian history. Second, as well as establishing the fact of gathering, they explored the changing modes of participation in that gathering. Third, they explored the liturgical assembly as a theological reality. In particular, they were interested in the biblical and theological foundations of the assembly and in its significance in ecclesial life. These liturgical scholars brought to all these issues a critical concern for present and past practice and a desire to retrieve the best of the tradition regarding assembling. They also sought to move beyond the limitations of the past through a constructive application of the tradition to their contemporary ecclesial situation. The following is a summary of their findings on each of these issues.

Critical Reflections on Theory and Practice

A major criticism of the scholars under review was that the church community had lost a sense of itself as an assembly and of the connection between liturgical assembling and ecclesial identity. Chirat argued that the ties that bind Christians to one another and that penetrate to the very heart of their existence are given birth and reinforced in liturgical assemblies. In his analysis, Christians needed to reclaim their sense of being people of prayer, not only as individuals but as a group, and to recapture the apostolic dynamism that is the fruit of the prayer of the assembly.[3] Arguing from a similar position, Martimort considered many of the liturgical problems facing the church at mid-century to be the result of a gradual but unrelenting decline in the value of the assembly and a failure to understand the effects of this decline on the life and worship of the church.

Among the factors detrimental to the assembly that Martimort cited were changes in church population and changes in ecclesial organization over time. Martimort argued that the liturgical assembly was an essential dimension of the apostolic definition and practice of the church: no church without assembly. In the first centuries, however, the church had to adjust its priority of a single weekly gathering of the whole community due to a significant increase in its population. In the urban church of Rome, for example, which had grown beyond the possibility of a single gathering, the rite of *fermentum* and stational liturgies[4] were attempts to maintain the ties between assemblies and to preserve the relationship between the growing number of assemblies and the bishop.[5]

The circumstances of rural churches were slightly different. Distances and difficulties of travel made small celebrations practical, and "private chapels" were built to accommodate these small gatherings. Martimort argued that the establishment of the "private chapels" endangered the primacy of the assembly since, in his analysis, they worked against an understanding of church that by definition included "gathering together in one place." Two issues were at stake: the actual gathering of members of a local church and gathering around the bishop. The solution to this fragmentation of the local church and loss of contact with the bishop was legislation forbidding or limiting use of these oratories for major feasts, favoring larger gatherings. Martimort claimed that this legislation is evidence that the church recognized that the assembly revealed something of the mystery of the church and must therefore be upheld.[6]

The rise of the mendicant orders and the establishment of their churches alongside parish churches likewise threatened to fragment the local church and, therefore, to undermine the role of the assembly to gather the local church into unity. Martimort argued that legislation attempted to remedy this problem by prescribing attendance at parish churches on Sundays and major feasts. The commitment to this principle weakened over time, as indicated by the Council of Trent's modification of the prescription to a simple exhortation.[7] Martimort's judgment was that the church did not adequately maintain the primacy of the assembly in the face of these and other changes.

The structure of the liturgical assembly and patterns of participation in the assembly were also Martimort's concern. Just as increased numbers and the movement of the church from urban to rural areas changed the way in which the liturgical assembly related to the local church, other changes in the church affected the structure and the participation within the assembly itself. The results were clear: the liturgy became clericalized, participation by the laity decreased if not ceased altogether, and an individualistic piety replaced collective liturgical prayer. Martimort believed that an exploration of the roots of these problems would provide the key to their resolution.

The first problematic change was the development of prayer by deputation. Without tracing its complex and gradual evolution, Martimort noted that the prayer of monks or other distinct groups within the church began to be considered as "liturgical prayer," i.e., prayer of the church. In his view this posed a serious threat to the understanding of the liturgical assembly and of its prayer because of the select nature of the group. Prayer by deputation or prayer "in the name of the church" was, not prayer of the whole church, but only of a segment of it. When the monastic office displaced the cathedral office and conventual Masses moved to cathedral churches, liturgical practice reinforced the idea that liturgy did not necessarily involve the work of all the people.[8]

If prayer "in the name of the church" contributed to the demise of the assembly, Martimort claimed that the development of the private Mass in the ninth century delivered the final blow. Private Masses were celebrated on days when the assembly was not convoked, and even communities of priests were splintered as individual priests celebrated "their" Masses simultaneously in the same church. The Christian assembly was reduced to a symbolic presence in the person of the assisting minister or even in the person of the priest celebrant.[9]

Martimort also argued that private Masses distorted the self-understanding of all members of the assembly. The priest lost the sense that his ministry was one of presiding over an assembly, an assembly that exercised a variety of ministries different from his own. Other members of the community lost the sense that Sunday obligated them to gather around the Word and Eucharist and that their full but differentiated participation was essential to the accomplishment of the liturgy.[10]

There were other factors that also contributed to the demise of the liturgical assembly. These factors included the failure to distinguish the liturgical assembly from the liturgical acts of the assembly and to consider the assembly in and of itself.[11] The loss of the "assembly" contributed to a loss of the biblical heritage connected with this word.[12] The liturgical assembly had also suffered because of the changes in eucharistic theology and piety. Gantoy, for example, argued that an overemphasis on the Eucharist itself led to a neglect of the assembly, while this impoverished the understanding of the Eucharist.[13] Nicolas Afanasieff, an Orthodox theologian, suggested that the Eucharist had lost its ecclesiological character by being viewed as a sacrament *in* the church rather than as a sacrament *of* the church, while Maertens suggested that the medieval preoccupation with the eucharistic "real presence" overshadowed the "real presence" in the assembly itself.[14]

Retrieval of the Tradition

As noted above, a critique by Martimort, Gantoy, Maertens, and others was that the Christian community, to its detriment, had forgotten the rich biblical heritage of the liturgical assembly. A major task for these scholars, therefore, was to retrieve this heritage in order to reinvigorate the Christian assembly at the level of self-understanding and liturgical practice.

Louis Bouyer and Maertens were primarily responsible for taking the biblical scholarship on *qahal* (the assembly) and applying it directly to the study of the Christian liturgical assembly.[15] In his work *L'Assemblée chrétienne*, Maertens provides an extensive treatment of *qahal* in the Old Testament traditions.[16] He recognized that *qahal* was not a monolithic concept but that changing historical and cultural factors shaped and reshaped both the concept and practice of the assembly in Israel during the period from the seventh to the third centuries BCE.

While not attempting to summarize all of Maertens' text, it is possible to highlight some of his significant findings. The assembly itself could be understood in two ways: it was the *gathered people*, but it was also an *event* in the life of this people, and it had a recognizable structure and content. Israel's theology of the assembly, in sum, provided insight into who God was and who Israel was in relation to God, and God's concern for all humanity.

God was ultimately the one who convoked the assembly. It was God who took the initiative and who extended the invitation. God was the great "assembler," the shepherd who called from every corner to good pasture.

In its solemn assemblies Israel could take cognizance of itself as a people called by God, the *qahal Yahweh*. In this sense, the assembly could be understood as the gathering of the people themselves. It was in physically coming together that their identity as God's assembly was instilled and strengthened. Their identity was tied to God and God's intention for them; God's holiness was communicated to them in the assembly.

Once the assembly was convoked, the reading of the Law and the Prophets constituted an essential element of the celebration. The Scriptures not only testified to God's action in history, they constituted the divine presence in the local assembly. Understanding the Scriptures was also needed, so instruction was incorporated in the assembly event. The assembly was a dialogical event. God's initiative and revelation in the Scriptures constituted one aspect of the assembly; the people's response in a profession of faith, sacrifice, or in a presidential prayer of blessing or thanksgiving completed the action.

God's invitation extended to all peoples, although Maertens argued that this ecumenical dimension suffered the most at the hands of Israel's national fate. The assembly also took on eschatological overtones. Vision shifted from memory of past events toward future promise, to the ultimate assembly. Out of this insight grew a sense of mission to work with God in its accomplishment. Dismissals sent the assembly out to participate in this mission.

The change from national assemblies to small, local assemblies was also instrumental in transforming the theology of assembly. What once applied to national assemblies now applied to the local level. The local assembly ultimately became a sign of the eschatological assembly yet to be convoked.

The task of retrieval also brought pre–Vatican II liturgical scholars to the New Testament. Among them Maertens again provided the most extended study of the assembly in the gospels.[17] His purpose was to explore how Jesus redefined the fundamental structure and meaning of the assembly through his own person and through his actions, if indeed he did.

In summary, Maertens found significant development in the theology of assembly from the testimony of the gospels. Jesus, the Risen Christ, has become the initiator of the assembly and the focus of it. He is the new Word of disclosure and the means through which other "words" are interpreted. Christ's presence in the assembly is promised and is continued through sign and rite. As he is the great assembler, he is also the one who dismisses so that his ministry may be continued. The gospel traditions also redefined the limits of inclusion and exclusion in the assembly: all are invited, especially those who are marginalized. The sick are healed, sinners are forgiven, while barriers that excluded whole classes are broken down. The ministry to summon and to include all in the assembly is the church's as well.

When French liturgical scholars turned toward the rest of the New Testament witness, two questions guided their inquiry in the liturgical assembly: Did the early church understand itself as a continuation or even a fulfillment of the *qahal Yahweh* or the Septuagint equivalent *ekklesia tou Theou*? What, if anything, did Christian communities add to the meaning and practice of the assembly?

The consensus of the authors surveyed here is that the apostolic church clearly understood itself as the continuation of Israel in general and of the *qahal Yahweh* in particular. A typological reading of the Hebrew Scriptures allowed the apostolic church to see itself (both universal and local) as the new "people of God," "a chosen race," "a holy nation," "a people set apart." Prayers of praise, thanksgiving, and supplication were common to both Jewish and Christian assemblies, as were scriptural readings and instruction. What was obviously different in Christian assemblies was prayer in and through Christ, the proclamation of his death and resurrection, and the celebration of the Lord's Supper.[18]

Martimort argued that both the gospels and Acts of the Apostles express the priority the apostolic church placed on gathering together. This began even prior to Pentecost and came to be understood as an essential dimension of Christian identity. The common Greek phrase *epi to auto*, to be in one place, became a technical term for solemn Christian assemblies. The meaning of this term was not limited to physical proximity, however; it also implied a profound unity of mind and heart.[19]

Maertens argued that another characteristic of these early gatherings was that their leadership was tied to "witness to the Risen Christ." This leadership was not only internally focused but outwardly directed as well. Barnabas and Saul, leaders of the church at Antioch, were called from a liturgical assembly and sent out as missionary witnesses. Maertens claimed that the importance of this action is that it directly connected the missionary task with a local community, with the leadership of that community, and with the liturgical assembly itself.[20]

The collection for Jerusalem constitutes another important characteristic of the Christian assembly developed at Antioch. While local churches were developing, means were also being found to establish and deepen the bonds of *koinonia,* of mutual care, between them. In this case, it was the contribution of the whole community that maintained the ecumenical character of the assembly, even while its universality was underlined by the choice of Paul and Barnabas as the bearers of the gift.[21]

The liturgical assembly also has eschatological meaning and is a sign of the ultimate assembly. Just as the final assembly gathers all peoples from all nations and languages and overcomes all human divisions, so too must the liturgical assembly show forth these same characteristics, even if imperfectly. The liturgical assembly anticipates the heavenly assembly of joyous praise of the risen Lord and itself constitutes a feast. It also points to the eschatological assembly in the sense that it proclaims the fullness yet to be revealed.[22]

The retrieval process also involved these scholars in a study of early church documents and patristic authors. They found that the writing of the postapostolic period contained considerable reflection on the liturgical assembly, particularly regarding the place of the assembly in Christian life and further specification of the characteristics of the assembly.

Martimort noted that the postapostolic writers continued to exhort the community to attend the liturgical assembly, just as Paul and the author of Hebrews had done before them. He concluded that in early Christianity motivation to attend liturgical assemblies was not to fulfill a purely legal obligation; rather, it arose from a profound need within Christianity that impelled the faithful toward these common gatherings.[23]

Patristic authors also elucidated the advantages of gathering into assembly. If absence from the assembly damaged the Body of Christ, attendance was of mutual benefit to all concerned. All members of the church owed it to one another and to themselves to attend the liturgical assembly in order that the whole Body might be built up and that individual faith might be nourished and strengthened. Failure to attend was not simply a neutral act or one that affected only the individual; it harmed the whole Body of Christ.[24]

The patristic writers also stressed the connection of the Eucharist and the assembly and the Christian assembling and Sunday. Although not all Christian assemblies are eucharistic, Martimort argued that even from antiquity the assembly par excellence is the eucharistic assembly and that all other assemblies are ordered toward the Eucharist.[25] Martimort claimed too that it is the unanimous testimony of postapostolic letters, apologies, and ecclesial legislation that solemn liturgical assemblies punctuated Christian life on Sunday, while Philippe Rouillard suggested that the Fathers developed a rich and complex understanding of Sunday. It served as the memorial of the resurrection; the sacrament of the presence of Christ in the midst of his own; and, as the eighth day, a sign of the world to come.[26]

Reconstructive Efforts

Building upon their historical and biblical studies, these scholars consciously addressed contemporary issues, offering new insights into both the theology and practice of the assembly. The first major concern of the constructive work of this preconciliar period was to clarify how the liturgical assembly and its liturgy related to the life and understanding of the church. A second concern was to clarify the characteristics of the assembly. This involved an exploration of the dialogical character of the assembly and its liturgy, the membership of the assembly, the demands exacted for entrance into it and departure from it, and the assembly's communal nature. It also involved looking at how the assembly is ordered, how roles are differentiated, how the assembly is convoked, and what constitutes liturgical and nonliturgical assemblies. Finally, it involved exploring the presence of Christ in the assembly and in its actions. For present purposes it will be possible to review only a few of these issues.

Several scholars pursued the notion of the liturgical assembly as a sign of the church. Although the church is in the realm of mystery, Martimort stressed that it is also a visible reality and must therefore realize itself materially. In other words, the church must manifest itself in the realm of signs. From this initial position, Martimort argued that the liturgical assembly is the most common, ordinary, and accessible manifestation of the church. Anselme Robeyns called the assembly "the efficacious sign of the church acting in the world," while Jean Hild called the assembly the "Epiphany of the Church."[27]

For Martimort this epiphany is more than just a way of showing forth what already is or what will continue to be whether or not it ever meets in assembly. Rather, occasional gatherings of the church in assembly are absolutely essential for the continuing existence of the church. The liturgical assembly is the church in act, the church becoming itself and expressing the fullness of its being.[28] The liturgical assembly, consequently, will obey the same laws that govern church structure, i.e., as a sign/mystery of salvation.[29] In addition, Martimort suggested that although the church is both universal and local, participation in the universal church is by means of the local church. In his analysis, "the liturgical assembly expresses the local church, and participates in the whole mystery of the church."[30]

In order to gain further insight into the assembly understood as sign, Martimort turned to the sacramental categories of *sacramentum, res et sacramentum,* and *res sacramenti.*[31] Although acknowledging that the assembly is not a true sacrament, nonetheless he maintained that these sacramental categories do shed light on its meaning.

The use of *sacramentum* in this discussion is clear enough: the *sacramentum,* the sign is the assembly itself, and it is the sign of an invisible reality, the unity and charity of all in God (*res sacramenti*). Martimort's constant refrain is that the assembly is not the gathering of like-minded individuals but the motley mixture (*bigarrure*) that God has called into unity and charity.[32] The *res et sacramentum* is that intermediate, invisible reality caused by the sign and producing in its turn the ultimate grace of the sacrament; for Martimort it is the presence of Christ and the power of the Holy Spirit.[33] While clearly struggling with these classical sacramental categories (particularly the last), Martimort was able to use them to argue the theological significance of the assembly, while at the same time stretching those categories beyond their previous use.

Participation in the assembly was also an area of concern and reflection. Martimort considered that participation is limited only by faith and baptism (or preparation for baptism). Beyond these restrictions, the assembly is accepting of "all comers." "The liturgical assembly," he said, "is only able to be a visible manifestation of the church if it, like the church, is variegated."[34] Likewise the liturgical assembly is not made up of the perfect but of sinners who willingly acknowledge their sin and their need of God's mercy. For Martimort the assembly, like the church, is able to transform those who are not holy into a holy people through the grace promised.

Especially for Martimort, diversity in the assembly is not an obstacle to be overcome but a gift to be respected and even celebrated. Since the assembly is of a local church, it will reflect the cultural and historical context of the local church. The grace of the assembly is the achievement of unity and charity in the midst of diversity.

It would be a misreading of Martimort to assume that the achievement of unity and charity in the midst of this diversity, and even its sin, is merely the easy accomplishment of God's grace, "cheap grace," as it were. Rather, Martimort argued that the liturgical assembly precisely as sign makes painful demands on the participants. The assembly at the level of sign, of gesture, of sight, and of sound must manifest to the greatest degree possible the unity and charity to which it points. Martimort maintained that the assembly invites, calls, and challenges the participants to move toward the ultimate grace of the assembly. For this reason, Martimort suggested that the first pastoral task is "to make the signs more significant, more clear and more evocative."[35]

This insight is perhaps Martimort's most provocative thesis. He is offering the suggestion that we begin with the *sign* of the assembly and not with the *concept* of community or gathering in order to understand it and to live it. To become a member of the assembly is to participate in the dynamism of the symbol, to interpret it and to be interpreted by it. In Paul Ricoeur's language, the symbol *"donne à penser"* and it demands that we enter into the wager of belief through participation in the symbol in order that we might understand.[36]

The wager that Martimort claimed is involved in the liturgical assembly is the willingness to undergo the violent rupture required for entrance into the assembly and for dismissal from it. Entrance into the assembly demands that we disavow the separations and discriminations that mark daily life and surmount the enmity that mars our relationships. A second rupture is exacted when we are dismissed from the assembly to return to daily tasks, to the missionary work of the church, and to the work of charity. Although the liturgical assembly is a sign and pledge of the ultimate gathering of all people in God, the two do not coincide. The grace of the assembly, unity and charity, remains a task for the community, both within its own boundaries and beyond them.

These preconciliar writers frequently stressed the communal nature of the assembly. Martimort, for example, hoped to counter the minimalizing and clericalizing tendencies of liturgical practice of the time through this emphasis. In his view, all members of the community are called together in assembly as their first act and then all are called to active but differentiated participation in the liturgical actions of the assembly. As an organic body, not everyone does everything or the same thing, but everyone has some vital part to play.[37]

Martimort is largely responsible for reclaiming the ordained minister's role as "president" or "presider" of the assembly. Maertens, for his part, explored the patristic theory on the role of the bishop in relation to the assembly, emphasizing his role to bear witness, to ensure the unity within a local church and between local churches.

There are other special ministers in the assembly who are distinct from the presider and the people. In Martimort's analysis, assisting ministers focus their ministry in two directions: on the one hand, they assist the presiding minister in the celebration of the rites, and on the other, they assist the congregation in their participation.[38]

The establishment in the mid-fifties of a commentator whose ministry was to assist the people in their participation constituted a major change in ecclesial practice.[39] The significance of this ministry directed toward the gathered community was that it refocused attention on the whole assembly as active subjects of the celebration. The preferred persons for this ministry were either the ordained or members of the clerical state, but in their absence laity could fulfill this role.[40]

While special liturgical ministries were opened to the laity during this period, both ecclesiastical legislation and theological opinion saw fit to distinguish between laymen and laywomen. According to the 1958 *Instruction on Sacred Music*, women were not permitted to be commentators and their part in the *schola* was by way of exception. As I indicated earlier, if they did participate in the *schola*, it had to move out of the sanctuary area. Arguing from 1 Corinthians 14:34 and the constant teaching of the tradition, Martimort stated with the 1958 *Instruction* that "no women are able to receive deputation for any ministerial service properly so-called in the assembly."[41] He also explained that the tradition of men having their heads uncovered and women having their heads covered during sacred functions was in continuity with the Pauline injunction and was "an expression of the harmonious hierarchicalization which characterizes the church."[42]

The final aspect of this scholarship that I would like to note is the attention several authors gave to the presence of Christ in the assembly itself. Both Roguet and Maertens expressed the need to enhance the sense that Christ is present in the liturgical assembly itself.[43] Martimort and Gantoy were more explicitly constructive in their work. Both treated the topic within the framework of the assembly as sign and sacrament. Gantoy wrote that "the presence of Christ, in the midst of the gathered community, is the grace proper to the assembly."[44] Martimort claimed that even beyond the presence of Christ in the sacraments, Christ is present in the liturgical assembly itself, basing his judgment on the text in Matthew 18:20: "Where two or three are gathered in my name, there am I in the midst of them."[45]

Critique and Reappraisal

At this point it is appropriate to make some comments on the major contributions and limitations of this work. While making no claims for either list being exhaustive, I will focus more fully on the constructive aspects of their work.

The retrieval of the biblical heritage on the assembly by these liturgical scholars provides a rich resource from which we can continue to draw new insights, even as we expand our own skills in critical biblical interpretation. Maertens' insight into the way Jesus redefined the theology of the assembly is a neglected but potentially fruitful area of exploration. The critical review by these scholars on the fortunes of the liturgical assembly throughout Christian history serves as a reminder of the distortion that can reshape even our most valued practices.

At the level of constructive work, the contribution of these authors included the deliberated separation (for purposes of analysis) of the assembly from the actions of the assembly. The assembly as a liturgical subject is distinct from its acts; the assembly is the presupposition and the context for its acts, but it can be considered in and of itself. Without this distinction, consideration of the assembly as a sign would have been impossible, thus losing the opportunity to explore this aspect of the assembly's theological meaning and significance. The distinction also opened the way for more extensive consideration of the assembly as a corporate ritual subject.

The consideration of the liturgical assembly in direct relationship to the church must be counted as a valuable contribution of the scholars of this period. By relating the assembly and its worship to the existence and expression of the church, these scholars held liturgical concerns within the larger context of ecclesial life, and they offered an ecclesiology that explicitly included worship. By considering the liturgical assembly as the manifestation of the church, they were able to explore the assembly as a sign and mystery of salvation. They underlined the importance of the assembly to establish ecclesial identity and noted that the assembly is the place where faith is nourished and passed on. By acknowledging that the church precedes and supersedes the assembly and its worship, they also left enough room to claim that the work of the church includes far more than worship.

The third contribution of these scholars was their exploration of the characteristics of the assembly. Of particular importance was their emphasis on the inclusive nature of the assembly, the demands made by the assembly, and the ultimate grace and goal of the assembly. They also stressed the communal nature of the assembly and its actions, and the differentiation and ordering of functions within the assembly. These authors expanded previous notions of God's presence in word and sacrament by insisting that God is present in the very assembly itself.

While the contributions of these scholars are significant, there are a number of criticisms that must be leveled at their work. They were so concerned with expounding the attributes of the assembly as a mystery and as the gift of God that surpasses all human limitation that they failed to explore the ways in which the liturgical assembly is similar to other human gatherings. By doing so, they succumbed to a kind of theological reductionism. All the issues they examined were "theological" issues, and the methods they employed for analysis were strictly within the theological sciences. Exploration of the dynamics of social gatherings; the role of ritual in the social process; cultural, historical, and political influences were outside their concern, as were the social and human sciences that could have aided such an exploration. Such an interdisciplinary approach to the study of the assembly has been the task of post-conciliar scholars.

The entire project can also be characterized as lacking critical suspicion. The scholars under review presented the church and the liturgical assembly very idealistically. Even Martimort's "organic" metaphor for the differentiated nature of the assembly contributed to an idealization of the forms of the church and assembly. Organic metaphors always grant too much "givenness" to ecclesial structures and deflect attention from the human decision-making factors that generate those structures.

These liturgical scholars made some real criticism of ecclesial practice, but the issues were quite limited. For example, they held participation of the laity in the liturgy in high regard and severely criticized clericalizing tendencies. However, they continued to support uncritically the position that all participation was determined by one's rank in the ecclesiastical hierarchy. There was no awareness or suspicion that the organizing principle might have been problematic.

The exclusion of women even from the responsibilities of the laity, e.g., participation in special ministerial roles, did not pose a problem to these scholars. In spite of Martimort's extravagant claims for the assembly's inclusivity, its nondiscrimination, and its ability to overcome all separations, he continued to support the exclusion, discrimination, and segregation of women regarding special ministries. He even deemed the hierarchicalization of women and men in the church harmonious. Maertens likewise failed to draw the connection between the inclusion of women and other marginalized persons in Jesus' ministry and contemporary ecclesial practice.

Martimort's use of the classical sacramental categories had both advantages and disadvantages. Positively, his consideration of the sacramentality of the assembly was a significant new insight but one he could have developed further. One of the difficulties of remaining within these categories was that Martimort became caught in accounting for every part of the analogy. Rather than looking for a new model, he tried to force the assembly into the categories as given. There is no evidence that Martimort was aware of the new directions that Edward Schillebeeckx and Karl Rahner were setting in ecclesiology and sacramental theology. Mutual consideration of one another's work could have broadened and strengthened all positions.

The Assembly in Conciliar and Postconciliar Writings

In chapter 1, I argued that the liturgical movement of the nineteenth and twentieth centuries had a direct influence on the liturgical reform agenda of the Second Vatican Council. As we saw, individuals of the liturgical movement were largely the same individuals who served as consulters and theological *periti* at the council and as members on the postconciliar commissions. It seems logical to ask, then, did the council fathers incorporate into the Liturgy Constitution the developments of a theology of the assembly? In addition, we might also ask how the insights into the theology and character of the assembly were worked into later ecclesial teaching and practice, if indeed they were.

The Assembly as Subject of the Liturgy

In the previous chapter I noted that while the "assembly" was not explicitly mentioned in the conciliar constitution, it was the implied subject of the liturgy. The ecclesiology of *Mediator Dei* (*MD*) spoke of the Body of Christ, head and members, as the subject of liturgical action. The constitution states that all those who gather and celebrate the liturgy proclaim the paschal mystery, read the Scriptures, celebrate the Eucharist, praise God, express in their lives and manifest to others the mystery of Christ and the real nature of the true church (*CSL* 2, 6, 10).

The difference between *CSL* and *MD* is shown in what *CSL* does not say about the subject of the liturgy. It does not repeat *MD*'s teaching that it is the priest chiefly who performs the sacred liturgy (*MD* 44); it does not repeat that "as often as a priest repeats what the divine Redeemer did at the Last Supper the sacrifice is really completed" (*MD* 96); it does not repeat that "the integrity of the sacrifice only requires that the priest partake of the heavenly food" (*MD* 112).

The positive statements of the conciliar text on participation are even more important. Article 14 of *CSL* states that the "full and active participation by all the people is the aim to be considered before all else" in the reform and promotion of the liturgy. Both texts and rites are to be reformed to facilitate this participation (*CSL* 21). The whole assembly participates through acclamations, responses, psalmody, antiphons, etc., while special ministers have their own responsibilities that are not to be duplicated by the presiding celebrant (or any other minister) (*CSL* 28, 30).

Regarding eucharistic celebration, *CSL* outlines the role of the whole assembly. They are to offer the "immaculate Victim, not only through the hands of the priest, but also with him" (*CSL* 48). The faithful are to be able to say or to sing "those parts of the Ordinary of the Mass belonging to them" (*CSL* 54). The communion of the faithful is strongly recommended as "that more complete form of participation in the Mass" (*CSL* 55). All these statements lead to the conclusion that the liturgy is a corporate activity celebrated by a corporate and differentiated subject.

In the documents on the liturgical reform that followed the council, there is a noticeable change from "Body of Christ" imagery to that of "people of God" in the discussion of the liturgy as ecclesial action. For example, *Liturgicae Instaurationes*[46] states that one of the aims of the contemporary reform is to make the liturgical prayer of the tradition more available to the community. Once made available, however, "this prayer must appear clearly as the work of the entire people of God in all their orders and ministries."[47] The *General Instruction of the Roman Missal* (*GIRM*)[48] makes a similar point. In describing the Eucharist as the "action of the whole church," *GIRM* states that participation should be based on one's place in the people of God. After using this image, *GIRM* then expounds upon this people's character and mission. They are a people purchased by Christ's Blood, gathered and nourished by the Lord; they are a people called to offer God prayers, giving thanks in Christ, growing into unity; they are a people holy by their origin, made so by their conscious, active, and fruitful participation.[49] Slightly later in the same document, the celebration of the Mass is described as "the action of Christ and the People of God arrayed hierarchically" (16). *GIRM* comes close to an explicit statement that the assembly is the subject of the liturgy in its description of the Mass where it employs the people of God image. It states that "At Mass—that is, the Lord's Supper—the People of God is called together . . . to celebrate the memorial of the Lord, the Eucharistic

Sacrifice" (27). Immediately after this it states that "Christ is really present in the very liturgical assembly gathered in his name" (27).

Later documents of the United State bishops explicitly claim the liturgical assembly as the subject of liturgical celebrations. The Bishops' Committee on the Liturgy published a short statement on the assembly in its *Newsletter* of 1977. It uses both the Body of Christ and the people of God images, but it states unequivocally that the assembly is the subject of the celebration. It says,

> the greatest liturgical symbol is the assembly of the Christian community transformed into the body of Christ. As such it is the subject of liturgical celebration. . . . Since this is the case, then the primary responsibility for good liturgy rests in the ability of the primary symbol to function as the praying people of God, the assembly of the faithful.[50]

Environment & Art (*E&A*) of 1978 is equally forthright in its specification of the assembly as the subject of liturgical action. The title of chapter 2 is "The subject of the liturgical action: the Church," but the document quickly specifies the church at worship as the assembly. *E&A* draws a clear distinction between the subject and its actions when it speaks of the experience of the sacred. It states that "the most powerful experience of the sacred is found in the celebration and the persons celebrating, that is, it is found in the action of the assembly . . ." (*E&A* 29). While the assembly that gathers always comes together with the intention of engaging in liturgical action, this document suggests, as did the liturgical scholars reviewed above, that the subject can be distinguished from its actions. That subject according to *E&A* is a concretely gathered community.

Built of Living Stones: Art, Architecture and Worship, published in 2000 and thus a more recent document of the USCCB Committee on the Liturgy, continues to speak of the church gathered as a liturgical assembly, although not with as much emphasis. Christians build churches "to shelter the liturgical assembly that praises God and celebrates the sacraments" (20). Speaking of the church building, this document states that "the church building manifests the baptismal unity of all who gather for the celebration of liturgy and 'conveys the image of the gathered assembly'" (50).

In summary, the Liturgy Constitution introduced a dynamic understanding of the liturgy as the action of the church. While never explicitly naming the liturgical assembly as subject of the liturgy, its insistence on the presence and participation of all suggests such an interpretation. Postconciliar documents developed *CSL*'s position in two areas. First, Roman documents such as *Liturgicae Instaurationes* and *GIRM* incorporated an ecclesiology of the people of God not available to the authors of *CSL*. Thus they had an ecclesial foundation explicitly specifying both ordained and laity upon which to base their considerations of the liturgical subject. Second, postconciliar texts gradually came to name the liturgical assembly as the subject of the liturgy more and more explicitly. This is particularly clear in select documents of the United States magisterium that state unequivocally that the liturgical assembly is the subject of the liturgy.

The Assembly and the Presence of Christ

Earlier I spoke of the Liturgy Constitution's statement that Christ is present when the church prays and sings (*CSL* 7). The presence of Christ in the assembly as liturgical subject begins to be more clearly articulated in postconciliar documents. The 1965 encyclical of Paul VI, *Mysterium Fidei* (*MF*), sharpens the focus on the church as a subject of liturgical action, although not explicitly naming the assembly. This document contextualizes the sacramental presence of Christ by noting that the church has multiple ministries and that Christ is present in the church as it performs each of these various actions: Christ is present when the church performs acts of charity, when it preaches, when it shepherds and guides the people of God. To the point, Christ is present in the church when it prays, when it offers sacrifice, when it administers the sacraments.[51]

Three later documents attend more deliberately to the church as gathered, and they separate more clearly the assembly and its actions. In doing so, they note that Christ is present in the assembly itself and that Christ is present in the actions of the assembly. *Eucharisticum Mysterium* (*EM*) states that "He [Christ] is always present in an assembly of the faithful gathered in his name."[52] Paragraph 55 states explicitly that, in the celebration of the Mass, Christ is present in various modes, the first of which is the gathered assembly, and then the assembly's liturgical actions.[53] The *GIRM* makes a similar point in its discussion of the Mass as the action of an intentional community, an assembly. It is in this assembly that Christ is present. "For in the celebration of Mass . . . Christ is really present in the very liturgical assembly gathered in his name"

(27). *Built of Living Stones* likewise notes the presence of Christ in the gathered community: "In the liturgical assembly, Christ's presence is realized in all *the baptized* who gather in his name" (22).

In summary, the discussion of the presence of Christ in the assembly and in its liturgical actions supports the insight that the assembly is the subject of the liturgy. The liturgical assembly itself constitutes a special mode of Christ's presence. *CSL* focused more explicitly on Christ's presence in the church's liturgical actions, while postconciliar texts were more specific regarding the presence of Christ in the assembly distinct from its acts.

The Liturgical Assembly as Event

In the preceding parts of this chapter, the liturgical assembly was explored as the gathering of the Christian community, as a people called together by God. In other words, the focus was on the assembly as "people." This has allowed us to speak of the assembly as a liturgical subject, a corporate liturgical subject.

Members of a local church gather periodically for the purpose of liturgical celebrations, and it is the event of gathering that also can be called the liturgical assembly. While there are many different occasions that call a local community to assemble, the concern here is the Sunday eucharistic assembly. It is the primary liturgical event in the life of a community and the normal context for other sacramental celebrations. Consideration of the Sunday assembly allows access to conciliar and postconciliar teaching on the priority of gathering, the relationship of gathering to Christian identity, and the principal components of that event.

The original schema of the Liturgy Constitution provided only a very brief reference to Sunday. During the conciliar debate, several fathers requested that a better description of the Lord's Day be provided.[54] Accordingly, the conciliar liturgical commission introduced a new paragraph (106) that became incorporated into the final text. In four sentences the Constitution presents a theology of Sunday, a rationale for Christian gathering on this day, and the principal elements of the Christian assembly. This exceedingly compact article is supported by Article 6, which traces in very broad strokes the Constitution's theology of the liturgy, and by Article 102, which serves as a general introduction to chapter 5 on the Liturgical Year.

Articles 6, 102, and 106 taken together provide the council's teaching on Sunday and the Sunday assembly. It is worth quoting them at length.

> From that time [Pentecost] onward the Church has never failed to come together to celebrate the paschal mystery. (*CSL* 6)

> Every week, on the day which the Church has called the Lord's Day, it keeps the memory of the Lord's resurrection. (*CSL* 102)

> By a tradition handed down from the apostles and having its origin from the very day of Christ's resurrection, the Church celebrates the paschal mystery every eighth day, which, with good reason, bears the name of the Lord's Day or Sunday. For on this day Christ's faithful must gather together so that, by hearing the word of God and taking part in the eucharist, they may call to mind the passion, the resurrection, and the glorification of the Lord Jesus and may thank God, who "has begotten them again unto a living hope through the resurrection of Jesus Christ from the dead" (1 Pt 1:3). Hence the Lord's Day is the first holyday of all and should be proposed to the devotion of the faithful and taught to them in such a way that it may become in fact a day of joy and of freedom from work. Other celebrations, unless they be truly of greatest importance, shall not have precedence over the Sunday, the foundation and core of the whole liturgical year. (*CSL* 106)

The council texts propose that Sunday is the day that the church has kept as the Lord's Day because Sunday is the day of the resurrection. It is a day for keeping the memory of the whole paschal mystery and for giving thanks for our participation in that saving event. As the primary holy day, it takes precedence over all other feasts; as the eighth day, it has eschatological significance; it is a feast of joy.

The first thing that can be said about these texts is that they retrieve ecclesial teaching and practice regarding Sunday. It is important to recall that immediately before the council significant work had been done in bringing to light the history and significance of Sunday. As indicated earlier, by the end of the first century Sunday had become known as the Lord's Day; the early church clearly connected Sunday with the resurrection; patristic authors used the "eighth day" as a way of stressing the relationship between Sunday and the world to come as well as the day of new creation. The festal character of Sunday was also important in patristic writings. These elements were incorporated into the theology of the assembly developed in the period prior to the council, and, as can be seen above, they were also incorporated into the Constitution.

These paragraphs quoted above constitute the clearest statement in the Liturgy Constitution regarding the gathering of the community into liturgical assembly. The Constitution introduces neither an individualistic piety nor a legal sense of obligation into its concept of the Sunday assembly. Rather, it maintains a communal sense of the church, and suggests that attendance at this event is called forth by the nature of the Sunday assembly as participation in the work of salvation.[55]

Having established the fact and necessity of assembling on Sunday, the Constitution then goes on to explicate what takes place in this event. Primarily, it is a celebration of the passion, resurrection, and glorification of the Lord; the gathered church remembers and gives thanks. Articles 6 and 106 explain how that is done: through proclamation of the word and celebration of the Eucharist. Again recalling Martimort's work, there is no Sunday without the assembly and no assembly without the proclamation of the word and celebration of the Eucharist.[56]

The *General Norms for the Liturgical Year and the Calendar* (GNLYC) promulgated March 21, 1969, summarily repeats the Constitution's teaching on Sunday, but its specific contribution is to rank all celebrations and their relationship to Sunday.[57] In 1977 Paul VI sent a letter on the occasion of the 19th National Eucharistic Congress of Italy whose theme was "The Lord's Day." Commenting on Article 106 of the Constitution, the pope incorporates into the theology of Sunday an element of a theology of the assembly that had not yet appeared in magisterial statements. He says, "thus on the Lord's Day the ecclesial community, gathered as one around the Lord who called its members out of darkness into his sublime light, not only must devoutly call those saving events to mind, but, with the help of divine grace, bring them to bear on its members."[58] In this text the centrality of Christ in the assembly and his role as assembler is presented in a way that had not been done before in magisterial texts and recalls the work of Maertens. The pope also uses the text from the *Didascalia Apostolorum* that was so important in the work of the preconciliar liturgical theologians. "Because you are Christ's members, do not scatter from the church by not coming together. . . . Do not shatter or scatter the Body of Christ. . . . Instead on the Lord's Day, putting all else aside, run together to the church."[59] Here the accent is placed on the act of gathering itself and the responsibility each member has to participate in this event for the well-being of the community.

Cardinal Villot, in his capacity as Secretary of State, also wrote a letter on the same topic to the 28th National Liturgical Week of Italy in 1977. He incorporated even more themes central to the theology of the assembly.

> First of all is the basic meaning that Sunday has always had for
> Christians: that they come together in a worship assembly to hear
> the word of God and to take part in the eucharist. The paschal
> mystery includes and requires such a gathering together because
> it is the mystery of Christ the Redeemer and he came to gather
> again the children of God who had been scattered (see Jn
> 11:52). . . .

> There is no Sunday without a worshiping assembly and no as-
> sembly without the word of God and the eucharist.[60]

The *Directory for Sunday Celebrations in the Absence of a Priest* dedicates
an entire chapter to the meaning of Sunday, the Sunday assembly, and
their history in the Christian community.[61] It highlights especially the
church's continuing practice of gathering to celebrate the paschal mystery (1). It outlines the requisites for the Sunday assembly: (a) gathering
of the faithful, (b) proclamation of the word and preaching, (c) celebration of the eucharistic sacrifice. When this document presents a history
of the Sunday assembly in early church practice and the priority it held
in Christian life, it does so by quoting from many of the same sources
cited by the French scholars reviewed in the first part of this chapter:
Acta Martyrum Bytiniae, *Didache* 14, Justin's *Apology*, *Didascalia Apostolorum*,
and the letter of Ignatius *Ad Magnesios* (8–11). The *Directory* also stresses
that the assembly is gathered through divine initiative and that the assembly manifests the church. Sunday calls for "[t]he gathering of the
faithful to manifest the church, not simply on their own initiative but as
called together by God, that is, as the people of God in their organic
structure, presided over by a priest, who acts in the person of Christ"
(12 a). While this document retrieves many elements of a theology of the
Sunday assembly, it does not integrate an ecclesiology that more consciously unites the ordained minister with the rest of the assembly in
eucharistic celebration.

Finally, we need to mention the 1998 document *Dies Domini* (*DD*), On
Keeping the Lord's Day Holy.[62] It devotes chapter 3 to the "day of the
church," and expresses a significantly developed theology of the assembly, particularly regarding the notion of unity. It speaks of Sunday as "a
celebration of the living presence of the Risen Lord in the midst of his
own people" (31). Arguing that an individualistic piety is not sufficient,
it states that: "It is important therefore that [the People of God] come
together to express fully the very identity of the church, the *ekklesia*, the
assembly called together by the Risen Lord who offered his life 'to reunite
the scattered children of God' (Jn 11:52)". It states that the "Sunday as-

sembly is the privileged place of unity: It is the setting for the celebration of the *sacramentum unitatis* which profoundly marked the church as a people gathered "by" and "in" the unity of the Father, of the Son and of the Holy Spirit" (36). Recalling the work of our French scholars, *Dies Domini* speaks often of the link between the assembly, the church and the Eucharist. "By its very nature, the eucharist is an epiphany of the church" (34). And further on it declares that "each community, gathering all its members for the 'breaking of the bread,' becomes the place where the mystery of the church is concretely made present" (34).

In summary, these magisterial texts on the Sunday assembly have incorporated many elements discussed in the preconciliar period. As well as presenting a general teaching on Sunday, *CSL* noted that the essential elements of the Sunday assembly are the gathering of the community, and the acts of remembering and giving thanks through proclamation of the word and celebration of Eucharist. The letters of Paul VI and Villot stressed the divine initiative and the centrality of Christ. Villot's letter also tried to strike a balance between the church's ministry in liturgy and its ministry beyond the liturgical event. The *Directory* brought together many of these strains on the Sunday assembly as well as presented considerable testimony from the early church on the issue. Finally, *Dies Domini* stressed the Sunday assembly as the epiphany of the church and the importance of unity.

Roles in the Liturgical Assembly

The purpose of this section is to set out more systematically the offices and ministries of the church's liturgical celebrations and to explore how these various offices and ministries are filled by members of the assembly. Magisterial treatment of these issues is particularly important because it is through liturgical legislation that new roles and changing patterns of participation are mandated for the universal and the local church. As such, a review of this material reveals how the concerns of preconciliar scholars for full and diversified participation have been received into ecclesial practice.

LITURGICAL MINISTRIES AS SERVICE TO THE CELEBRATION
AND SERVICE TO THE SUBJECT OF THE CELEBRATION

Liturgy is a differentiated action. It proceeds through the progressive unfolding of prayers said or sung, actions performed, stories told, dialogue exchanged, gestures given and received, etc. The Liturgy Constitution makes some specific comment on several of these component parts. It speaks of the ministry of liturgical presiding, which includes among other things speaking prayers in the name of the church (33), giving liturgical catechesis within the rites (35.3), offering sacrifice in the eucharistic liturgy (48). Instruction on the word is also cited several times as an important element in the revised liturgies (35.2 and 52). "Acclamation, responses, psalmody, antiphons and song" (30) are the kinds of participation assigned to the assembly, while "servers, readers, commentators, and members of the choir also exercise a genuine liturgical function" (29) through their action, proclamation, explanation, or song.

Liturgical ministries are about the doing of these various actions in order that the liturgy may be actualized and the ultimate term of the action accomplished. In this sense, liturgical ministries serve the liturgical celebration; the exercise of these ministries is the performance of the celebration.

The liturgy is also the action of a subject, the local church gathered in assembly. That subject interacts amongst itself and with the tradition as expressed in officially promulgated liturgical books, in liturgical space designated for worship, in music and art, and in all the symbolic forms that make up the liturgy. The assembly as subject does/celebrates the liturgy and becomes itself through its celebration. Liturgical ministries are also about serving this assembly as it actualizes itself as church and they help the assembly to accomplish its ultimate intentions. Liturgical ministries are about serving the assembly in a diversity of ways as it celebrates the liturgy.

Several postconciliar texts by the U.S. bishops address this aspect of liturgical ministry as service to the assembly. They indicate the degree to which the retrieval of the presider's role vis-à-vis the assembly so stressed by preconciliar scholars has become incorporated into magisterial teaching. The NCCB's statement *Called and Gifted: The American Catholic Laity* of 1980 highlights the presider's role to coordinate the various liturgical ministries of an assembly. "As lay persons assume their roles in liturgical celebration according to the gifts of the Spirit bestowed on them for that purpose, the ordained celebrant will be more clearly seen as the one who presides over the community, bringing together the diverse talents of the community as gift to the Father."[63] Cardinal Bernardin's Pastoral Letter on the Liturgy emphasizes throughout the service that liturgical ministries render to the assembly, but expresses the point most succinctly regarding the ministry of bishops, priests, and deacons. These, he says, "have unique roles in celebrating the liturgy, but they act as persons who serve the assembled people."[64]

Environment & Art best expresses the twofold focus of liturgical ministry. Article 37 states that different ministries do not imply superiority or inferiority, but are necessary to facilitate worship, just as they do in any human, social activity. In addition to the service they render to the celebration, these ministries are services to the assembly, making the ministers servants of the assembly. "These [ministries] are services to the assembly and those who perform them are servants of God who render services to the assembly. Those who perform such ministries are indeed servants of the assembly" (37). Keeping in mind this twofold focus of liturgical ministries, let us explore the major roles and responsibilities exercised by members of the assembly and the criteria used for determining participation in these roles and responsibilities.

DISTRIBUTION OF ROLES IN THE LITURGICAL ASSEMBLY

The Liturgy Constitution states the "liturgical services involve the whole Body of the church," although "in different ways, according to their different orders, offices, and actual participation" (26). Those preparing for baptism are in the order of catechumens, while the fully initiated belong to the order of the baptized. Some among these latter are also ordained, while others remain in the order of the baptized but are installed in offices and/or receive special designation for the exercise of particular ministries.

CSL does not give a clear specification of the office and ministries of the whole people in liturgical celebrations, but it does give some general indications. It repeatedly encourages their participation by means of "acclamations, responses, psalmody, antiphons, and songs, as well as by actions, gestures, and bearing" (30). It describes the role of the faithful in the Eucharist as receiving nourishment from the table of the word and the Eucharist; giving thanks to God; offering Christ through and with the priest; and offering themselves as well (48). Criteria for the exercises of this participation are by virtue of baptism (6), while the actual assignment of individual parts is given in each of the revised liturgical books (31).

Eucharisticum Mysterium makes several brief comments on the role of the faithful in the Mass. It states that all who gather for Eucharist have a part in the sacred rites, and that when the faithful recognize the parts they are to fulfill, their participation will be more conscious and fruitful.[65]

The *GIRM* provides a very deliberate treatment of the "Duties and Ministries in the Mass." They are organized in this document according to two criteria: the distinction of orders within the church and the distinction of functions that are not assigned exclusively to the ordained or the whole assembly.[66] The role of the people of God in the Mass is to give thanks to God, to offer the sacrifice together with the priest, to act in unity with one another through common participation either in words, song, or gesture (95 and 96).

GIRM makes several comments regarding music and church architecture that address the role and responsibility of the assembly. First it deliberately places the schola cantorum and the cantor with the assembly, and describes one of their principal functions as enabling the assembly to participate in singing those parts that belong to it (103, 104, 294). Second, *GIRM* stresses the need to design liturgical space according to the needs of all members of the assembly. A design of the church building "must be such that in some way it conveys the image of the gathered assembly and allows the appropriate ordering of all the participants, as well as facilitating each in the proper carrying out of his function" (294).

ROLES OF ORDAINED MINISTERS

Through its sacramental rites of ordination and specifically the laying on of hands, the church designates men for permanent roles of leadership in the church and in the liturgical assembly. During the council there was a great deal of concern regarding the sacramental nature of the episcopacy and the relationship of other ordained ministries to it. Developments in a theology of the local church and episcopal collegiality also caused a reevaluation of the role of the bishop in relation to liturgical celebration. The Liturgy Constitution places the bishop at the center of the liturgical life of the local church. At least in the ideal, he is to preside over the liturgical assembly of his local church with the assistance of his presbyters and other ministers (41). Liturgical preaching is another principal responsibility of bishops. Both of these liturgical roles are "proper" to the bishop by virtue of his office as pastor and teacher.

Ecclesiae Imago (EI) of 1973 further specifies the ministry of the bishop in liturgical celebration.[67] His first task is that of "assembler": he is to gather the church together to worship God through prayer and the celebration of the Eucharist. Within that gathered assembly he stands as High Priest and presider, and exercises his office of teaching in the homily.[68] The bishop together with the local church, but all in the way proper to them, exercise the church's priestly office in the liturgical assembly of the "new people of God, the holy nation, the Royal priesthood."[69]

Because of the size of contemporary dioceses, it is usually impossible for the bishop to preside regularly over liturgical assemblies of the local church. *CSL* notes then that lesser groupings of the faithful are formed into parishes under the leadership of presbyters (42). Under the authority of the bishop and through their ordination, presbyters also share in the office of sanctifying. Accordingly, they exercise certain liturgical ministries.

CSL states that presbyters preside over an assembly and address prayer to God in the name of the whole church and of all present. Their ministry is further specified in the *GIRM*: to preside over the assembly, lead it in prayer, proclaim the gospel, associate the people with himself in offering sacrifice, and share with the community the bread of salvation (93). The presbyter is also to shape the instructions, introductions, and conclusions to the situation of the community, thus highlighting the presider's relationship to the gathered assembly (31).

In summary, because of their position of permanent leadership in the community, certain liturgical roles are "proper" to those who have been ordained. With the order of the ministerial priesthood, certain liturgical roles pertain to bishop, to presbyters and to deacons respectively. Of particular importance for our concerns is the centrality of the role of "presidency" throughout the various texts surveyed. This accent must be seen as a genuine retrieval of the ordained celebrant's role as a presider not only over a rite, but over a community that together celebrates a rite.

OTHER LITURGICAL MINISTRIES

In addition to the roles of the assembly and those proper to the ordained, other ministries also serve the accomplishment of the liturgy and render service to the assembly. The Liturgy Constitution made an important clarification regarding the exercise of liturgical ministries by the laity. As we indicated earlier, the 1958 *Instruction on Sacred Music* had introduced the notion that when those ordained or members of the clerical state performed liturgical ministries, they exercised "a true and proper ministerial service." Male laity, on the other hand, exercised a direct but only delegated liturgical service whenever they performed those same ministries (93). In contrast to this position, the conciliar liturgy document states explicitly that "servers, readers, commentators, and members of the choir also exercise a genuine liturgical function" (29). While not everyone does the same thing, there is no a priori quali-fication in the kind of liturgical service rendered between those baptized and those ordained or in the clerical state.[70]

Beyond the general statement of *CSL* mentioned above, no explana-tion or specification about participation in these ministries was given in the conciliar text. It was left to the postconciliar period to introduce, describe and develop new ministries in light of changing pastoral needs and in the face of challenges posed by changing cultural insights into the dignity of all persons—women and men.

Office of Reader and Acolyte

The *motu proprio* of Paul VI, *Ministeria Quaedam* (*MQ*), substantially changed the church's discipline and theology concerning minor orders and the liturgical ministries therefore proper to these orders. Paul VI suppressed tonsure, the minor orders of porter and exorcist, and the major order of the subdiaconate.[71] This left the office of reader and acolyte as the only two liturgical offices with canonical status and a rite of insti-tution besides those of the sacrament of order.

The pope also eliminated the term "order" (entrance into which was by *ordinatio*) in favor of "ministries" (entrance into which will now be by *institutio*) for what had been the minor orders of lector and acolyte. His stated intention was to remove these ministries from direct connec-tion to the clerical state, although those who will be ordained do receive institution into these ministries. These ministries are exercised by the laity and are proper to them by virtue of their baptism. Arguing from tradition, however, he reserved these ministries exclusively for men.[72]

The reader's proper liturgical function is to proclaim the word of God, read the intentions if necessary, and assist the faithful in their participa-tion. The acolyte's liturgical responsibilities are to assist the deacon or the priest at the altar and assist with the distribution of Communion. The assignment of roles to the reader and acolyte clearly reflects the twofold focus of liturgical ministries outlined above, i.e., that of serving the liturgy and the assembly.

Non-instituted Ministries of Reader and Acolyte

Alongside the canonical office of reader, there is also temporary dele-gation of both women and men for the reading of Scripture in the litur-gical assembly. The *GIRM* underlines the importance and integrity of this ministry whether exercised by one installed in the office or by another. While stressing its integrity, the first four editions of *GIRM* reflect the different conditions that govern the participation of women and men in this ministry.

The 1970 text reads: "The conference of bishops may grant that when there is no man present capable of carrying out the reader's function, a suitable woman, standing outside the sanctuary, may proclaim the readings preceding the gospel."[73] *Liturgicae Instaurationes*, the third Instruction published between the second and third editions of the *GIRM*, also addresses the participation of women. Positively, it is not explicit in its preference for male readers, although it presumes more difficulties in the adequate exercise of this ministry by female than by male readers. Negatively, it continues to treat placement of women performing this ministry as a problem, and leaves the issue to the discretion of the conference of bishops. The document states that women are allowed to "proclaim the readings, except the gospel. They are to make sure that . . . they can be comfortably heard by all. The conferences of bishops are to give specific directions on the place best suited for women to read the word of God in the liturgical assembly."[74]

The 1972 and 1975 editions of the *GIRM* take into account the changes inaugurated by *Ministeria Quaedam* and state that laymen may perform all functions below those reserved to deacons, while women may be appointed to ministries that are performed outside the sanctuary at the discretion of the rector. Qualified women may proclaim the readings before the gospel, but it again leaves to the conferences of bishops to determine a suitable place for that proclamation.[75] In both documents (*LI* and *GIRM*) men's participation is unconditionally granted, while women's participation is permitted, but carefully circumscribed by those in authority.

The statement on the "Place of Women in the Liturgy" by the United States Bishops' Committee on the Liturgy in 1971 makes two recommendations regarding the participation of women in liturgical ministries. Both pertain to the priority of the liturgical action over any discrimination between persons. First, it states that women who read should do so from the lectern or ambo, since "the reservation of a single place for all the biblical readings is more significant than the person of the reader, whether ordained or lay, whether woman or man." Second, it states that women are not to be barred from the sanctuary area, but should perform all their ministries in a place suitable to the "circumstances or convenience."[76] This was added to the fourth-edition Appendix of *GIRM* for the United States Church. In the most recent edition (2002) distinctions by gender have been removed except in the case of installed acolytes and readers.

In magisterial documents women's exercise of the role of acolyte has been even more limited than that of reader. Issued in 1970, the instruction *Liturgicae Instaurationes* (*LI*) specifies the extent of women's liturgical ministry and repeats tradition's norm barring women from service at the altar. "In conformity with norms traditional in the Church, women (single, married, religious), whether in churches, homes, convents, schools, or institutions for women, are barred from serving the priest at the altar."[77] This remained the case until a 1994 letter from the Congregation for Divine Worship and the Sacraments clarified that women and girls may serve at the altar.[78] Once again the most recent edition of *GIRM* has taken this into account and voices no preference by gender on this issue.

Extraordinary Ministers of Communion

Between 1966 and 1973 disciplinary changes were made in eucharistic ministry that significantly increased lay participation. The instruction *Fidei Custos* of 1966/69 extended the ministry of distribution of Communion to the laity both within the Mass and in the pastoral care of the sick at home.[79] While permission could be granted to all nonordained, an order of preference clearly distinguished rank both among those in orders and among the laity. "A suitable person . . . is to be chosen in this order of preference: subdeacons, clerics in minor orders, those who have received tonsure, men religious, women religious, male catechists (unless, in the prudent judgment of the pastor, a male catechist is preferable to a woman religious)."[80] Later in the same document it states, "a woman of outstanding piety may be chosen in cases of necessity, that is, whenever another fit person cannot be found."[81] Later documents soften this exclusion. *Immensae Caritatis* of 1973 is another instruction on facilitating the reception of Communion.[82] It takes into account *Ministeria Quaedam* and provides guidelines for both permanent and temporary naming of special ministers of the Eucharist. While it continues to prioritize participation in this ministry, it loosens some of the restrictions on women's participation. "The fit person . . . will be designated according to the order of this listing (which may be changed at the prudent discretion of the local Ordinary): reader, major seminarian, men religious, woman religious, catechists, one of the faithful—a man or a woman."[83] The most recent edition of *GIRM* does not make any comment regarding gender distinction of extraordinary eucharistic ministers.

In summary, since the time of the council the ministry of distribution of the Eucharist has been opened once more to the laity in response to pastoral need. Rather than opening such ministry to all the laity, participation has been carefully prescribed and ordered for most of the period since the council. Recently, however, all concerns of ranking and ordering of ministers have ceased except the distinction of ordained ministers as "ordinary" ministers of Communion and instituted acolytes and lay persons as "extraordinary" ministers of Communion.[84]

Conclusions

It is clear that consideration of the liturgical assembly is a crucial element of any review of the liturgical reform of the council. It is equally clear that an articulation of a theology of the liturgical assembly came to light gradually and took its time to reach ecclesial consciousness. We might review a few of its key components. Simply by using the word "assembly," one invokes its biblical heritage, a factor of considerable importance in an ecclesial community that honors its foundations in the Scriptures. Consideration of the assembly as a corporate subject allows one to focus on the communal nature of liturgical prayer, something that was in much need at the time of the council and one might argue is still quite important today. The assembly's identity as a mystery of the church and its constitution by God in Christ and the Holy Spirit reminds us of the importance of gathering. Once gathered we have work to do: praise, thanksgiving, invocation, the work of giving God glory and increasing human sanctification. We noted how tied a theology of the assembly is to a theology of the church and how ordering in the church is reflected in ordering of the assembly. We remarked throughout the text how fuller participation mitigated some of the clericalism that shaped the liturgy, but that gender issues continued to limit and even prohibit women's participation in lay roles and ministries until the very recent past (and still do in certain dioceses).

We might mention some of the issues that still need to be addressed. The biblical foundations of the assembly still could use more emphasis, particularly the aspect of Christ the "assembler" and the priority on God's gathering of the people. In spite of Martimort's strong insistence on the *bigarrure* nature of the assembly and the challenge such diversity poses for believers, we are still struggling with issues of diversity and unity. Our multicultural communities have yet to find adequate expression in liturgical gatherings. Perhaps a topic that remains ever present is the relationship between justice within the assembly and justice outside of liturgy. The American liturgical reformers of the twentieth century would not be pleased that we have lost touch with the idea of liturgical reform for the sake of social regeneration. While noting the relationship between ecclesiology and a theology of the assembly, we have yet to address how the evolution of lay ecclesial ministers in our church will change the complexion of the liturgical assembly (especially regarding leadership roles). We will address some of these issues in ensuing chapters, but I hope that it is now clear to the reader how central the liturgical assembly is to any liturgical theology or any efforts at liturgical reform.

CHAPTER THREE

Liturgy as a Divine Human Dialogue

In the last chapter we traced the history of a very important dimension of the liturgical reform movement, the retrieval of a theology of the liturgical assembly. We saw that in part it was a response to the clericalizing tendencies that had marked the liturgy from the medieval period to the eve of the council. Thus the retrieval of the whole body, clergy and laity together, as the subject of liturgical action was a necessary and important countermeasure to repair this distortion. We also saw that a theology of the assembly provided the background for a corporate understanding of liturgical prayer, an understanding that was lacking in the pre–Vatican II church. An emphasis on the corporate nature of liturgical prayer countered an individualistic approach to the liturgy and sacraments, and sought to dwell on the unity of the Body gathered together for the glorification of God and sanctification of the Body.

While there is still much work to be done in these areas, the reform of the liturgical books has institutionalized a corporate approach to the liturgy, and efforts have been made to foster a corporate spirituality through liturgical celebration. One of the effects of this change has been the disappearance of personal pious practices during the liturgy and the retrieval of active participation in the liturgy itself.

Some of the critics of the modern liturgical reform movement have noted that the attention to the liturgy as the action of the church assembled has deflected attention away from the liturgy as the action of God in Christ and the Holy Spirit. Sometimes that gets expressed in comments that we have lost a "sense of the holy" in our liturgical celebrations. Others say that the mystery has gone out of the liturgy. There are several presuppositions involved in these judgments that could be addressed at length, but I want to focus my attention on who is the subject of the liturgy because, beyond the polemics of the liturgy wars, there is something important in their critique.

The liturgy must be understood as the joint action of God and the people of God. To negate or diminish either side of this equation does an injustice to the tradition and deprives the contemporary community of the fulsomeness of Christian liturgical practice. I believe that the retrieval of the assembly's role was a necessary response to a liturgy that was focused almost solely on God's action. Sometimes the impression was given that the liturgy as we know it is a direct institution of Christ himself, whole and entire, without due regard to the church's role in the formation of the scriptural canon in the first place and in the shaping of the sacraments we have, East and West. What we celebrate now as the Mass is the fruit of many generations' efforts to be faithful to the Lord's command to gather and remember what God has done. The variety of eucharistic prayers, for example, gives evidence of the church's role in shaping Christ's remembrance. The creation of our liturgical forms is a work of the church from one perspective, and the celebration of these liturgies is the work of the church from another. If we have dwelt on these aspects in recent years, it is understandable and has been pastorally important. The liturgy is not only this, as I will argue below, but it is at least this. If we have neglected to stress the liturgy as God's work, it is not that we no longer believe that to be true, but that we needed to emphasize the church's role to repair the imbalance that had existed. Perhaps the time has come to attend to liturgy as God's work, trying this time to keep in balance the ecclesial and divine dimensions. Only an approach that keeps both realties in mind is faithful to our tradition and is what we owe future believers as we pass on the tradition to them. In the rest of the chapter I will address this issue from two perspectives: the dialogical nature of the liturgy and liturgy as God's gift to us.

The Dialogical Nature of the Liturgy

I have gone to great lengths to stress the importance of a theology of the assembly and suggested that the contemporary church has integrated many, but not all, dimensions of this theology. As the critics of the liturgical movement have indicated, we have retrieved to a significant degree the importance of the assembly in the liturgical event, and I count that as a great accomplishment. However, there is another dimension to the biblical foundations of a theology of the assembly that has not received as much attention as it should. It is precisely God's role in calling the assembly into being and what God does in that assembly event that we have perhaps overlooked to this point.

If you recall, the French scholars doing research on the liturgical assembly in the Hebrew Scriptures noted that it was divine initiative that drew a disparate people into assembly and fashioned them into the *qahal Yahweh*. It was not human decision making that created the assembly of God. Quite to the contrary, it was because God chose (for reasons beyond all human logic) to gather a covenant people to announce the salvation of God among the nations. At the heart of this covenant was a call to gather periodically in assembly so that God's word would be proclaimed and broken open and that God's own holiness would be shared among the gathered. There is no other way to characterize this phenomenon outside of the theological categories of grace and mystery.

There is a gratuity to grace that cannot be logically accounted for. Simply by definition grace is the free offer of God to the human community to engage in a relationship of knowledge and love. There is nothing we have done or can do to earn this grace. It is simply the effect of God's desire to share life with us. That is the mystery of salvation, first revealed to Israel, then brought to fullness in Jesus Christ, and now lived out in the church. This is why it was so important that the French scholars rooted their theology of assembly in a theology of election and in an ecclesiology. The very existence of the covenanted people, and now the church, rests in God's unambiguous call to divine/human encounter in love. The very existence of the church constitutes a mystery of God's love. By extension the assembly, as Martimort reminded us, shares in the very mystery of the church in this respect. God draws a people who have no reason to gather together into a people of God. The liturgical assembly is as much a mystery of God's salvific will as is the church and the covenanted community of Israel. To reduce the liturgical assembly to a mere human gathering for strictly human purposes is to reduce it beyond its essential nature. We are and will always be a community called into being by God, and called into specific liturgical assemblies for God's own purpose.

Before we explore the purposes of the assembly, it is important to note that the gathering of the people of God into assembly follows the dynamic of call and response. The very existence of the assembly is dialogic. The initiative comes from God; the response to gather comes from us. Enabled by God's grace, we choose to join that "motley mixture" that

Martimort spoke of so appropriately. This coming together is no simple task nor does it come without price. There is, as he suggested, something of violence attached to this act of gathering. That is, we are invited to set aside those prejudices and the bias that divide the human community into the "haves" and "have-nots," those above from those below, those of difference we would prefer to set apart. We are called and graced to move from being a "people who were no people" to becoming God's own people. There is nothing frivolous about this response to divine initiative; there is nothing easy about living out the demands of the assembly.

As there would be no assembly without God's call, so too there would be no assembly without the community's response. To an extent even the community's response is done with the grace of God, yet the element of human freedom remains essential. God so respects what God has made that even God waits upon human freedom to respond to the divine offer of love and relationship. This is true in general; it is likewise true regarding the liturgical assembly. The event of the assembly cannot happen unless the church responds to the divine call to gather under the name of God; in doing so it becomes the new *qahal Yahweh*.

The assembly, as a people, is the fruit of the divine human dialogue; it is now appropriate to explore the dialogical nature of the assembly as event. As we reviewed in chapter 2, there is a purposefulness to gathering into liturgical assembly. First and foremost, we are called together to hear a word from our God, in particular a word that saves. For Israel, readings from the Law and the Prophets were central to their assembly gatherings. For Christians we add to these readings the witness to the Christ event in the gospels and in the writings of the apostles. Beyond the revelation of God to the world through creation and to individual peoples through their particular history, Jews and Christians believe that their Scriptures are privileged means of God's self-revelation and of discerning their own identity as a covenanted people. Thus the reading of the Scriptures is central to the understanding of the assembly event of Israel and of Christianity. Note how the emphasis is on the action of God: God's own sharing of self is accomplished in the reading of and preaching on the Scriptures.

The dialogical nature of this event is also writ large as we move from God's action to the assembly's response. The proclamation is to a people whose ears and hearts must be open to this ongoing revelation of life and love. We know this openness was an ongoing task of Israel and one that it failed quite often. The prophets railed against those whose hearts had turned to stone and would not hear the word of God and act upon it. Jesus' parables were often addressed to those who had "ears but could not hear and eyes that could not see." To these the word comes as judgment; for those willing to listen and allow themselves to be transformed by the revelation, the word comes as salvation. Divine gift is met with human response.

Even within the assembly event itself, there was need for immediate response to the spoken word. That was why the assembly included prayers of thanksgiving and sometimes sacrifice. In some way, it could be said that if the assembly could not respond positively to God immediately after the proclamation, there was little hope that it would do so later. Response needs to come to expression both in ritual form and in action outside of ritual. There is an intrinsic connection between the two that we ignore at our own peril. It appears from the prophet's perspective that God is pleased with ritual only to the extent that it correlates with the people's action for justice outside of ritual time. Thus we hear in Amos, "I hate, I despise your festivals, and I take no delight in your solemn assemblies. Even though you offer me your burnt offerings and grain offerings, I will not accept them . . . But let justice roll down like waters, and righteousness like an ever-flowing stream" (Amos 5:21-24). We will return to this theme later, but for now it is enough to point out the dialogical nature of proclamation and response in some form, in ritual and in ethical behavior.

Within the assembly event, the proclamation of the word was met with praise, thanksgiving, and sacrifice. In Israel's assembly this meant that a prayer of thanksgiving was offered and/or a sacrifice by the priests, to which the assembly added its "amen." The dynamic of the Christian assembly is no different. The council stressed that there is a connection between the word and the Eucharist, and indeed that the Mass was to be revised to "bring out more clearly the intrinsic nature and purpose of its several parts, as also the connection between them" (*CSL* 50). The *GIRM* also makes an effort to connect the various parts of the Mass. Speaking directly of the word, the *GIRM* says that "God speaks to his people, opening up to them the mystery of redemption and salvation, and offering them spiritual nourishment; and Christ himself is present in the midst of the faithful through his word" (*GIRM* 55). Within the ritual unit of the Liturgy of the Word, there is room for the assembly's response. Speaking of the profession of faith, *GIRM* goes on further to say that its purpose is so that "the whole gathered people may respond to the word of God proclaimed in the readings" (*GIRM* 67). This relationship of the

Creed to the Word can be understood as a "mini-dialogue" in that it constitutes an offer of God's very self to us and our response, all within the Liturgy of the Word. Note how essential both partners are in the dialogue. Even within the small structures of the Liturgy of the Word, both God's action and the assembly's are required to constitute the event. We now need to turn our attention to larger structures within the Christian assembly's principal event—the Mass.

During the very important 1956 Assisi liturgy meeting (The First International Congress of Pastoral Liturgy), Father Augustine Bea addressed the pastoral function of the word of God in the liturgy; he wondered about its importance and its efficacy.[1] His address was important because it greatly influenced the emphasis on the word in the conciliar constitution on the liturgy. Bea spoke of the need of the faithful to be fed with the bread of God's word as well as the bread of the Eucharist. The word would put before them the great figures of the faith, most especially Christ himself, as guides to their faith and their models in life. Its efficacy was based on the fact that the Scriptures "*are* the word of God through that singular charism of inspiration."[2] In this sense the word of God constitutes a primary means through which the faithful are "gifted" with God's very revelation of self. Other parts of the Mass (e.g., the *Confiteor* and *Kyrie*) prepare for a receptive hearing of the word, and its power is made more efficacious by its union with the eucharistic sacrifice. The word serves with the Eucharist as spiritual nourishment given to us as God's gift.[3] Bea also treats the word as preparation for the eucharistic sacrifice and the sacrifice as a response to that offer given in the word. Although his language seems a little dated, nonetheless, it gives voice to the relationship between word and Eucharist.

> Man, listening to the word of God and welcoming it, prepares and fits his soul to render to God, his Lord and Creator, that sublime worship in spirit and in truth, that most perfect gift, the immeasurable sacrifice of the Man-God, and in return receives from God the precious gift of the grace which flows from the eucharistic Sacrifice.[4]

We need now to address in more detail this larger dialogue, namely, the relationship between the Liturgy of the Word and the Liturgy of the Eucharist. Indeed, as Bea suggested, the Liturgy of the Eucharist can be understood as a response of thanksgiving and sacrifice to the word. The *GIRM* speaks of the meaning of the eucharistic prayer in this way: "The entire congregation of the faithful should join itself with Christ in confessing the great deeds of God and in the offering of Sacrifice" (*GIRM* 78). In other words, in response to the proclamation of a saving word, the whole community joins Christ in responding with its own word of praise, thanksgiving, and offering. The whole structure of the Mass, in other words, is that of divine offer and human response, a dialogue between God and God's people. And in all parts of this there is the promise of mutual presencing. Christ is present when the assembly gathers in praise and thanksgiving, in the word, in the leadership of the priest, and in a most excellent way in the eucharistic sharing itself. The assembly, through the grace of God, also makes its personal presence felt. Through the gift of human freedom, the assembly openly places itself before this divine offer of presencing and responds with its own acts of love and devotion. At the level of large structures—the Word and the Eucharist—the whole Liturgy of the Eucharist can be seen as the assembly's response to the offer of divine love given in the Liturgy of the Word.

There is also a dialogical dimension to the Liturgy of the Eucharist itself. It is the "holy exchange," the *divinum commercium*, of gifts that constitutes the eucharistic rite. We take bread and wine, gifts of the earth and work of human hands, and offer them to God. God receives those gifts, and through prayers of sanctification and consecration, the gifts become in a new way the presencing of Christ to the assembly. Receiving back these gifts, now consecrated and made holy, we offer them to the Father in union with Christ. Eucharistic Prayer II speaks of our offering "this life-giving bread, this saving cup." The second Prayer of Reconciliation offers the "gift you have given us, the sacrifice of reconciliation." Not to be outdone in generosity, God gives back this offering to the assembled people. But the gift of the Body and Blood is not just to "be there," it is given to be received in faith. Thus the Communion rite constitutes the high point of the eucharistic liturgy, fulfilling in a sacramental way the circle of divine and human exchange. This sharing of divine life, we may call this "holiness," is one of the primary purposes of the assembly event—participation in the very holiness of God.

There is another "exchange of gifts" in the Liturgy of the Eucharist. It is the offer of ourselves. The *GIRM* speaks of the "offering" section of the eucharistic prayer as an "offer[ing] in the Holy Spirit [of] the spotless Victim to the Father. The Church's intention, however, is that the faithful not only offer this spotless Victim but also learn to offer themselves" (*GIRM* 79f.). We too are subject to prayers of consecration and epiclesis (a prayer calling down the Holy Spirit) that we may be transformed, become one church, one body in the Holy Spirit (Eucharistic Prayers II and III). This too is a "holy exchange of gifts." It is the dialogue of human offer and divine response. The fruit of this exchange is transformation into Christ by the power of the Holy Spirit, once again, holiness by any other name. All that remains is the response to the divine offer in Word and Eucharist with lives of justice and mercy to all people and to the earth itself in all dimensions of our lives.

In summary, dialogue is the nature of the liturgy. The community comes together in response to divine call; and in the unfolding of the liturgy, in small structures and in large, it responds with affirmation, with praise, and with offering. Through mutual presencing, God and the assembly engage in a "holy exchange of gifts," most important, the gift of themselves given and received in love. It is a relationship initiated by God but expressed in mutuality of exchange where we receive always more than we have to offer. As we said at the beginning of this chapter, the liturgy must be understood as the joint action of God and the people of God. It is only in keeping both dimensions in balance that we account for the full dynamic of the liturgy.

Liturgy and Sacrament as God's Gift

A bit more needs to be said of the kind of giving that is the reality of liturgy and sacrament. Rather than beginning with the specifics of liturgy and sacrament, we need to cast our gaze much wider in order to properly contextualize these terms. We need to begin with God's self-emptying in Christ, the Word made flesh. This is the original and foundational "gift exchange" or *divinum commercium*; it is the exchange between the divine and the human that we celebrate in sacrament. David Power has written extensively on this. To the point here he says:

> From the earth, the Word takes human nature, but brings it into an exchange with the divine, and so sanctifies it by the gifts of grace. The exchange therefore is not rooted in the bringing of gifts by the community, but in the gift that comes forth from God in the incarnation and that constitutes an exchange, or a *commercium* between the divine and the human.[5]

This foundational exchange is what comes to visibility in Christian liturgy and sacrament. Through remembrance in language and rite of the self-emptying of God in Christ and the power of the Spirit, God's continuing presencing to us and gifting of us takes form. The initiative is from God, not humanity; any giving that we do is a consequence of God's initial desire to reach out toward us in self-emptying love. Power goes on to say:

> Whatever gifts the people may bring, they are taken up into the celebration of the wonderful exchange between God and humans enacted in the fleshly mysteries of the Word. They do not so much bring gifts as lift up that which is to be transformed into the symbol of the one wondrous gift that stems from God.[6]

From this perspective, when the church speaks of the foundation of the sacraments by Christ, it is speaking of Christ giving us the symbols that make that original gift visible. Thus we have in the Eucharist, the symbols of bread, cup, and equal table-sharing handed over to us as a share in the divine gift-giving of God's very self, all done in the context of memorial thanksgiving. In baptism we have the waters of new life, the waters of womb and tomb showing forth the "spilling out" of the Word of life for our sake and for our salvation. How we shape the rituals and create the narratives of remembrance, however, are the work of the church contextualized as it always is in history and culture. Once again, beyond all logic, Christ has left to a very human church the responsibility of remembering his saving offer of self in language and rite.[7]

In speaking of liturgy and sacraments as "God's gift," we find ourselves using analogical language. That is, we are using personalistic terms for God and ideas of gift-giving to speak of what must remain mystery. Traditionally, sacramental theology has allowed the use of such analogies so long as certain parameters were kept. The act of creating analogies is the effort to move from an understanding of something we do know to something we do not know. Essential to this process is the belief that the differences in the analogy are always greater than the similarities. Thus we can speak of God in personalistic terms and we can speak of sacrament as a gift of God. God is at least personal and is at least capable of acts of giving. God is certainly more than that, but it seems important that we continue to use some personalistic terms for God so that the very idea of God's self-giving can be at least minimally comprehensible.

That being said, in using the analogy of sacrament as the gift of God, we need to be aware of certain dangers of reductionism. In this sacramental offer of gift, we receive an offer of life that is given freely and is not to be identified with the giver. There is always a danger that we domesticate God and even identify sacraments of God's self-giving as objects to be possessed. However, there is no absolute identification of the gift with the giver. Even as we speak of God's gift as a giving of "self," God always remains "unpossessed" and remains mystery. In the offer of self, God remains distinct; so too do we—the recipients of that gift. God and humanity do not merge in sacrament; we meet in sacrament. But it is never the meeting of two equal "persons." Categories of person and being cannot adequately capture the reality of who God is, but it is a place to start as long as we are constantly aware of its limits.

In contemporary sacramental theology there is an effort to go beyond language of ontology (being) and causality. In other words, language about the "being" of God has, it is argued, been taken too much from the human and the created to ever adequately express the otherness of God. Thus we have Jean-Luc Marion's efforts to speak of "God beyond being," which suggests that God is inconceivable within the range of concepts that belong within metaphysical systems.[8] To move beyond these categories of metaphysics and causality, Power suggests that we turn to the iconic to understand how God gifts us with self in sacraments. Drawn from Eastern practice and theology, the icon allows us to look at sacraments as making visible the reality they signify without positing that the icon "reproduces" the divine action. In other words, the icon does take part in "the reality of the imaged, makes it indeed present as communicable, but it does not reproduce it."[9] Indeed, as Power suggests, working from the primordial reference of Christ as image of the Father, the icon takes on the dynamic of imaging in difference. Christ empties himself of glory and so makes visible the unseen God. The icon moves us from the visible to the invisible; it works through "hiddenness." Understanding sacrament in this way, Power suggests that "at its core the power of sacrament to reveal lies in the unlike, in the concealment needed to make known what is revealed. An icon is a coming to presence of the divine, without it being present as knowable in 'it'self."[10] Drawing upon Marion, Power continues, "the iconic is the visible mirror of the invisible, a visible reality suffused with divine light while leaving the divine itself incomprehensible."[11] This is how the divine offer of self is made known to the believing community. In sacramental symbols of bread, wine, water, and oil, icons if you will, the invisible, unknowable God comes to expression as divine offer as did the eternal Word.

We can speak of sacraments, then, as an "eventing" of this divine offer of God's self to us in Christ and the Spirit. The offer of God's giving of self continues to happen in the church when the community gathers and keeps memory of the one in whom it finds life. As the church is ever new in every generation, so too, the self-giving of God continues to be an ongoing offer of self to us. As Power says,

> A sacramental action is the showing forth of the gift given by God through Word and Spirit, present/ing now through the medium of signs, that is, rites and language. In the remembrance of the Church, in all its appropriation of what has been said and revealed, the original event of the Pasch, in all its complexity of passion, act, and proclamation, keeps showing forth and eventing. In this showing forth, there is the continued outflow, the continued giving of the Word and the Spirit, in whose power the gift of God takes form among peoples of different times, places, and cultures.[12]

It is in this very large sense of sacrament as icon of the self-giving of God that we can speak of the Eucharist, for example, as God's gift to us. Through words of remembrance spoken by the church, with scriptural warrants spoken in the context of blessing, through ritual actions of breaking and sharing, the church assembled together stands in an attitude of receptivity. It opens its hands to receive what could never be imagined or expected, the gratuitous offer of God's very self in freedom and love. It is to this offer that the assembly responds with its own offer of self.

Unlike human gift-giving that is so often, if not always, marked with expectations of reciprocity, the divine offer of life is presented to our freedom. Divine gift is truly presented to us as offer, awaiting our response. If we do respond with openness, our humanity is somehow not overwhelmed with the offer of divine life but is transformed through participation in divine life in a way that paradoxically makes us more fully human. Our capacity for goodness, for acts of justice and mercy, for working for the full humanity of others, is enlarged as a result of the receptivity of divine gift. We cannot engage in this holy exchange of gifts without a transformation of life. We are transformed in liturgy, but not only for liturgy. We are a single person in and out of ritual space. Our transformation seeks its own expression in ethical and loving lives. Failure to act so *outside* of ritual space gives lie to any claims of transformation *within* ritual space. In the dialogical terms that we introduced above, we can speak of this large dynamic of divine offer in ritual space and human response outside of ritual space as a dialogical understanding of liturgy and sacrament in the widest sense.

One of the mysteries of divine grace is that in communicating with us God reaches out to us in ways that are absolutely personal. In a sense this is the flip side of the communal nature of the liturgy; it never ceases to be individual and personal. By that I mean that the offer of grace in the sacraments is always uniquely suited to our reality at a given time and place. God takes us so seriously that not a single element of our life is left untouched by the reaches of grace. No matter what our history, what hurts and failings that we bring to the table, the offer of divine love is always tailored to our needs, individual and communal. That is why we are never overwhelmed by God's presence and God's gifting, although we should make no mistake and attempt to domesticate God into bite-sized pieces. Rather, liturgy does its job in buffering us from the magnitude of God even as it mediates God's presence. Through the mediation of divine love in icons of bread and cup, sharing and bathing, anointing and forgiving, we are invited into the divine orb of relationship in ways suitable to our situation at every moment.

If the gift of God's self is given in the moment, it is a gift that always reaches out to future fulfillment. There is a fullness of life that God has promised us not only in this life but also in the next that is the fruit of the offer of divine life. In a sense sacrament is less about a particular "gift" than about being drawn into an infinite relationship of mutuality of self-gifting. It is in this sense that the future holds more than a particular moment can show. Sacrament is always about the time-bound human community who until the end time lives only with symbols of divine mystery.

Conclusions

In summary, we suggested that the liturgy and sacraments are dialogical by nature. The assembly itself is a fruit of divine call and human response. The assembly as event is likewise a dialogue of offer and response. In structures small and large, we engage with Divine love in a "holy exchange" of gifts—primarily the gift of self mediated by ritual actions. Paradoxically, the liturgy and sacraments are acts of God and acts of the church at the same time. It is not as if God speaks first and then sequentially the church speaks. Rather, in both word and Eucharist we have both divine offer and human response. God gifts us with word and sacrament that the church itself has shaped under the influence of the Holy Spirit.

We also saw how liturgy and sacraments can be understood within the category of gift. Here the stress is placed on God's action through the mediation of sacramental signs. Using the icons of bread, cup, water, and oil, God's self-emptying in Christ is rehearsed again and again in a community that lives one day at a time under the dispensation of signs and symbols. Careful not to reduce God to concepts too small to bear the weight of mystery, we nevertheless used metaphors of personhood and gift to describe the mystery of God's love for humankind. The liturgy and sacraments are indeed God's action in Christ and in the Holy Spirit, but they are only that in dialogue with the church assembled in a posture of active receptivity. We end where we began: the liturgy and sacraments are both the work of God and the work of the church.

CHAPTER FOUR

The Paschal Mystery and
Liturgical Anamnesis

In chapter 1 we reviewed the framework of the Constitution on the Sacred Liturgy of Vatican II. We suggested that in the Constitution there was a deliberate attempt to connect the mystery of Christ, the mystery of the church, and the mystery of the liturgy. We saw that what was revealed in Christ is to be proclaimed by the church and celebrated in the liturgy. We return once again to these themes but from a different perspective. Our attention now is on the Christ mystery and the proclamation of that mystery by the church in the liturgy. As the Constitution reminded us so clearly, it is through the liturgy that "the faithful may express in their lives and manifest to others the mystery of Christ and the real nature of the true Church" (*CSL* 2).

The Paschal Mystery[1]

There is nothing more central or more profound for either the Jewish or Christian communities than the belief that God has entered into human history with an offer of salvation from all that binds us to death in any of its dimensions. The Israelites celebrated in feast and liturgy the memory of God's action on their behalf. Of paradigmatic importance to them was the saving action of God in freeing them from their Egyptian overlords and in their passage through the Red Sea into a land of freedom. Today we know the celebration of this divine action as the feast of Passover; in ancient Israel it was known as *pesach* in Hebrew and *pascha* in Aramaic.[2] Passover had its roots in two celebrations. One was the celebration of the "passage" of the angel of death over the houses of the Hebrews with its sacrifice of a lamb needed for the blood to be placed over the doorposts. A second feast, that of unleavened bread, was an agricultural feast marking the beginning of the barley harvest that Israel celebrated in the land of Canaan. Using only the newest grain without leaven, it celebrated fresh beginnings and became a suitable feast to commemorate Israel's redemption from slavery in Egypt, the new start Israel had after crossing the Red Sea. Not incidentally, this feast also had messianic expectations and hopes for the final redemption. Sometime between the reform of Josiah (621) and the Exile (587–39) it became joined to the Passover feast.

The early church found in the coincidence of Jesus' death and resurrection within the general ambit of the Passover feast ample room to explore his significance within the great plan of salvation. The Synoptics place the Last Supper as a Passover meal on the evening of the fourteenth of the Jewish month Nisan (our March–April) and his death on the fifteenth of Nisan. John's gospel, on the other hand, situates Jesus' death at the sacrifice of the lambs on the preparation day of the Passover, the afternoon of the fourteenth of Nisan. Whatever the difference on dating, the early Christian community took advantage of both meanings connected with the Passover feast, the sacrifice of the lambs and the passage to freedom.

The connection of Jesus' death with the slaying of the paschal lambs appears early on in the Christian tradition even before John's gospel. Already in Paul's letter to the Corinthians we hear the connection he makes between Christ and the paschal lamb: "For our paschal lamb, Christ, has been sacrificed" (1 Cor 5:7). Postapostolic writers pick up this theme and develop it. Justin Martyr, in his *Dialogue with Trypho* (ca. 135), speaks of the Passover lamb as "truly a type of Christ, with whose Blood the believers . . . anoint their homes (cf. Exod 12:7), that is, themselves."[3] Melito of Sardis' homily on the Pasch (last half of the second century) constantly emphasizes Christ as the new lamb, slain for all, "For the sacrifice of the Lamb . . . has been fulfilled in Christ" and [Christ] is "born as Son, and led to slaughter as a lamb, and sacrificed as a sheep."[4] Even with such a strong emphasis on Christ's death as the Paschal Lamb, Melito's homily is instructive in how he is able to hold the whole redemptive mystery together. Melito proclaims of the Christ, "I (am) the Pascha of salvation, I (am) the lamb slain for you, I (am) your ransom, I (*am*) your *life* . . . *light* . . . salvation . . . *resurrection*."[5] Nonetheless, at this early point in the tradition the emphasis is on Christ's suffering.

It is interesting to point out that even in the earliest layers of the tradition there was an effort to connect the understanding of Christ our Pasch with the ritual celebrations of the community. We hear in Paul that the remembrance of our salvation in Christ is celebrated in terms of the Passover meal rituals of bread and cup, now in the Eucharist: "For as often as you eat this bread and drink the cup, you proclaim the Lord's death until he comes" (1 Cor 11:26). Pseudo-Chrysostom's homily on the Pasch (387) continues this line of thought, "Wherefore, since the Only-Begotten was sacrificed once for all . . . the lamb is no longer sacrificed, but the Savior . . . gives bread and a cup as a representation of the most excellent sacrifice . . . and command[s] (us) to perform the Pascha with these symbols."[6] Thus, on the one hand, the early church was able to connect the remembrance of Christ with a yearly Passover, and on the other to celebrate his memorial in Eucharist more frequently, especially on Sunday, outside the Passover context proper in eucharistic table-sharing. Beginning with the Pauline tradition of Romans 5, the early church also connected keeping memorial of the death and resurrection of the Lord in baptism.

Before exploring this sacramental memorializing of the paschal mystery any further, it is helpful to consider more clearly the two distinct ways in which the church understood the paschal imagery it inherited—Pasch as *passio* and Pasch as *transitus*. As I indicated above, in the Hebrew tradition the Pascha could refer to the *sacrifice of the lambs*, the blood of which was a sign for God to preserve the children of Israel (Exod 12), or to the passing over of the Hebrews themselves as they crossed the Red Sea into freedom (Exod 14). The application to Christ of the paschal lamb imagery sacrificed for the sake of the people, as well as the association of the fourteenth and fifteenth of Nisan with the actual suffering and death of the Lord, led to an understanding of Pascha as "suffering." As we saw above, this appears to be the older layer of interpretation for the Christian community. In a paschal homily Melito of Sardis argues that the term *pascha* derives from the Greek verb *pathein*, meaning "to suffer." "What is the Pascha? Its name is taken from an accompanying circumstance: *paschein* (to keep Pascha) comes from *pathein* (to suffer). Therefore learn who the sufferer is."[7] While Melito is counted among the Quartodecimans of the East,[8] the connection between Pascha and the suffering of the Lord also spread to the Latin West. In an anti-Jewish polemic Pseudo-Tertullian explicitly makes the connection between the Pascha of Unleavened Bread and the passion of Christ.[9] Pseudo-Cyprian likewise explains that "we, who celebrate the Pascha, no longer symbolically, as [the Jews] did, but in truth, to commemorate the passion of the son of God."[10] These early sources show us that there was originally an emphasis on Christ's suffering rather than on the resurrection, a development that would come just a bit later.

With Origen of Alexandria we see a shift in the understanding of the Pascha. He explains, "Most, if not all, of the brethren think that the Pascha is named Pascha from the passion of the Savior. However, the feast in question is not called precisely Pascha by the Hebrews, but *phas[h]*. . . . Translated, it means 'passage'" or in Latin, *transitus*.[11] According to liturgical scholar Thomas Talley, Origen "is the first Christian writer . . . to apply that understanding to Christ's passage into the kingdom."[12] Such a change shifted the emphasis from the day of Christ's death to the Sunday following his suffering, more clearly highlighting the resurrection aspect of the paschal event.

During the third and fourth centuries, while maintaining its practice of celebrating the Pascha on Sunday following the fourteenth and fifteenth of Nisan, the Latin West combined the earlier Asiatic tradition of Pascha as *passio* with Origen's understanding of it as passage or *transitus*. Traditions were combined, but also developed. Ambrose took the understanding of Pascha as *transitus* and its connection with Exodus 13–14 as the passage of the people, and applied it in a moralizing way to the transformation of the Christian who needs to pass over from sin to grace, from the world to God. Once again we see the connection the church made between the paschal mystery and that of its sacramental celebrations. In this case, as Raniero Cantalamessa suggests, "the paschal sacrament *par excellence* tends to be baptism rather than the Eucharist."[13]

Augustine would accomplish the synthesis of these two traditions of suffering and passage in a new way and develop them in conjunction with his concern for christology/anthropology and Eucharist/baptism. He first treats suffering and passage in its christological context not by opposing the meanings but by integrating them: "For by suffering the Lord made the passage from death to life."[14] He then speaks about the annual celebration of the Pascha in sacramental terms (that it signifies something else), and suggests that what happens to Christ is what happens to us in the sacraments: "For by suffering . . . [he] made the passage from death to life and opened a way for us who believe in his resurrection by which we too might pass from death to life."[15]

Up to this point we have been concentrating on the "paschal" dimension of the paschal mystery, particularly the christological dimension. Christ is our Pasch; he is the Word made flesh for our salvation. He suffered for our sake and passed over from death to life showing us the way. It is time now to spend a moment on the "mystery" dimension of this phrase before we transition to a consideration of the church's liturgy as a celebration of the paschal mystery.

In the most basic biblical sense, the great mystery is that of God and secondarily the saving plan of God for humankind. This plan is a hidden reality made known only through revelation and therefore available only in faith. For the Hebrews that revelation is made known in law and covenant, through chosen leaders and prophets, through the people's experience of rescue and redemption. In the Pauline corpus *mysterion* refers to the whole redemptive plan of God that culminates in the union of Christ with humankind in a relationship that is redemptive (Eph 1:3-14). He equates in 1 Corinthians 2 the mystery of God with Christ crucified made known to us through the power of the Spirit: "'What no eye has seen, nor ear heard, nor the human heart conceived, what God has prepared for those who love him,' these things God has revealed to us through the Spirit" (1 Cor 2:9). Christ in us, the hope of our glory, is a *mysterion*. The election of the gentiles is a *mysterion* (Eph 3:3), and Paul himself has been named minister or steward of the mysteries of God (1 Cor 4:1). The mystery comes to fullness in Christ, but there awaits a final revelation in the eschaton when Christ will be all in all.

Christ, then, is the *mysterion* of God, the wisdom of God revealed through the Incarnation and paradoxically through the Cross. But death does not have the last word; the resurrection serves as further revelation of what God desires for us in Christ. As James Empereur notes in his article on the paschal mystery, it is in this second level of meaning that the word *paschal* joins the word *mystery*. "For Christians, Jesus Christ brings to a new order the passover of the Hebrew scriptures. He is the new covenant with God. The mystery which had been hidden for so many centuries now takes human form."[16]

After Pentecost the church takes up the announcement of this paschal mystery. That mystery made known to the Hebrews, expressed in Christ now becomes mediated by the church whose ministry it is to proclaim this saving Word to all the world. It does this through its proclamation of the kerygma, through the celebrations of the sacraments, and through living the Christian life. To speak of the church as continuing the mission of Jesus Christ is to say that its life is *paschal* and that it too is a manifestation of *mystery* in the Pauline sense. For those plunged into the paschal mystery in baptism and fed at the eucharistic table, which is its memorial, all life is a participation in God's ongoing revelation of life and love. It now remains to show how our liturgies mediate the paschal mystery.

Liturgical Anamnesis/Keeping Memorial

Remembering the Mystery

Throughout the Hebrew Scriptures there is a rich use of memorial. God remembers the people (and thereby holds them in life), and the people remember God's deeds and promises. For the Jews remembrance or memorial of God's mighty deeds was and is essential to their identity. They were called into covenant by God and then expected to be forever mindful of those covenants and to respond with blessing, thanksgiving, and commitment. We spoke earlier of the Passover meal; it serves as the paradigmatic celebration of remembrance wherein those who celebrated it are caught up in its significance. It is a story of the past, but celebrated in the present, and awaits future fulfillment. Most important, remembrance connects those celebrating to the salvific event memorialized in that ritual. Sofia Cavaletti writes,

> According to the Mishnah, every Jew must "consider himself as having come forth from Egypt." The liberation worked by God at the time of Moses is the same as the liberation worked by him for each and every Jew. The Passover rite enables all Jews to become conscious of this liberation and share in it.[17]

Note her emphasis on participation. The act of remembrance is not just a reminiscence of the past but a memorial action done in obedience to divine command and guaranteed by God. Memorial rituals, in fact, connect their participants with the reality signified. In other words, we can speak of the Passover meal as "efficacious" or as "achieving" what it set out to do. According to Patrick McGoldrick, "In the case of the Passover, scholars tend to conclude that in this memorial God acts in a salvific way to somehow join past event and present situation so that the saving deed is made actual or effective for participants today."[18] For those of us used to speaking of Christian sacraments in terms of efficaciousness, this profound sense of memorial in the Hebrew Scriptures may appear unfamiliar to us. Yet, we must recall that both Judaism and Christianity base their faith in divine compassion in the same living God. Both traditions ritualize their beliefs and thus it is not surprising that both would make similar claims about the power of our rituals. In addition, as we have indicated earlier in this chapter, the roots of Christian ritual lie in the Jewish tradition, and even if Jews and Christians have differed over the centuries in the manner of interpreting their cultic behavior, they share much in common. Since the 1950s biblical and liturgical scholarship has at least agreed that memorial is central to both traditions.

It is clear that Jesus was acutely conscious of the role of memory and of the significance of the Passover feast. While external forces determined his betrayal and execution at the time of Passover, he intentionally used the Passover meal to recast the tradition and to provide an interpretation of his own significance within it. Using the familiar blessing pattern of the Passover meal, Jesus inserts himself into this memorial with the interpretive words, "Take, eat; this is my body," and taking the cup he gave thanks and gave it to the disciples saying "Drink from it, all of you; for this is my blood of the covenant, which is poured out for many for the forgiveness of sins" (Matt 26:26-29). The Lukan text continues after the cup, "Do this in remembrance of me" (Luke 22:19). We might say that Jesus was announcing that he is the new turning point of history, the new manifestation of the great mysterion, superseding the Exodus event. He states that he is the new covenant and that his blood shall be given for the forgiveness of sins. This new act of divine redemption would call for a new form of cultic remembrance, one that the church would shape over time.

That memorial of Christ, of his suffering, death, and resurrection, came to be called Eucharist; said in another way, the principal context in which the paschal mystery was remembered and celebrated was in that ritual we have come to call the Eucharist. One early example of how the Eucharist was understood as a memorial thanksgiving for the paschal mystery is given in Justin Martyr's *Dialogue with Trypho*.

> The offering of fine flour . . . which was handed down to be offered by those who were cleansed from leprosy, was a type of the *bread of the thanksgiving, which our Lord Jesus Christ handed down to us to do for a remembrance of the suffering which he suffered* for those who are cleansed in their souls from all wickedness of men, so that we might give thanks to God, both for creating the world with all things that are in it for the sake of [humanity], and for freeing us from the evil in which we were born, and for accomplishing a complete destruction of the principalities and powers through him who suffered according to [God's] will.[19] (emphasis added)

It is clear from this reading that the early church understood that its memorial action was to be done in obedience to Jesus' command as he articulated it at the Last Supper. Justin also notes in his *First Apology* that the bread and cup that we receive (called "thanksgiving") are really the Body and Blood of the incarnate Son and that this action of memorial thanksgiving is done because of Jesus' command.

> For we do not receive these things as common bread or common drink; but just as our Savior Jesus Christ, being incarnate through the word of God, took flesh and blood for our salvation, so too we have been taught that the food over which thanks have been given by a word of prayer which is from him, (the food) from which our flesh and blood are fed by transformation, is both the flesh and blood of that incarnate Jesus.

> For the apostles in the records composed by them which are called gospels, have handed down thus what was commanded of them: that Jesus took bread. . . .[20]

We need to notice both the "why" and the "what" of the church's action. The church does what it does in fidelity to the Lord's command, but what it does is an act of ritual memory keeping. In participating in these ritual actions, the church participates in the saving action symbolized. By eating and drinking the Lord's Body and Blood, we are incorporated ever more deeply into Christ's Body and made participants in his redemption.

All forms of the liturgy are at heart acts of remembrance or of liturgical anamnesis. We have been concentrating on the Eucharist as the church's principal celebration, but it is no less true for the other sacraments. Baptism has clearly been understood since the time of Paul as a plunging into the death and resurrection of Christ (Rom 5:12). The fourth- and fifth-century mystagogues speak repeatedly of participation in the sacramental signs of baptism as participation in the reality they signify. Syrian bishop Theodore of Mopsuestia suggests that as we await the final eschaton we participate in sacraments which are its symbols.

> Baptism contains the signs of the new birth which will be manifested in reality when you rise from the dead and recover all that death has stolen from you. . . . While you are waiting for the resurrection you must be content with receiving symbols and signs of it in this awesome sacrament which affords you certainty of sharing in the blessings to come.[21]

Commenting further on Paul's theology of baptism, Theodore says that

> believing this we come to him for baptism, because we wish now to share in his death so as to share like him in the resurrection from the dead. So when I am baptized and put my head under the water, I wish to receive the death and burial of Christ our

Lord, and I solemnly profess my faith in his resurrection; when I come up out of the water, this is a sign that I believe I am already risen.[22]

Cyril of Jerusalem speaks eloquently of our participation in the paschal mystery by means of sacramental symbols.

The strange, the extraordinary, thing is that we did not really die, nor were really buried or really crucified; nor did we really rise again: this was figurative and symbolic; yet our salvation was real. Christ's crucifixion was real, his burial was . . . made ours, that by sharing his sufferings in a symbolic enactment we may really and truly gain salvation.[23]

Ambrose, fourth-century bishop of Milan, likewise speaks of how our celebration of the sacraments joins us to the reality of Christ's salvific mystery. In a slightly anti-Jewish polemic Ambrose notes the superiority of Christian sacraments over Jewish practice.

What superiority is there over the people of the Jews having passed through the sea. . . . Yet the Jews who passed through, all died in the desert. But he who passes through this font, that is from the earthly to the heavenly—for there is a passage here, thus Easter, that is "his passage" [Exod 12:10], the passage from sin to life, from fault to grace, from defilement to sanctification—he who passes through this font does not die but rises.[24]

The alert reader will recognize in these selections the beginnings of a sacramental theology. By participating in the symbols of our redemption, we participate in the reality signified. While the authors quoted here would not have used the term "liturgical anamnesis," the parallels with present-day use of the term are unmistakable. The church, through her sacraments, ritually keeps memory of what God has done in Christ and in the power of the Spirit. Like other aspects of the liturgy, this action of keeping memorial is dialogical: we remember and give thanks for the mighty works of God, and God keeps mindful of us, catching us up in the reality of what the memorial rituals symbolize. The guarantee of their efficaciousness is God's fidelity.

We can speak also of other liturgical celebrations as acts of liturgical anamnesis. Consider, for example, the liturgical year. There is no peculiar sense of time in Hebrew thought or in the New Testament, strictly speaking. What is true, however, is that in both Judaism and Christianity we use time as a symbolic marker or as a cultic memorial of God's work. Not only do we celebrate Passover or Easter with festive meals (i.e., for Christians—Eucharist), we celebrate the day itself as a form of memorial. What these feast days do is to present to the living community a way of keeping memorial God's active intervention in human life through the symbol of time. In other words, what constituted an encounter with the living God in the past is presented now in the present as another opportunity for encounter. The present encounter in faith is the heart of it all. The events cannot be repeated—they are once and for all—but the reality they signify is made operative in the lives of the present believing community. As liturgical scholar Robert Taft says

> They [the historical events] created and manifested and remain the bearers of a new and permanent quality of existence called salvation, initiating a permanent dialectic of call and response between God and his people. . . . The reality it initiates and signifies, however, is neither past nor contingent but ever present in God, and through faith to us.[25]

So through yearly festivals such as the paschal celebration at Easter, the weekly Sunday, or individual feasts of the Lord such as the Ascension or the Baptism the church community gathers and keeps memorial of what God has done in Christ. There is a way in which "the New Testament recapitulates and 'personalizes' all of salvation history in Christ. . . . He is God's eternal Word (Jn 1:1-14); . . . his new creation (2 Cor 5:17, Gal 6:15, Rom 8:19ff., Apoc 21–22) . . . ; the new Pasch and its lamb (1 Cor 5:7, Jn 1:29, 36; 19:36, 1 Pet 1:19, Apoc 5ff. *passim*); . . . the new sacrifice, and its priest (Eph 5:2, Heb 2:17–3:2; 4:14–10:14); . . . and the Messianic Age that was to come (Lk 4:16-21, Acts 2:14-36)."[26] So when we celebrate Christ in feast and season, we celebrate the revelation of what God has done for us throughout time and what God desires for us as a present event and as a personal presence. The act of liturgical anamnesis is an act of proclamation, a faithful recalling of the whole Christ mystery, and our making a commitment once again to that Gospel. We "remind" God of past covenants and promises; we remind ourselves of those same covenants and our commitment in their regard. In the act of memory we place ourselves in an open posture, we make ourselves ready to receive the offer of God's very self to us in ever changing circumstances. As the

Constitution on the Sacred Liturgy stated, that is a presencing in word, in ministers, in the assembly, and in a most excellent way in eucharistic table-sharing (*CSL* 7). Not being able to live all at once or to decide once for all time, we need to engage again and again with the Gospel and God's abiding presence.

All liturgy does this: the sacraments, the Liturgy of the Hours, feasts and seasons, celebrations of the word. As Taft says so succinctly,

> The focus is not on the story, not on the past, but on Paul's "power of God unto salvation, first for the Jew, then for the Greek," and right now for you and me. This is what we do in liturgy. We make anamnesis, memorial, of this dynamic saving power in our lives, to make it penetrate ever more into the depths of our being, for the building up of the Body of Christ.[27]

We have been speaking up to this point about fidelity to keeping God's memory alive through word and symbol, feast and fast. The Christian community has done this "memory keeping" differently in East and West and over time. One need only review the eucharistic prayers of the various ancient and contemporary Christian churches to see how rich this act of liturgical anamnesis can be. The actual shape and content of the eucharistic memorial was determined by doctrinal controversies, by the particular circumstances and the genius of the celebrating communities. Various doctrinal controversies helped to shape that memory with an emphasis on Christ's humanity at one time or his divinity at another, for example. Various schools of biblical interpretation such as that of Antioch and Alexandria likewise made a difference in how memory was kept. Differences in metaphors such as sacrifice or the descent into hell have likewise shaped memorial action. So it is quite legitimate to ask how well have we remembered across Christian denominations and across time. Having used the Roman Canon as the principal form of eucharistic remembrance for some 1600 years, the Roman Catholic Church decided after Vatican II to add a number of additional prayers. They include Eucharistic Prayers II, III, and IV as well as prayers for children and reconciliation and the recently added prayers for various needs and occasions. The church has apparently judged that we were not well served with only a single way of keeping eucharistic memorial and so has enlarged our ritual vocabulary significantly. A review of the other revised sacramental rituals likewise shows an effort to provide a variety of prayers on many occasions for naming the mystery; where before only one was provided, now there are six or seven, each taken from a different church tradition. Still, in spite of these additions and changes, we must constantly question how well we have remembered, because each generation needs to appropriate the faith anew, and what appeared satisfactory for one age is inadequate for another. This is a never-ending task. The mystery in question is infinite; our efforts to keep mindful of it are ever so finite.

Remembering the Church

We have been speaking of liturgical anamnesis or memorial as the ritual act of remembrance of God's great works of redemption. But there is another dimension of memorial that has become important in our day. The question is "how well have we remembered the community?" This is important because we believe that God is present in the lives of those who keep the Gospel. If we are looking for a "presencing of Christ" we need to extend our gaze and consider those persons and situations that do not usually come into our line of vision. The vision metaphor is quite appropriate. One of the characteristics of keeping memory is that the act is necessarily selective. We do not remember everything or everyone. We have blind spots in our vision, sometimes by choice, by habit, or by social location. In any case such selective memory keeping gives evidence of bias, either personal or group bias, and can be very destructive both for those overlooked and for those doing the memory keeping. Several examples will help to make the point. In the past we have tended to speak of the "Christian West" or even identified Europe with the church and the church with Europe. Such language makes the Jews and other minority groups invisible and unaccounted for in that history. Christians have tolerated having such a blind spot, while European Jewry has paid a terrible price for it. Similar examples could be taken from American history as well, such as when European monarchs "claimed" territories in the Americas without any effort to negotiate with the native peoples who already lived on this land. Once again, such bias decimated indigenous peoples as first European governments and then the U.S. government rode roughshod over their human and civil rights, reneging on treaty after treaty—if any had been made. While such bias has obvious ill effects on those marginalized or forgotten, the dominant community loses out as well. Its vision of reality is skewed and therefore its response to it is inadequate, and it misses out on the contributions and gifts of those marginalized. Christianity is less because of its bias; the United States is less because of its bias.

A group that has been on the margins of ecclesial life over two millennia is the women of the church, even though they make up more than half the population. While this is neither the time nor the place to do a thorough review of this history (such work has already been done), it is enough to mention that the church has been a patriarchal institution and has, like the society in which it lived, exhibited a strong bias against women. Once again some examples may enlighten those who are not familiar with the critique of the tradition. Women have been blamed unfairly for the persistence of evil and called the devil's gateway (Tertullian); women have been declared as not possessing the image of God in themselves (Augustine); women have been defined as defective (Aquinas); women have been unevenly and unfairly treated in canon and liturgical law; and women have remained outside decision-making structures of the church until very recently and now only in a limited way. In addition to the very negative perspective the church has had on women, what has been forgotten of women's lives and contributions is massive. Women have traditionally received less education than men; those who were educated found their work more keenly scrutinized or rejected or, more likely, forgotten. Volumes more could be said and I would refer the reader to many of the Christian and Catholic feminist authors who have been doing the critical, retrieval, and creative work since the 1970s.[28]

While much more could be said of the patriarchal bias of the tradition in areas of spirituality, systematic theology, ethics, and so on, I turn now to the presence (or absence) of women in the liturgical tradition. Here a word must be said regarding women and the Scriptures since this has direct effect on the liturgy. Significant work has been done both in critiquing the presentation of women in the Bible and in retrieving the contributions of women in the Hebrew and Christian Scriptures. The bibliography is too massive to include here, but reference should be made to the works of Phyllis Trible and Elisabeth Schüssler Fiorenza and the fulsome bibliographies available in their texts.[29] The result of the research is quite mixed. First, the absence of women in the biblical record is striking; second, the presentation of those women mentioned is often problematic. Women are mentioned sometimes in a positive framework, at other times quite negatively. Women are often referred to exclusively in relationship to men and often presented as a problem. Despite Jesus' claim that the woman who anointed him would be remembered, her name, like countless others, has been forgotten. The most serious critique of the biblical material is whether the Scriptures with their biased presentation of women constitute "good news" to the community—whether women or men.

This biblical work has direct impact on liturgical matters in that our lectionaries are selective collections of biblical texts. Is there an additional layer of bias involved in the selection process and interpretation of biblical texts in the Lectionary? As Elizabeth Smith notes, "groups doing feminist liberation theology approach lectionaries with a hermeneutics of suspicion, and experience the liturgical proclamation of Scripture as a mixed blessing."[30] A few examples will suffice to make the point. While the presence of women in the biblical texts is limited at best, the selective nature of lectionaries only exaggerates the problem. Three issues are at stake: are they included, how are they included, and where are they included—on Sundays or weekdays? Deborah; Tamar; Shiphrah and Puah; Rahab; Jael; Sapphira; Rhoda; Philip's prophetic daughters, Euodia and Syntayche; and Phoebe, to name a few, are never mentioned in the Lectionary. Eve is presented only as coming from Adam's rib or as sinning. Sarah is included in one Sunday reading and there she does not speak; she is only spoken about. Rachel, on her part, is never named and mentioned only in one weekday reading as a wife of Jacob. Mary appears frequently in the Lectionary, but even such an important text as the *Magnificat* appears only in a weekday reading. There is the additional problem of excising women from the stories. In some examples, such as the mother of the martyred sons in Maccabees, the mother is excluded from the reading, as is the prophetess Anna in the Lukan account of the presentation. In other places where the Lectionary allows a shorter reading to be done, the results often exclude the women, such as the woman with the hemorrhage and the woman who anointed Jesus at the beginning of the Passion text. A further problem is the cultural context within which lectionary readings are proclaimed. By that I mean that while a reading may appear harmless to those not being oppressed, it has a very different effect on those who are. Women being abused hear the message of women's submissiveness in Ephesians and 1 Timothy very differently from those not in this position. This is only a small insight into the problems of the Lectionary regarding women and their participation in the biblical witness.[31]

Another liturgical issue regarding the presence, absence, and interpretation of women is that of the Roman calendar of saints. Of the thirty-three doctors of the church, only three are women—St. Teresa of Avila, St. Catherine of Siena, and St. Thérèse of Lisieux, and these have been added only since 1970. In the Roman calendar there are one hundred forty-four male saints, while only twenty-eight female saints are included. In the U.S. calendar there are an additional ten men and seven women. The ranking of the feasts is also a problem. Women are included only as memorials or lower. In addition, forty-two male saints have proper readings compared with only eight women.

In order to address this lopsided view of the Hebrew and Christian traditions, much more biblical work needs to be done at the level of critique, while an imaginative reconstruction of the past would help to fill in the missing pieces of women's past participation in the biblical traditions. A retrieval of biblical women is not enough, however. Much historical work needs to be done to uncover the actual contributions of women to Jewish and Christian traditions. It simply is not true that men have been the normative Christians, the normative models of holiness, the normative models of ecclesial ministry. Historians have done significant work to bring to the forefront outstanding women of the tradition. The enormous popularity of Hildegard of Bingen is but one example of an outstanding woman of multiple talents finally coming into recognition by the community. Much more historical work also needs to be done to uncover the actual history of women specifically in Christian worship, although some of that history has come to light.[32]

While looking backward would do much to redress the missing history of women in the tradition, means need to be found to include this material in the present experience of communities. Since in the Roman Catholic tradition change happens slowly and liturgical books are revised only once every several hundred years, it is obvious that not only forms of remembrance are needed. Celebrations honoring the contributions of women in the tradition are needed; forums for disseminating the huge historical work that has been done are necessary; new rituals remembering and honoring women are needed. All these would serve not only women's groups but also the community at large. Women's gifts and contributions need to be honored in the present so that we do not find ourselves in a similar place a hundred years from now with a continued biased view of our history.

Patriarchy is a major blind spot in the Christian tradition. The church is not well served by a one-sided view of its membership. Inclusion of all members in processes of remembrance is a matter of justice for the whole community and is not to be dismissed as the concern of a few radical feminists. Opening up blind spots is inevitably painful for those at home with the status quo, but it is no excuse for a church that seeks the face of Christ in all its members. Those who have been overlooked, dismissed, or oppressed have already experienced too much pain at the hands of a church they love. The rest of the church community, on the other hand, has also suffered by the loss of so many gifts and lives left in the shadows.

Liturgical anamnesis is a moral issue. We are bound to remember the God who has created and redeemed us. We are held accountable for keeping fidelity to the covenants, old and new. We are responsible for remembering all that God has done for us, especially in Christ and in the power of the Spirit. We are likewise bound to remember the whole community with fairness and justice. Such a stand demands that we engage in a process of critique, retrieval, and reconstruction of the tradition to open up what has been lost or distorted and to set ourselves on a new path. We must have the courage to be critical of what has distorted the humanity of women and imaginative in ways that can restore such humanity.

Conclusions

From earliest times the church has celebrated the paschal mystery or the saving death-resurrection-glorification of Christ as its core belief. That is not to say that it has always interpreted the paschal mystery in the same way. At times the church emphasized the suffering aspect; at other times, the emphasis was on the passage of Christ to the kingdom. These differences had an impact on the church's choice of Christ's death date or his resurrection as the primary Christian festival. In time, both meanings became fused. The Pasch accounts only for the first half of the term, however; mystery accounts for the other. Above all the great *mysterion* is God's saving love for us made known especially in Christ and in the Spirit. The paschal mystery is what the sacraments celebrate; the paschal mystery is what we participate in when we celebrate the sacraments.

To speak of celebration is to speak of memorial and anamnesis. Like our Jewish forebears, the Christian community takes deliberate care to remember the great works of God in creation and redemption. We have come to speak about such remembering as efficacious. By remembering the paschal mystery, Christians are actually caught up into the saving acts of God. The liturgy of the church, from the sacraments to the liturgical year, is an efficacious way that the church keeps faithful memorial of God and enters into the salvation offered by God. To be the church is to be a community of remembrance.

I also noted that while anamnesis is a remembrance of God's work, it is also about remembering the church and all its members. I spoke about blind spots that we as a church have had over the course of our history. At times we have been blind to our Jewish sisters and brothers and to the indigenous peoples of the Americas, but we have also been blind to the members of our own community. In particular we spoke of the church's bias toward women and its forgetfulness of women and women's deeds. I drew attention to the absence of women in the liturgical tradition, particularly in the Lectionary and the liturgical year. Critique of the tradition is important, but so too are retrieval and reconstructive efforts to redress the imbalance in the treat of women and men. I have closed by suggesting that liturgical memorial is a moral issue. We are bound to keep memory of the God who created and redeemed us; we are bound to keep memorial of all those whose lives have mediated that saving presence.

CHAPTER FIVE

Naming Toward God

The Problem

The Jewish and Christian traditions, among others, believe in a living God who has manifested self in human history. Christians, in particular, express the specific belief that God is most clearly manifested in Jesus Christ, one who is fully human and fully divine. Divinity, our faith tradition believes, has "emptied self out" and has chosen to take on human form for our sake and the sake of our salvation. Further, the Spirit of God abides in the world and in us, closer to us than we are to ourselves. Whether Jews or Christians, we believe that we are bound to this God through covenanted love. Initiated by God, these covenants call the human community to respond in word and deed to divine mercy.

If we are able to use covenant language to speak of the divine/human relationship, we, Jewish or Christian, monotheistic or with trinitarian faith, are left with the dilemma of how to speak to this God and about this God. But what words are adequate and do not betray an all-too-human positing of divine mystery? Moses struggled with God because the people wanted to call God by a name. But naming is no easy business. Genesis speaks about the human act of naming in terms of having dominion over the plants and animals of the earth, and there is truth to this claim. Naming exerts control over the named. For humans to attempt to name God is to exhibit extraordinary arrogance in relationship to divine mystery and the creator of the universe. One solution to this dilemma is to ask what God wishes to be called. And so Moses did, only to be given a name that is no name: ʿehyeh ʿasher ʿehyeh, "I AM who I AM" (Exod 3:14).[1]

Perhaps understandably, Jewish and Christian communities have been unsatisfied with this answer and have tried again and again to name this holy mystery. Because we believe that God desires to be in dialogue with us, we are almost forced to address this God to the best of our ability, even while understanding that by doing so we exert no power over divine mystery. We also must admit that whatever names we do apply are feeble human attempts to speak about the unspeakable. The Holy One whose essence is beyond the limits of human conceptualization cannot be named as one object next to other objects, because God is the ground, the source, the origin, and term of all being. God cannot be named adequately by anything that arises in human, earthly, or cosmic experience. In actuality we can only name "toward God" with halting and stumbling efforts. Our language and our images bear the finitude of human existence, and holy mystery exceeds even our grandest ideas of goodness and love.

Yet, if our language is too limited to use for speaking of God, we seem to be relegated to silence. We would need to stop raising our voices in song and prayer in community or individually. Perhaps silence is the only appropriate response to ineffable mystery, but it is a response that is not to be reached too prematurely. I would argue that silence is the last response we should make after reaching the limits of our language and the limits of our search for the divine. Since this would seem to imply rarely, if ever, perhaps we should say that silence should punctuate our speech about God at key moments when we seem to have reached our limits. Silence should chasten us and be an ascetical practice, reminding us of our finitude in relation to holy mystery. But even silence has its limits, and after dwelling there for some time we are forced back to name the unnameable and find words and images for what calls our hearts beyond its limits. Speech about God is a legitimate, even necessary, human effort but one that stands in constant need of review lest we absolutize our names and images and fall into idolatry.

The task for this chapter is to explore some theological issues and methods of "naming toward" divine mystery and to look at some of the recent efforts to stretch our naming and imaging of God beyond the limits of the recent past. The theological foundation upon which all the following rests is that God is incomprehensible. Neither in this world nor in the next will we fully know the height and depth of divine mystery. A second principle is that naming toward God is a legitimate and necessary human enterprise but one that has absolute limits. Nothing we can say of divinity is sufficient and thus our naming is always provisional, indeed, can even be problematic.

While we have argued theologically that no name for God is ever adequate, pastorally we have fallen into the trap of absolutizing or at least privileging certain names and images for God. This has led us to slip from the understandable and legitimate effort to name what we know is nameless to a position of literalizing certain names: God is this and no other. Such practice needs constant review because it is theologically indefensible as far as God is concerned, and it has negative repercussions on human self-understanding and relationships. In Elizabeth Johnson's felicitous phrase, God-language "functions." "Neither abstract in content nor neutral in its effect, speaking about God sums up, unifies, and expresses a faith community's sense of ultimate mystery, the world view and expectation of order devolving from this, and the concomitant orientation of human life and devotion."[2] Speaking more explicitly of the implications of misnaming God, liberation theologian Juan Luis Segundo suggests that "by deforming God we protect our own egotism." Going further, he says, "Our falsified and inauthentic ways of dealing with our fellow [human beings] are allied to our falsifications of the idea of God. Our unjust society and our perverted idea of God are in close and terrible alliance."[3]

Using an example from the U.S. church with its mobility and its constantly changing demographics, what do African American communities do when they begin using church buildings originally built and decorated by white Christians of European descent and find church murals or statuary depicting a God very much in the image of a white European male? With the history of slavery and white racism in this country, what can such imaging reveal about the nature of God for this community? What does it say about the privileging of a certain race? Does not such imaging of God reinforce white privilege and subordinate all others? A second example is like the first. In light of the gender bias that also marks our culture and the violence that is disproportionately visited upon women, what do the women of our church do when the God-language in worship and theology is almost exclusively masculine? Again, what does it say about the nature of God and the ordering of the human community? Does not such imaging privilege the male and subordinate the female? These are only two examples of the disconnect communities find with the culturally limited naming and imaging of divine mystery. Such culturally bound imaging is understandable, perhaps even necessary, but never adequate to encompass and reveal the God who will not be so limited. Every community and every segment of the community has the right to offer its own efforts of naming toward God as long as they all acknowledge the limits of such naming for God's sake and the sake of human flourishing. When we realize our God-language on the one hand duplicates distorted human relationship and, on the other, is used to justify such, we are obligated to step back and try once again to speak of God more adequately.

Theological Issues of Naming Toward God

Starting with the Human

One of the results of the "anthropocentric turn" of the mid-twentieth century in theology is that we realized that we can and ought to begin with known human experience and extrapolate out toward what is unknown. Writers like Karl Rahner and Edward Schillebeeckx, among others, argued that there is an inherent drive within humanity toward self-transcendence. The human person by nature strives to reach beyond the limits of human experience to the unknown limits of the infinite. Rahner named this drive toward the infinite the "supernatural existential" and the infinite toward which we long, the "whither of our self-transcendence"—in a more prosaic term, "God." This is another way of saying that the infinite is a dimension of human being. We have, as it were, been gifted with divine life that makes us stretch out to our own infinite future and, to the divine, which is our source and end.

The implications of this are many. One of them is that the human person has a capacity for seeking the truth and knowing the truth. Related to our topic of naming toward God, we can say that part of our effort to name God is to seek the truth of God's being and God's relationship with us. There is, then, an imperative to use our intellect and imaginations, indeed all our capacities, to learn as much as we can of God before being content to rest in silence in the face of divine mystery. A second implication follows this first imperative: it is legitimate—even necessary—to speak the truth as we have come to know it. The question remains then of the relationship between what I know of divine mystery and what I can speak.

Discourse about Divine Mystery

What we have moved into here is an exploration of our knowledge of God. Our experience of divine mystery is a gift; it is "given" to us. It is given first in our creation as finite beings with an infinite horizon that we call God. Part of our experience of faith is to accept this orientation and with it the relationship with the ground and end of our being. There is a sense in which this realization of who we are and with whom we relate is a revelation of God who comes to us as gift but remains mystery and beyond our grasp or control. As Rahner says,

> The concept "God" is not a grasp of God by which a person masters the mystery, but it is letting oneself be grasped by the mystery which is present and yet ever distant. This mystery remains a mystery even though it reveals itself to man and thus continually grounds the possibility of man being a subject.[4]

Traditionally, we have spoken of a kind of natural revelation of God made known to us through our ability to reason. We have also spoken about the revelation of God through God's own self- communication, or the self-revelation known to us through salvation history.[5] All this revelation gives to us a certain knowledge of God who is paradoxically beyond all knowing, but it is not knowledge that controls or dominates the known. In other words, according to Rahner, human "subjectivity is always a transcendence which listens, which does not control, which is overwhelmed by mystery and opened up by mystery."[6]

Because we are oriented toward God by nature, we can say that there is an original experience of God before there is any effort to discourse about that experience, although we naturally want to bring our experience to reflection. It is a fact of human existence that speech and our experiences do not coincide. Our words, images, and symbols can lay claim to being truthful, but they cannot claim to express the fullness of our experiences. If this is the case with even the most basic human experiences of creaturely life, how much more so is our experience of divine mystery? We need always remember that our primary experience of the ground of our being and the term of our existence is not to be fully identified with our discourse about it. This is true whether we are talking about the reflection that is theology or the reflection that is prayer as articulated in our liturgical forms. We may begin with human experience and acknowledge that our experience of God is true, but the divine exceeds every human attempt to know it fully or to speak about it adequately.

Whenever we speak of God, from our experience of our own transcendence or from explicit revelation in salvation history, our speaking of God is always an exceptional use of what we normally refer to as naming. God is always out of our control, and even our best efforts to speak of our knowledge of God are limited by the finitude of our language and limits of our ability to reflect about this most basic experience of absolute transcendence. Theologically we can say that this transcendence for which we are constantly seeking a name is always present as nameless and indefinable, for to give something a name is to define it within the limited categories of creation. The infinite horizon that holds everything that is in being, itself cannot be given a name because we never want to objectify divinity. We never want to reduce it to less than the absolute that is its essential nature. Even calling God a "being" poses a danger of limiting the ground of all "being" to one "being" among many others, even if we insist that God is the greatest of all beings.

And so the struggle of how to speak of the unspeakable continues. The alert reader will have noticed that even when arguing against the adequacy of divine naming, I have continued to use the appellation "God." Is this justifiable and what do we mean when we say the term?

Rahner provides some important insights regarding how we humans can speak of absolute mystery.[7] He begins first by asking what we mean by the term *God* itself. God is not a name per se, he suggests, but a reference to "the 'ineffable one,' the 'nameless one' who does not enter into the world we can name as a part of it."[8] Rather, as Rahner says, "it is the final word before we become silent, the word which allows all the individual things we can name to disappear into the background, the word in which we are dealing with the totality which grounds them all."[9] God is not an object among other objects, even the most exalted, but the ground and foundation of them all. Before God we must fall silent lest we reduce God to another creature like something of this world. God is a word that brings the human person face-to-face with the whole of reality and with the source and term of our own existence. Rahner repeats again and again that God is the ground of all reality, including language. What we designate when we use the word *God* is not just any word, "but is the word in which language, that is, the self-expression of the self-presence of world and human existence together, grasps itself in its ground."[10] While Rahner's philosophical language may be difficult to grasp, his theological point is clear: that which we call *God* is not contained, limited, or described by the term *God*. The word *God* does not function as a name, but it is the last thing we can speak prior to our resting in silence before the darkness of holy mystery.

At the same time, however, the continued use of the word *God* does cause significant concern because it has not been used as neutrally as Rahner would have us think. While some progress has been made in shifting away from exclusively masculine language for the divine by replacing masculine terms with the seemingly more generic *God*, we have still neither completely removed the gendered connotations of the term nor come up with another word to replace it. As Johnson has demonstrated, the term has been so affected by a male-gendered understanding of the divine that it is almost impossible to say it or write it without implying a male image.[11] Rosemary Radford Ruether has suggested for the written word using the term "God/ess." For her, it combines both masculine and feminine images while preserving the Judeo-Christian affirmation that divinity is one. However, since it is unpronounceable it cannot assist us in liturgical speech. As she says, "It serves here as an analytic sign to point toward that yet unnamable understanding of the divine that would transcend patriarchal limitations and signal redemptive experience for women as well as men."[12] I applaud her creative efforts and agree with her project, but my concern is with language that we can use in worship that must be spoken. While waiting for more adequate speech, I have chosen to continue to use the term *God* in these pages to designate the divine, but not in the sense that it functions as a name for the divine.

While the term *God* may serve as a suitable reference word for divine mystery, it is not very disclosive of the truth of this mystery nor does it serve well in our praise and worship. Therefore, before we rest in silence, we have the right and even the duty of "naming toward God" rather than naming God per se. As I have argued above, it is part of human nature to reach out toward the ineffable, and it is part of biblical faith to speak of the disclosure of God. However, I want us to recall at all times the limits of our language in speaking of holy mystery. I want us to recall that even our best efforts of reflection upon the revelation of the holy One remain tentative at best. As Aquinas says, "all affirmations we can make about God are not such that our minds may rest in them, nor of such sort that we may suppose God does not transcend them."[13] However, if we are not to remain in silence, we must conclude that there is some truth to be found in our naming toward God. Even if our naming touches only the surface of what we understand by our use of the term *God*, our belief in the self-revelation of God experienced both through personal transcendence and in salvation history suggests that something true can be said of this God, even if it is not the whole truth. Thus we are left with a tradition of naming toward God in our Scriptures, in our prayer, and in our theological reflection. It remains our task now to speak of some of the ways we have used language to name toward God.

NAMING BY ANALOGY

> Joyful is the dark,
> holy, hidden God,
> rolling cloud of night beyond all naming,
> Majesty in darkness,
> Energy of love,
> Word-in-flesh, the mystery proclaiming.[14]

Classical Christianity has long dealt with the dilemma of how to name the "unnameable One." It has made use of the very helpful category of analogy to prevent speech about God from slipping into the identification of its speech with God. Analogy, simply put, is the setting up of a relationship of likeness and difference.[15] David Tracy speaks of analogy as "a language of ordered relationships articulating similarity-in-difference."[16] In other words, working from our human experience, we use a term that is true of us and, in this case, apply it to God noting that the difference between God and ourselves is as least as significant as is the likeness. The dynamic of analogy is that of affirmation, negation, and then eminence. We affirm that God is good, for example, but not in the same way that creatures are good. Finally, we say that God is eminently good beyond all human conception. As Elizabeth Johnson describes the use of analogy in early Christian thought, she says, "A word whose meaning is known and prized from human experience is first affirmed of God. The same word is then critically negated to remove any association with creaturely modes of being. Finally, the word is predicated of God in a supereminent way that transcends all cognitive capabilities."[17] Thus there is a twofold negation. First there is a negation of the positive attribute, and then a negation of the negation by claiming the preeminence of God beyond all created being. The ultimate aim, as we described above, is to speak truthfully of God while maintaining God's incomprehensibility. What is implied here is that there is a relationship between God and humanity that is marked by a sharing of God's own nature with us while maintaining the absoluteness of God. This means that by reflecting upon human experience, we can know something of the divine in whose image we are made. This assures us that there is some element of truth in the analogical naming of God. We can use such terms as good, loving, and wise (or as our hymn quoted above suggests, joyful, holy and majestic) for God, but not in the way humans are good, loving, and wise (joyful, holy, and majestic); God is eminently good, loving, and wise (joyful, holy, and majestic) beyond anything we can imagine from human experience.

Whatever we can know of God's disclosure, even by way of analogy, there is infinitely more that escapes us. Borrowing from David Tracy, there is in our naming God a "similarity-in-difference, the negation of any univocity, the manifestation in the event of sheer giftedness, the concealment in every disclosure, the absence in every presence, the incomprehensibility in every moment of genuine comprehensibility, the radical mystery empowering all intelligibility."[18] It is this tension of presence/absence, disclosure/hiddenness that we must keep in mind in all naming of God, lest our naming become idolatry. History has shown how easy it is to create idols of the living God, projecting our own biases upon divine mystery. We have also fought against tendency. Late Judaism was hesitant to name God because of the fear of making God into its own image. Johnson speaks of their hesitancy to name the living God as "reverential abstinence." It does not indicate, she says, a divine aloofness, but that "at the end of the process the mystery of the living God is evoked while the human thinker ends up, intellectually and existentially, in religious awe and adoration."[19] Christianity needs to keep this dynamic in mind as well. Whether giving God names by the use of analogy or in abstaining from naming God, we want to end up raising our voices in prayer and praise of holy mystery, knowing that regardless of what we choose to say or not say, the divine far exceeds our grasp.

NAMING BY NEGATION

> Ascending higher we say:
> It [the Godhead] is
> Not soul, not intellect,
> Not imagination, opinion, reason and
>   not understanding,
> not logos, not intellection,
> not spoken, not thought, . . .
> not being,
> not eternity, not time, . . .
> not spirit (as we know spirit) . . .
> It is not dark nor light,
> Not error, and not truth.[20]

Related to the negation of analogy, the Christian community has chosen to speak of God by saying what God is not in order to maintain God's incomprehensibility. Theologians of no less stature than Aquinas have reminded us that "now we cannot know what God is, but only what God is not; we must therefore consider the ways in which God does not exist, rather than the ways in which God does."[21] The quote used at the head of this section is from the sixth-century mystic writer Pseudo-Dionysius and represents the so-called apophatic tradition. This tradition more consciously reminds us of the limits of our knowledge and the limits of our language when speaking of divine mystery. The liturgical tradition has made use of this technique more so in the East than in the West. In the early Egyptian anaphora (eucharistic prayer) of Bishop Sarapion of Thmuis, we find God addressed as "uncreated God, unsearchable, ineffable, incomprehensible by all created being."[22] The Orthodox Liturgy of St. John Chrysostom likewise uses similar appellations for God: "For you are God, ineffable, inconceivable, invisible, incomprehensible, existing always and in the same way."[23] What is interesting, of course, is that even when using these negative images for God, one image is not sufficient. An abundance of names is necessary to more adequately speak of God even when one is describing what God is not. We will speak more of this tendency to multiply names for God below.

NAMING BY METAPHOR

> So I will become like a lion to them,
>   like a leopard I will lurk beside the way.
> I will fall upon them like a bear
>   robbed of her cubs,
> and will tear open the
>   covering of their heart;
> there I will devour them like a lion,
>   as a wild animal would mangle them. (Hos 13:7-8)

Not unlike analogy, metaphoric speech seeks to bring insight by pairing dissimilar things.

God and lion are clearly not related, yet by their pairing of similarity in difference, new insight is brought both to God and to lion. If analogy works by affirmation, negation, and eminence, metaphor works by holding is/is not in creative tension; affirmation and negation yield new understanding. Metaphor creates a shock by this pairing of the is/is not, and the shock is felt most clearly when the pairing is first made. It follows, then, that metaphors can die; they can lose their disclosive potential when they become worn out by constant use. We have said earlier that continued naming of God is required because of God's own essence and because of the continuing effort of humanity to reach beyond its own limits; now we must suggest that the creation of new metaphors is also required by the nature of metaphoric speech.

Lutheran liturgical theologian Gail Ramshaw speaks of metaphor as a mind-expanding experience; the new is imagined and the old renovated. "Metaphor," she says, "does not label: it connects in a revolutionary way . . . metaphor forms a comparison where none previously existed. Metaphor alters perception by superimposing disparate images."[24] Thus metaphoric speech is particularly apt to speak of the divine. By definition metaphor reaches out beyond conventional understandings and limits. It forces the hearer to constantly reassess previous understandings and move forward with new insights that will color the future—until the next metaphor breaks through even these.

Our ancestors in the faith have long recognized the power and suitability of metaphoric speech for the divine, and thus our Scriptures are filled with metaphors. They are drawn from the world around us and from human experience. God's voice is like thunder or a mighty torrent, God's spirit is like the wind, and God's justice and wisdom are like the deep ocean and an irrigating river.[25] God is a rock, a spring, a fortress, a shield. Like the Hosea passage quoted above, God is panther, leopard, and she-bear, at other times a raging lion or a soaring eagle. Using anthropomorphic images, God has a voice, a strong and outstretched arm, a heart, a palm upon which our names are written, a face and eyes, bosom and bowels. Human trades and roles are also fertile images for divinity. God is shepherd, hero, potter, builder, warrior, midwife, woman in labor, king, husband, and father. Clearly, holy mystery is none of these, yet by their juxtaposition we learn something true of divine mystery. The challenge of all metaphoric speech is to refuse to literalize these images, to be willing to allow dead metaphors to fade away even as the poets among us find new and provocative ones that open our imaginations again and again.

Clearly, the tradition has both privileged and literalized certain metaphors for God. It is no surprise that the biblical texts, coming as they do out of a patriarchal culture, have favored masculine, majestic names for God. God stands as Father, Lord of the universe, king, enthroned in glory, ruler of the earth and its inhabitants. These favored images have made other equally tensive images invisible and so less able to test the prevailing notions of divinity that all speech about God must do. Thanks to the scholarship of the last decades, less common biblical images for the divine are coming to light and are providing rich counterpoint to these patriarchal images. God as wisdom has become far more prominent, as have other feminine images for God: lover, friend, woman with a womb, woman giving birth, a hen gathering her brood, a she-bear fighting for her offspring. God can be referred to equally as mother or father, as she or he. The strong reaction of many people, positive or negative, to female imaging of God gives testimony to the shock of new metaphors. Rather than being dismayed by these reactions, we should be grateful that metaphoric speech is doing its job, startling our consciousness and bringing fresh insight to light.

As we said earlier, God-language functions; that is, it serves both to reveal and to sustain the worldview and values of the authors. Even when such language appears in the Scriptures, we have been careful to note that it speaks truthfully of God only when it is salvific for the community.[26] While slavery remained an acceptable form of life (as it is in both Hebrew and Christian Scriptures and in the Christian tradition up to the nineteenth century), we felt free to rationalize it from the biblical text. However, once our understanding of the dignity of all persons led us to conclude that all forms of slavery are abhorrently evil, we set aside those texts as a rule for life and as disclosive of God's desire for the human community. We are coming to the same conclusion regarding the patriarchal texts of Scripture and tradition that diminish, subordinate, treat as temptation or as evil, or relegate to the margins of society (and the church) women who are equally made in the image of God. This includes not just readings about women but readings about God that posit the divine as more appropriately masculine than feminine and thus uphold a patriarchal ordering of society. Neither feminine nor masculine language for the divine is to be absolutized or literalized. All speech of God is metaphoric or analogical; that is, the difference between God and us is truer than any perceived similarities. On the other hand, both feminine and masculine speech about God can be liberating in that each allows either women or men to see themselves as made in the image and likeness of God, and as equally capable of symbolizing holy mystery.

The Christian theological tradition has suffered the same fate as our biblical tradition in absolutizing select names for God. While arguing that all God-language ultimately fails to speak adequately of God, even our most esteemed theologians have fallen prey to absolutizing male images for God. Augustine writes explicitly of the poverty of our God-talk, yet he inevitably ends with male pronouns for the divine that he uses uncritically.

> Have I spoken of God, or uttered His praise, in any worthy way? Nay, I feel that I have done nothing more than desire to speak; and if I have said anything, it is not what I desired to say. How do I know this, except from the fact that God is unspeakable? But what I have said, if it had been unspeakable, could not have been spoken. And so God is not even to be called "unspeakable," because to say even this is to speak of Him.[27]

Our mystical tradition fares not much better, even when it urges one to silence. Meister Eckhart, speaking of divine naming says, "Now pay attention: God is nameless, because no one can say anything or understand anything about him. . . . So be silent, and do not chatter about God; for when you do chatter about him, you are telling lies and sinning."[28] Even as we become tongue-tied in naming toward the incomprehensible God, we find that we can do so only provisionally and with well-thought-out methods that insist upon the inadequacy of our God-talk.

Christianity must shoulder its blame for a patriarchal worldview that marginalizes and subordinates women, that grants them less dignity and esteem than their male counterparts. Christianity can likewise be responsible for the creation of an alternative world where the equal flourishing of women is regarded as God's desire "for us and for our salvation." God-language plays a part in this movement toward liberation, so we all have a vested interest in our God-talk. Whether we are personally interested in overcoming racism, sexism, or any other "ism," we need to realize that our God-talk makes its own contribution to creating a world with just patterns of relationships. The contribution of current theological reflection on naming God is a reminder that there is an ethical imperative in our naming God; it matters deeply how we name the living God. This leads us to the fourth technique we use in daring to speak of the unnameable.

NAMING BY ABUNDANCE

> O eternal Father! O fiery abyss of charity! O eternal beauty, O eternal wisdom, O eternal goodness, O eternal mercy! O hope and refuge of sinners! O immeasurable generosity! O eternal, infinite Good! O mad lover! . . . And what shall I say? I will stutter, "A-a," because there is nothing else I know how to say.[29]

What Catherine of Siena has done is to use both analogical and metaphoric speech in her effort to speak of one of her visions. But she has done more; she has stacked up name after name lest anyone be deceived into thinking than any one of the names reveals adequately the holy mystery she has experienced. It appears as if two or three names are not sufficient to be persuasive. Rather, superabundance is needed so that the imagination literally overflows with images. Writing of this theological technique of "bringing many names," Johnson says,

> None alone or even all taken together can exhaust the reality of divine mystery. Each symbol has a unique intelligibility that adds its own significance to the small store of collected human wisdom about the divine. In addition, as a concrete term balances an abstract one, and so forth, each operates as a corrective to any other that would pretend to completeness.[30]

The key here is that the variety of naming acts as a corrective to the dominance of one, whatever that may be.

Some of my readers must be wondering whether there are privileged names for God from the Christian Scriptures that are more suitable than others, for example, Jesus' use of the Aramaic word ʿabbâ. One needs to be cautious here on several accounts. First, Jesus himself must be acknowledged as continuing the tradition of asceticism in his God-talk, and he has not literalized (and therefore we should not literalize) what should be properly metaphoric or analogical language for the divine. To the contrary, the evidence from the gospels displays a rich pattern of God-talk by Jesus. He used an abundance of metaphors to speak of God and God's reign. God is like a woman who lost a coin and swept the whole house until she found it. God is like a good shepherd who searches for the lost. God is like yeast a bakerwoman mixes into the whole amount of dough. God is like an overgenerous employer. God's reign is like a kingdom where the first shall be last and the last first. It is like a net cast far and wide, a sheepfold, a banquet. Rather than absolutizing a single image, Jesus multiplies images so his hearers can catch a whiff of the new order of existence desired by God. True, as all scholars admit, Jesus does call God by the Aramaic term ʿabbâ, but there is much discussion regarding the centrality or the privileging of this name. Scholars like Joachim Jeremias writing in the 1960s emphasized Jesus' use of *abba*, but since then other scholars have challenged his insistence on the priority of this name.[31] As Johnson has shown, the data shows there is an increasing frequency of the use of *Father* in the gospels, starting with the earliest Gospel of Mark (4), then Luke (15), then Matthew (49), and finally in

John (109); but as James Dunn notes, these statements indicate "straight-forward evidence of a burgeoning tradition, of a manner of speaking about Jesus and his relation with God which became very popular in the last decades of the first century."[32] In other words, it was not Jesus who used this title so frequently but the early church. Aside from the sheer number of times Jesus used *abba*, two other issues need to be taken into account.

The first is how Jesus used the term *abba*. We must acknowledge that Jesus used this endearing term for God in stark contrast to the dominating, patriarchal reading of the term *Father*. Jesus' God was a compassionate figure who sided with the oppressed and understood leadership as a service. Even if one grants any privilege to the term *Father*, it cannot be used to support the domination of men over women in any form. Still less does it eliminate the church's ongoing need to find more adequate language for divine mystery. As the New Testament church continued searching for appropriate nomenclature for the divine, so the contemporary church also needs to engage in this reaching out toward divine mystery.

A second issue that should give us pause in privileging the term *abba* is the naming of God in the Fourth Gospel. In John's gospel we see a preference for the kind of naming that has a priority in the Hebrew Scriptures, namely, the I AM statements of Jesus. In other words, the self-naming of God in Exodus 3:14 (a name that is no name) is the same kind of naming Jesus uses for himself: I AM the bread of life, the light of the world, the resurrection and the life. Once again we have a chastened naming of God, a God who will not be limited by any human naming.

Liturgical Naming of God

Theologians may endlessly debate the proper way of speaking about and to God; however, those who serve as liturgical leaders, music ministers, and assemblies need to raise their voices in prayer and praise now—at this Wednesday night's prayer group or this Sunday's Eucharist. While theologians have an important role to play in the church, it is a fact that there are more people who go to worship than there are people who read theology. Even for those who do keep up with theological discourse, there is a decided difference between ruminating in private over appropriate language for God and actually bringing those words to speech in song or prayer. It is in worship that images, metaphors, and analogies take flight. God-talk ceases to be an interesting theological discussion; it is proclaimed as the faith of the church. What we have said in earlier chapters comes to bear on the situation here. Liturgy is expressive of the ecclesial community, and liturgy is formative of the community. As Suzanne Langer reminded us, in liturgy we "rehearse right attitudes." We repeat week in and week out our understanding of God and of the world. We repeat words placed in our mouths by our liturgical books until those words become our words, our praise. There is a personal investment in liturgical participation; we rehearse what we shall become and believe.

Our liturgical God-talk must be taken seriously because, as we have said earlier, God-talk aims at the truth of God, and it functions in human communities. It sets up our sense of holy mystery and the worldview and social ordering that devolve from this. Privileging certain images and metaphors privileges those who most nearly resemble those images. I began this chapter by speaking of the difficulties of white racial depictions of God and male-gendered language for God. I hope that it is clear by now that no matter what language or images we use, divinity far exceeds any of them. However, it is also clear that certain images have had the upper hand. God has been almost exclusively named in our official liturgical prayer in the image of the powerful male ruler—King, Lord, and Father. Speaking concretely, the opening prayer of the Eucharist, also known as the principal collect of the Mass, addresses the First Person of the Trinity approximately 730 times throughout the liturgical year and in various ritual Masses. In a review of the English translation of those terms, I found that 58 percent are addressed to Father, 25 percent to Lord, and 15 percent to God, with various adjectives such as ever living, merciful, all-powerful, etc.[33] Despite the claims the church has always made that God is beyond gender, it leaves the community listening to God imaged as male 83 percent of the time. Not a single appellation in anything close to female imagery is used. It is difficult to argue for the metaphoric nature of male God-talk when the same privilege is not granted to female God-talk. Neither male nor female images are to be literalized, but both may be used analogically or metaphorically. The resistance to female naming of God suggests that, indeed, male God-talk has been literalized. In addition, the variety of God-language necessary to keep us from absolutizing any single image, male or female, is very limited in our liturgical books.

Three things should be abundantly clear at this point. First, it is not surprising that the image makers have used themselves as the models, since, as I have argued, everyone and every culture may name God out of their own experience. Second, this androcentric naming has privileged those in whom those images were made. Third, such privileging cannot go on without further detriment to those left out of the imaging process. We are at the point when new images are required for truthfulness in naming toward God and for the flourishing of all members of the human community. As postmodern thinkers such as Emmanuel Levinas, Jacques Derrida, and Jean-Luc Marion have reminded us, "the problem of naming the unnameable God is necessarily linked to how we relate to fellow human beings, to the hungry in Levinas, justice in Derrida, and charity in Marion."[34]

Roman Catholic worship is shaped predominantly through officially approved liturgical Orders, be they for marriage, funerals, baptisms, or Eucharist. This means that our weekly and occasional services are not that malleable since liturgical leaders are expected to use most prayers as written. As I indicated above regarding the Eucharist, the vast majority of God-talk is male. Until such official Orders are modified to be inclusive of a richer palette of God-talk, we will have to depend on the soft parts of official liturgies and on newly created liturgical forms to include these changes.

By the "soft parts" of official liturgies I mean those places where the text says, "in these or similar words,"[35] in the homily, or in the music that is used. The first two situations call upon the creativity of the presiding celebrants, be they ordained or lay, and the last on creative composers and lyricists. Before creativity becomes an issue, however, these individuals need to undergo a conversion of mind and heart. They need to be convinced that inclusive, far-ranging, multiple images for God are necessary for truthfulness as far as God is concerned, on the one hand, and for human flourishing, on the other. This is where the work of theologians can be exceedingly helpful. Conversion, as Bernard Lonergan reminds us, takes place on multiple levels. Theological reflection helps prepare the ground for intellectual and religious conversion. Truly listening to those marginalized and negatively affected by current practice also plays a part in the impetus for change. As hymn writer Brian Wren says, "Reason cannot *rule* intuition, nor can clear ideas command the appearance of suitable metaphors. Yet analysis . . . often sets the poetic imagination in motion. Metaphors and phrases sometimes appear unbidden, but still have to be sifted, analyzed, and set in order."[36]

I have turned to hymnody as a particularly fertile place to look for more abundance and variety in God-talk because our hymn/lyric writers are the poets of our time, and they are making the most obvious contribution to new God-language in worship today. They are using all the techniques outlined above but are shaping them with a creativity that only the artists among us can truly do. We need to be extremely grateful to these poets for their contribution to our imaginations and to the ethical implications of such language use.

Not unlike the theologians and mystics we quoted above, many lyricists use multiple images of God that are metaphoric, analogical, or negative images for God. Seeking to expand our vocabulary, they mount image upon image, sometimes using familiar images and adding new and provocative images. Vince Ambrosetti, in his *Blest Are We*, refers to God as "light of the world, fire of love," and also as "Wisdom of God, Spirit of truth," all familiar images to us; but to these he adds, "flame never ending" and "fountain of newness."[37] Delores Dufner, in her *Pulsing Spirit*, clearly has the multiple naming of God as her central theme.

> Verse 1
> Pulsing Spirit, rippling river,
> Source of mercy's tender might,
> Gentle power, humble glory,
> Subtle, ever dancing light:
>
> Verse 2
> Spirit free, unbounded motion,
> Beauty's mirror, hearts delight,
> Gift abundant all around us,
> Flood the world with life and light.[38]

Brian Wren even writes into his lyrics the need to bring many names for God, but working off of such biblical texts as Isaiah 42:14-16, he also employs feminine imagery for the divine.

> God of many Names
> gathered into One,
> in your glory come and meet us,
> Moving, endlessly Becoming
> God of Hovering Wings,
> Womb and Birth of time,
> joyfully we sing your praises,
> Breath of life in every people.[39]

He also has tried to be explicit about naming the unnameable as he shows in his hymn *Name Unnamed*. Here he combines negative naming of God, metaphor, and multiple imaging of the divine.

> Name Unnamed, hidden and shown, knowing and known: Gloria!
>> Beautiful Movement,
>>> Ceaselessly forming,
>>> Growing, emerging with awesome delight . . .
>> Spinner of Chaos . . .
>> Weaver of Stories . . .
>> Nudging Discomforter . . .
>> Straight-talking Lover . . .
>> Midwife of Changes . . .
>> Mother of Wisdom . . .
>> Dare-devil Gambler . . .
>> Life-giving Loser . . .[40]

I could multiply examples, but these are enough to show the creative work that is going on at the moment by those taking seriously the ethical imperatives for truthfulness in God-talk.

Conclusions

In summary we can say that significant work has been done at the theological level and at the poetic level of naming toward God. We have shown that the tradition has been clear that God has no gender, that no single name or even multiple names for God are ever enough to name holy mystery. All naming is metaphoric or analogical, whether in theological reflection, prayer texts, or hymn texts. I have argued that human naming toward God is a permissible—even necessary—human effort based on the human capacity for transcendence. I have likewise argued that such God-talk can truthfully describe God but not in a way that ever eliminates God's utter incomprehensibility. Further, I have argued that God-language functions in human self-understanding and in the ordering of society; there are ethical implications in naming toward God. Finally, I have argued that while our official liturgical texts have limited images for God, even privileging male metaphors, current work in hymnody has deliberately taken the theological imperative for truthfulness in God-talk to the poetic level. Hymn writers are expanding our consciousness of the mystery of God and are doing so, not in the pages of theological journals, but in the assembly of believers.

CHAPTER SIX

Liturgy and Time

Time may be conceived as either cyclical or linear. Those who ascribe to a cyclical view of time conceive of it as a yearly cycle of new beginnings. For traditional societies the ingathering of crops often served as a suitable time for festival and rite. It was an opportunity for the community to repeat the myths and rituals of foundational events and thereby to renew itself and to set out once again on a new cycle of life and hope. In the contemporary West, whether or not agrarian, we continue to see remnants of this yearly cycle of new beginnings in our New Year's celebration when we make new resolutions for the upcoming year.

For biblical religion, however, time may also be conceived in a more linear perspective. Borrowing from agrarian and nomadic societies, Judaism took these cyclical feasts and connected them to historical saving events, events when YHWH intervened on their behalf. Speaking of this new concept of time, Mircea Eliade says,

> For the first time, we find affirmed, and increasingly accepted, the idea that historical events have a value in themselves, insofar as they are determined by the will of God. This God of the Jewish people is no longer an Oriental divinity, creator of archetypal gestures, but a personality who ceaselessly intervenes in history, who reveals his will through events.[1]

The Exodus was clearly such an event when YHWH led the people out of slavery in Egypt and into the Promised Land. This event was closely tied to their identity as a people, and so their yearly celebration of God's saving deed established them once more as a chosen people. Judaism's yearly festivals were also opportunities for the people to repent of having broken their covenant contract, or to renew that covenant. For Judaism, time had both a linear and a cyclical character. History became a way of salvation for this people, and they celebrated year after year those times when Yʜᴡʜ acted on their behalf.

It is important to note that Judaism's feasts were not about repeating the past; these historical events could not be repeated—only remembered. But the significance of the event could be re-presented in such a way as to allow the contemporary community to enter the saving event. Each year at Passover, Jews are reminded to celebrate the Passover, not as something that happened only to their ancestors, but as if they themselves were being freed from Egypt. It is also important to note that this linear sense of time not only presented past and present but also included hope for the future. The salvation celebrated in yearly, weekly, or daily rite was also a way of anticipating the future, the time of ultimate salvation.

Christianity became heir to this combination of cyclical and linear time. Continuing as a covenanted people, Christians began to celebrate in prayer and ritual daily, weekly, and yearly the new salvific events of God as made known through Jesus Christ. As in Judaism, Christian festival actualizes in the present the saving events of the past in such a way as the participants take part in the significance of those events. Again as in Judaism, the future is also celebrated in that the salvation earned for us in Christ Jesus awaits the end time when all will be brought to fullness. There is a sense that Christians are situated between the two comings of Christ: his first coming in history and his second coming in glory at the end of time. Between these two comings, Christians gather daily, weekly, and yearly to celebrate and remember the past saving events of the Cross and Resurrection and await in hope the final coming of Christ in glory. As with Judaism, we do not repeat these events but remember them or anticipate them through means of liturgical anamnesis as we described above. As Kevin Irwin says, "We do not redo Christ's paschal mystery; rather, through the liturgy, we continually share in his paschal triumph and joy."[2] It is the present encounter through liturgical celebration that is the point of Christian liturgy. Robert Taft says it best:

> The reality [liturgy] initiates and signifies, however, is neither past nor contingent but ever present in God, and through faith to us, at every moment of our lives. And if the past event is both permanent cause and contingent historical sign of salvation, the

ritual memorial is the present efficacious sign of the same eternal reality. The ritual moment, then, is a synthesis of past, present, and future, as is always true in "God's time."[3]

Based upon a biblical sense of time that is both linear and cyclical, the liturgy is the repeatable opportunity for believers to enter into the once-and-for-all event of Christ's saving victory over sin and death. Like our fellow Jews, we celebrate daily, weekly, and yearly the saving events of our faith.

The Daily Cycle of Prayer

To the best of our knowledge, at the time of Jesus there were patterns of daily prayer for observant Jews. The first was the pattern based on the daily natural rhythms of morning and nightfall. Deuteronomy states that "when you lie down and when you rise" you are to recite the Shema: "'Hear, O Israel: The LORD is our God, the LORD alone. You shall love the LORD your God with all your heart, and with all your soul, and with all your might'" (Deut 6:4-7). There was a second pattern that was attested to in Daniel of the third century BCE (Dan 6:11) and in the book of Judith (Judith 9:1; 12:5-6; 13:3). That was the practice of praying three times a day, evening, morning, and at noon.

The daily offerings of the Jerusalem Temple were another factor that influenced the daily prayer of Jews. Temple sacrifice was twice a day: once in the morning and once in the evening, although the evening sacrifice was moved up to the ninth hour (3 p.m.). The New Testament gives witness to the practice in Luke 1:10-21: "Now at the time of the incense offering, the whole assembly of the people was praying outside" while Zechariah was offering sacrifice in the Temple precincts; and in Acts 3:1: "One day Peter and John were going up to the temple at the hour of prayer, at three o'clock in the afternoon." For those not within the Temple grounds or outside Jerusalem proper, prayer was at the same hour that sacrifice was being offered in the Temple. The Acts of the Apostles 10:3-30 gives the account of Cornelius praying at the ninth hour when he received a vision.

The prayer of Jesus was also an important factor in determining the character of Christian prayer. From the gospels we have evidence that he participated in the Temple sacrifices and prayed at the prescribed times (see Luke 4:16; Mark 1:21; 12:29-30; Matt 6:5). But Jesus' prayer practices went beyond what was normally expected of the observant Jew. Luke's gospel especially speaks about the number of times Jesus went off to pray with or without his disciples (Luke 5:16; 6:12; 9:18; 9:28-29).

Luke continues the theme of prayer in the Acts of the Apostles where he speaks often of the disciples either going up to the Temple to pray or stopping and praying at the regular hours of prayer (Luke 24:53; Acts 2:46; 3:1-2; 5:42; 21:27). The *Didache* (a document from the last part of the first century) "formally prescribes that the faithful pray three times a day, although it replaces Jewish formulas with the Our Father."[4] In the Acts we also have other occasions when the disciples are noted at prayer, such as Paul and Silas praying at night in prison (16:25) or during the night at Paul's farewell liturgy (20:17-35). Finally, there is Paul's admonition to the Thessalonians to "pray without ceasing" (1 Thess 5:17). All this data suggests that "there were two ideals in particular that this prayer was to meet: it was to be an expression of unanimity and it was to be constant and persevering."[5]

The Christians of the third century were reminded by many of the church fathers of the command of Christ and Paul to be watchful in prayer. Clement, Tertullian, Hippolytus, and Cyprian all emphasized the need to "pray always" and at fixed hours. Origen, for example, wrote, "There is only one way of understanding how such a precept can be fulfilled: if the entire life of the saint is a single unbroken prayer and if part of this prayer is prayer in the stricter sense and is made at least (*ouk elaton*) three times a day."[6] Tertullian mentions prayer at dawn and twilight,[7] as does Hippolytus: "when the faithful arise from sleep in the morning, before they undertake any work," and "before you take your rest in bed."[8]

It is not only times of prayer that become traditional in Christianity, but the interpretation of those hours as well. Christ is unhesitantly connected with the sun and with the day. That Christ was the "light of the world" was already attested to by John in the Fourth Gospel, but early Christian writers extend this metaphor to the hours of prayer. Cyprian, for example, speaks of rising for morning prayer to celebrate the resurrection, but he also says,

> So too when the sun sets and the day is ending, we must pray again. Christ is the true Sun, the real Day. At the moment when the sun and day of this world disappear, we pray that light may nonetheless be ours. We ask for the coming of Christ and the gracious manifestation of eternal light. . . . Christ is the true Sun, the real Day.[9]

Evening prayer was also interpreted christologically, this time stressing the passion of Christ, which was to be understood as the "true evening sacrifice," and thus could be understood, according to John Cassian,

> either as the sacrifice which Christ taught his apostles in the evening at the Supper when he instituted the most holy mysteries of the Church, or as the sacrifice which he himself offered to the Father on the next day as an evening sacrifice—that is, a sacrifice at the end of the ages—by lifting up his hands for the salvation of the whole world.[10]

By the time of Constantine and the peace of the church, prayer at morning and evening became organized around two practices: the prayer of the Christian people assembled with their bishop (in what we would call parishes), called the "cathedral office"; and the prayer as celebrated by ascetics, monks, and nuns, who were beginning to organize themselves both in and out of the cities. What we know of the cathedral-style prayer from such fourth-century sources as Egeria and from Spanish and Gallican church councils of the fifth and sixth centuries was that there were two hours of prayer, morning and evening, and that the Psalms assigned for these hours were limited. Since books were quite rare, the people had to depend upon the memorization of morning psalms and evening psalms and so these did not vary. To these psalms were added hymns, biblical and nonbiblical canticles, intercessions, and a collect prayer.

The prayer of ascetics and monastics was determined more by the imperative to "pray always." They continued the practice of Morning and Evening Prayer, but to these they sometimes added prayer at the third (Terce), sixth (Sext), and ninth (None) hours as well as prayer during the night. To this already growing schedule was added a short office of prayer after supper (Compline) and prayer after morning Lauds (Prime). Because of the difference between common Christian life and that of the ascetics and monastics, the content of the prayer was also different. Rather than a fixed number of psalms and few readings, these communities added the whole Psalter to their repertoire as well as continuous readings from biblical and nonbiblical sources. It was the monasteries that were responsible "for the emergence of psalmody as the dominant element in the daily office."[11] In addition, we must include the fact that in the early church, the community interpreted the psalms christologically, contributing to their popularity.

These two forms of prayer, cathedral and monastic, did not remain as distinct as set out here; rather, they were joined by the practices of ascetics and priests living a communal life in the cities. There the ascetics and priests joined the people assembled around the bishop, while some laity stayed for the more prolonged prayer of the ascetics and priests. As the medieval period developed, monastic prayer continued to shape and reshape the Liturgy of the Hours. Some monasteries endeavored to follow the imperative to pray always by multiplying Hours and multiplying psalms within the Hours. In a religious community such as that of Cluny in the eleventh century, the entire Psalter was prayed each day, as well as an Office for the Dead, the Office of the Virgin Mary, and other Offices as well.

At the risk of skipping over a vast amount of history material, I will simply say the Liturgy of the Hours deteriorated significantly in the late medieval and early modern periods. Various factors contributed to the moving of various Hours in the practice of monastic communities and priests. For example, the desire to shorten the Lenten fast resulted in moving Vespers to as early as noon. Clerics, who were mandated to say all Hours, but were prevented from doing so because of apostolic work, celebrated the Hours whenever they could. All this contributed to a loss, in the words of Vatican II, of the "truth of the hours." Morning prayer was no longer prayer in the morning, night prayer was moved up to early afternoon, or in the most exaggerated abuse, all the Hours were said together simply in order to fulfill the obligation to choir. It was to these abuses that the Second Vatican Council addressed its reform agenda.

Sacrosanctum Concilium, the Constitution on the Sacred Liturgy, devoted eighteen paragraphs (83–101) to the reform of the Liturgy of the Hours, so important did it judge this form of prayer. Among other things, the Constitution mandated that the Psalter be spread out over a longer period than just a week (when modified, it was spread out over four weeks) and encouraged the singing of the psalms. The communal nature of the Hours was stressed. Morning Prayer and Evening Prayer again became the "hinge" Hours of the day, and the Hours were to be prayed only at the suitable time assigned (the so-called truth of the Hours). The Office of Prime was suppressed, and the night Office, which consisted of psalmody and readings, was to be revised so that it could be prayed at any hour. The readings were to be revised according to historical accuracy and suitability and were to be made longer.

Perhaps the most important part of the reform agenda was to restore the Liturgy of the Hours to the laity, at least for the major Hours. No longer was there to be a distinction between those who officially prayed "the public prayer of the Church" (*CSL* 98), i.e., those in the clerical state, and those who did not based upon their lay state. Monastics, religious, clerics, and laity who prayed the Hours all prayed the public prayer of the church. One of the greatest difficulties facing those who would re-configure the Hours after the council was how to make it suitable for these very distinct groups of people. There were those monastics who were bound by law to say the whole Office in choir, some religious whose Constitutions called for the recitation of part of the Hours, clerics who were bound to say the whole Hours in private, and the laity who were encouraged to gather when they could with their pastors, especially for Sunday Vespers and on special feasts. Some forty years after the council, all the above-mentioned groups are still trying to adapt the Hours to their particular circumstances. One thing that remains constant despite the difficulties of adaptation to different groups is that, through the Liturgy of the Hours, the church continues to celebrate the paschal mystery in the rhythm of daily prayer.

The Weekly Cycle of Prayer

Sunday is the original feast day. It was on the "first day of the week" that Christ rose from the dead and inaugurated a new age even as we await the fullness of time (Matt 28:1; Mark 16:9; Luke 24:1, 35; John 20:1). The appearances to the disciples occurred on Sunday, as did the sending of the Spirit and the sending of the apostles (Luke 24:41-43; John 20:21-23). Sunday marks two things: our core belief in Christ's resurrection and our encounter with him, and the identity of the community. As with all liturgical feasts, Sunday commemorates what happened to Christ, what happens to us because of his paschal mystery, and what we have to look forward to in the fullness of all time. Sunday is also about the church. Christians are those whose very identity is tied to gathering together to celebrate the Lord's passion, death, resurrection, and glory. The Second Vatican Council describes Sunday as follows:

> By a tradition handed down from the apostles and having its origin from the very day of Christ's resurrection, the Church celebrates the paschal mystery every eighth day, which, with good reason, bears the name of the Lord's Day or Sunday. For on this day Christ's faithful must gather together so that, by hearing the word of God and taking part in the eucharist, they may call

> to mind the passion, the resurrection, and the glorification of the
> Lord Jesus and may thank God, who "has begotten them again
> unto a living hope through the resurrection of Jesus Christ from
> the dead" (1 Pt 1:3). Hence the Lord's Day is the first holyday of
> all and should be proposed to the devotion of the faithful and
> taught to them in such a way that it may become in fact a day of
> joy and of freedom from work. (*CSL* 106)

Christians came to designate this "first day of the week" by several
titles. As early as Revelation 1:10, the term "Lord's Day" (*kyriakē*) came
into use in Greek-speaking churches and then in its Latin form (*dominicus
dies*) in the churches of the West (later to become *Dimanche, Domenica,
Domingo* in the Romance languages). Other traditions took the name
from the "day of the sun," as it was called in Roman culture (later to
become Sunday, *Sonntag, Zondag* in the Germanic languages). In the very
earliest days of the church, the followers of Jesus continued to celebrate
the Sabbath and added the celebration of Sunday to their practice. However, by the time of Ignatius of Antioch (ca. 107) the community had
ceased to celebrate the Sabbath and only celebrated Sunday. Ignatius
says, "Those who used to live according to the old order of things have
attained to a new hope and they observe no longer the Sabbath but
Sunday, the day on which Christ and his death raised up our life."[12] Note
how Ignatius emphasizes not what happened to Christ as much as what
happens to us because of Christ.

Justin Martyr, writing in 165, provides the first description we have
of the Sunday assembly and explains why Christians gather on
Sunday:

> On the day named after the sun, all who live in city or countryside
> assemble in the same place, and the memoirs of the apostles or
> the writings of the prophets are read. . . . The reason why we
> all assemble on Sunday is that it is the first day: the day on which
> God transformed darkness and matter and created the world,
> and the day on which Jesus Christ our Savior rose from the
> dead.[13]

Making the connection between the day of creation and the day of new
creation in Christ, Christians also began calling Sunday the "eighth day,"
which stressed its eschatological character. St. Augustine writes, "The
eighth [day] will be like the first, so that the first life will be restored, but
now as unending."[14]

Pierre Jounel, quoting Gregory of Nazianzus, sums up the theology of the names for Sunday by saying that

> the name "day of the resurrection" stresses more the commemorative aspect, the name "eighth day" the prophetic aspect, and the name "Lord's Day" the mysterious presence of the risen Lord in his Church. As memorial, prophecy, and presence, "our Lord's Day is truly the coming of the new creation and the breakthrough of the life from above."[15]

Pope John Paul II found Sunday to be of such importance in the life of the Christian community that he devoted an apostolic letter, *Dies Domini*, to the topic, and it will be helpful to summarize his main points here.[16] In it he stresses the centrality of Jesus' resurrection in our faith and therefore in the heart of the celebration of Sunday (1 and 2). He also suggests that the resurrection redefines the very notion of time itself. "For Christians," he says, "Sunday is 'the fundamental feast day,' established not only to mark the succession of time but to reveal time's deeper meaning" (2). In the letter he explores the day by addressing the *Dies Domini* (the Lord's Day) and the celebration of creation, the *Dies Christi* (the Day of Christ), *Dies Ecclesiae* (the Day of the Church), and the *Dies Hominis* (the Day of Humanity).

In the first of these considerations, the "Lord's Day," John Paul II stresses that the active presence of the Son in the creative work of God comes to fullness in the paschal mystery. "Christ, rising as 'the first fruits of those who had fallen asleep' (1 Corinthians 15:20), established the new creation and began the process which he himself will bring to completion when he returns in glory" (8). Thus there is a distinction between creation and redemption, but there is also a close link between the two (12). Working from the creation account in Genesis 2:3, John Paul II stresses that Sunday ought to be set aside as a privileged day of rest and a day of prayer and praise of God. "Our relationship with God also *demands times of explicit prayer.* . . . The Lord's Day is the day of this relationship *par excellence* when men and women raise their song to God and become the voice of all creation" (15). Through such celebration we declare that *"Everything belongs to God!"* (15). It is a day of remembering God's great works in creation and redemption.

The "Day of Christ" stresses the redemptive work of Christ. Certainly Sunday is the day of the resurrection, but it is also the day of the appearances to the disciples and the sending of the Spirit. It is the first day of the week and is linked with the first day in the cosmic week of creation in Genesis. This connection enabled the church community to understand Sunday as the day of the new creation, "the first fruits of which is the glorious Christ, 'the first born of all creation' (Colossians 1:15) and 'the first born from the dead' (Colossians 1:18)" (24). This also led the Christian community to connect Sunday with baptism since on that day we are baptized into his paschal mystery, and so baptism is encouraged on this day. The Pope also works with the metaphor of Christ as light, saying that "the theme of Sunday [is] the day illuminated by the triumph of the Risen Christ" (27). But Sunday can also be considered the day of fire, since the Holy Spirit was given on Easter Sunday and Pentecost (28).

As Justin Martyr reminded us, Sunday is the day when the church gathers from all places to celebrate its faith, and thus Sunday can justly be called the "Day of the Church." Earlier we spoke about the liturgical assembly as a day of gathering to remember God's salvific deeds and to share in God's own holiness; it was also a day to celebrate and participate with God's ingathering of all humanity. Sunday is this day of assembly for Christians. John Paul II says, "It is important therefore that they come together to express fully the very identity of the Church, the *ekklesia*, the assembly called together by the Risen Lord who offered his life 'to reunite the scattered children of God' (John 11:52)" (31). It is especially marked as a day to celebrate the sacrament of unity, the Eucharist. In chapter 2 we spoke of the eucharistic assembly as essential not only to the identity of the church but to its very existence. Reflecting this belief, the Pope says, "By its very nature, the eucharist is an epiphany of the Church. . . . Each community, gathering all its members for the 'breaking of the bread,' becomes the place where the mystery of the Church is concretely made present" (34).

Finally, Sunday is the "the Day of Humanity: Day of Joy, Rest and Solidarity." Because of its character of marking both the resurrection of Christ and the day of the new creation, Sunday is marked by joy in a very special way (57). Stretching the relationship of Sunday with the Sabbath, John Paul II suggests, "More than a 'replacement' for the Sabbath, therefore, Sunday is its fulfillment" (59). By doing this he tries to recapture the theology of the Sabbath and joins it with the theology of Sunday without pitting one against the other. Relying on this connection he suggests that Sunday is to be a day of rest for Christians as a way to challenge the cultural meaning of work and consumerism, or perhaps, better, to reset our priorities of the spiritual over the material (67). Finally, Sunday is a day when the church community should set aside time for the "works of mercy, charity, and apostolate" (69). It is to be a day of solidarity with the poor; where the sacrament of unity becomes a practical solidarity (71).

John Paul II closes his letter with a consideration of Sunday as a day that reveals the meaning of time (75). The Christian Sunday is the time between the two comings of Christ and it points toward the Second Coming. As he says, "it cuts through human time . . . like a directional arrow that points them toward their target: Christ's Second Coming" (75). All that we hope for in the parousia is already foreshadowed in Christ, and on Sunday we celebrate the hope of that for all creation.

The Yearly Cycle of Prayer

If the church uses the rhythms of the day and week to mark liturgical time, it does so on a grander scale during the entire year. Like the two periods discussed above, the point of the liturgical year is for the community to partake, in the present, in the paschal mystery of Christ, his dying, rising, and coming to glory. Once again, liturgical anamnesis is what we do by celebrating any particular feast or mystery throughout the year. We celebrate through the Eucharist and the Liturgy of the Hours what Christ has done once-and-for-all, but now applied to us as we enter into his mystery.

The Christian liturgical year is in some sense an experience of cyclical time: we gather year by year to celebrate foundational events. However, because these events are historical manifestations of God's eternal saving love for us, we do not repeat the past but celebrate their significance in the present and for the future. It is only in human time that we have a past, present, and future; in God there is only the eternal present. Since we are profoundly human and time is such an important element of our life, the church uses time and the yearly pattern of seasons to mark what once happened in history and what now concerns us.

The church year unfolds in two major seasons and their preparation, and in intervening weeks of Ordinary (read: "ordered") Time. The Easter Triduum is the feast par excellence and the high point of the liturgical year. It is a unitive feast of the passion, death, and resurrection of our Lord. For this reason, the liturgies of the Paschal Triduum are one continuous rite; there is no formal closing and reopening each day once we begin at the Mass of the Lord's Supper. This is a trace of the ancient celebration of the Pasch as one feast, either on Sunday or on the fourteenth or fifteenth of Nisan according to the Jewish calendar. Gradually, in the first four centuries of the church, the unitive feast of the Pasch becomes divided up into the three days of the Triduum. However, at that time, the Triduum comprised not Thursday, Friday, and Saturday, as we are accustomed to today, but Friday, Saturday, and Sunday. Origen explains that "For us the first day is the passion of the Savior; the second, on which he descended into hell; and the third, the day of resurrection."[17] At times the fathers of the fourth and early fifth centuries designate these three days sometimes individually and sometimes collectively as Christ's Pasch. After Leo in the late fifth century, however, the Pasch became the designation for the day of the resurrection only. Patrick Regan calls this the second stage of development: "The Pasch ceased being a three-day celebration of both the passion and passage of Christ, and became a one-day celebration of his resurrection alone on what is now called Easter Sunday."[18] Consequently the Triduum was moved back one day, now composed of Holy Thursday, Good Friday, and Holy Saturday. While the original Pasch was the celebration of the Lord's suffering (on Friday), his rest in the tomb or descent into hell (Saturday), and his resurrection (Sunday), now the Triduum became a preparation for the Sunday Pasch. Thus we have the first clear separation of Easter from the days preceding it, leading to the actual creation of Holy Week.

The great feast of Easter and its preparatory week called holy is preceded by another longer preparatory period known as Lent. The history of this period, as well as its meaning, is quite complex, and it is doubtful that we will find its exact origins. Some, such as Thomas Talley, argue that the Byzantine tradition of Lent had its origin in Alexandria. There, "until the patriarchate of Demetrius (189–ca. 232) the fast of forty days was begun on the day following the Epiphany, the commemoration of Christ's baptism in the Jordan."[19] This practice gradually died out as christological development emphasized the nativity rather than the baptism as the beginning of the gospel and as Easter baptisms grew in prominence. We also must attend to the meaning given to Lent in this period. In the case of Alexandria, Talley argues that "Lent in primitive Alexandria was both strict historical commemoration of the fast of Jesus and a time of preparation for baptism."[20] Other traditions followed a different development. As Maxwell Johnson notes, "the fifth-century historian Socrates describes his understanding of the variety of Lenten observances":

> The fasts before Easter will be found to be differently observed among different people. Those at Rome fast three successive

weeks before Easter, excepting Saturdays and Sundays. Those in
Illyrica and all over Greece and Alexandria observe a fast of six
weeks. . . . Others commencing their fast from the seventh week
before Easter, and fasting three to five days only. . . . It is indeed
surprising to me that thus differing in the number of days, they
should both give it one common appellation; but some assign
one reason for it, and others another, according to their several
fancies.[21]

Some have challenged his reading of Roman practice, but his comments
are enough to show the diversity of the early church. What seems to be
clear in this early period is that there first existed a forty-day Epiphany
fast in Alexandria, and a three-week preparatory period for baptisms,
which were not always celebrated on Easter. In such places as North
Africa and Rome, where Easter baptism became common, the preparation
for Easter and the preparation for baptism became one and the same.

What we currently know of a forty-day pre-paschal fast becomes
traditional only after Nicea (325). Still, different traditions calculated the
forty days differently; some included Holy Week, others not; some did
not fast on Sundays, and so a six-week Lent actually was thirty-six days
(Rome); accordingly, four days were added (starting at what would
become Ash Wednesday); still others, like the later Alexandria practice,
adopted a six-week period (ca. 330) but had no fasting on Saturday or
Sunday, and thus they eventually came to include an additional two
weeks (ca. 600). We need also to attend to the interpretation of Lent in
this post-Nicea period. According to Johnson, it becomes clear that Lent
has a threefold interpretation:

> this "forty days" was understood eventually as a time for the
> final preparation of catechumens for Easter baptism, for the
> preparation of those undergoing public penance for reconciliation
> on or before Easter (on the morning of Holy Thursday in Roman
> practice), and for the pre-paschal preparation of the whole Chris-
> tian community in general.[22]

In the *General Norms for the Liturgical Year and the Calendar* published
after Vatican II, Lent is described as a "preparation for the celebration
of Easter. For the Lenten liturgy disposes both catechumens and the
faithful to celebrate the paschal mystery" (27). This document takes into
account that public penance no longer exists, but that the period is still

geared to catechumens and the whole community as had been done in the early church. The fully initiated community is encouraged to remember their own baptisms and to engage in penitential practices, which were also practiced in the early church.

A word must be said about the Easter Season. The celebration of the Pasch is not limited to the Easter Triduum or even Easter Sunday itself; it lasts for an extended period of fifty days. The church is trying to have us mark the most important feast of the year with a prolonged period of celebration, but pastorally we are having difficulty in sustaining the joy of Easter for the fifty days until Pentecost. Through certain liturgical practices, such as singing the Alleluia and the *Gloria*, festive liturgical vesture and appropriate music, the church seeks to emphasize this most important feast. Mystagogical preaching, that is, preaching that breaks open the mysteries we have just celebrated is to mark these weeks after Easter as well, both for the newly baptized and the fully initiated community. Perhaps our inability to understand the character of such preaching works against the community's having a real sense of the seven weeks of Easter. As we will see elsewhere, one may question whether or not the liturgical year is actually the calendar that the Christian community follows.

The second great feast of the church's year is that of Christmas. The current *GNLYC* states that during this period "the Church holds most sacred the memorial of Christ's birth and early manifestations" (32). The Christmas season lasts from Evening Prayer I of Christmas until the Sunday after Epiphany or after January 6, inclusive. The history of Christmas and the Epiphany are tied together, and both their origins and content generate differing interpretations. It will serve our purposes to include a few words on the history and meaning of each feast.

Two schools of thought have their own hypotheses on the origin and dating of the feast of the Incarnation.[23] The "history of religions" theory suggests that in the fourth century, when Christianity in the West was competing with other religious groups for prominence, the birth of Christ was substituted for the celebration for the birth of the sun in the cult of *Sol Invictus*. This was seen as a way of weaning Christians away from this very popular practice. Since the winter solstice was considered to fall on December 25 at that time, the birth of Christ easily was connected with the birth of the sun. Christ was the true light of the world and the true Sun. Gradually this practice spread in (was imposed on?) the East, replacing the Epiphany as their celebration of the birth/manifestation of the Christ. A second hypothesis, known as the computation hypothesis, suggests that the date of December 25 was set on calendrical grounds.

Liturgical historian Louis Duchesne (of the nineteenth century) argued that, based upon the ancient practice of considering the lifespan of great figures only in whole years, the death of Jesus happened on the same date as his Incarnation (understood as his conception). Celebrating his conception on March 25 made calculating his birth quite simple—nine months later on December 25. Others, like Dom Frank Engberding in the mid-twentieth century, also aligned themselves with the calculation hypothesis but argued that the date was established first in the fourth century and then the rationale was established afterward.[24]

Epiphany has close ties to the celebration of Christmas. In fact, in the East it was the preferred date to celebrate the feast of the Incarnation and his early manifestations. In the East, in addition to his birth, the events connected with this feast were the adoration of the Magi, Jesus' baptism, and the wedding feast at Cana. "When Rome began to celebrate January 6 in the second half of the fourth century, it shifted to this date the remembrance of the adoration of the wise men," and it has remained such in the West.[25] When the East accepted December 25 as the feast of the Incarnation inclusive of the visiting of the shepherds and the coming of the Magi, it focused January 6 on the event of the Baptism.[26] Interestingly, the current Liturgy of the Hours includes an antiphon for the *Magnificat* on Epiphany Evening Prayer II that reveals a remnant of the complex content of the feast in the early church. The antiphon reads: "Three mysteries mark this holy day: today the star leads the Magi to the infant Christ; today water is changed into wine for the wedding feast; today Christ will to be baptized by John in the river Jordan to bring us salvation." In the current Roman Lectionary the readings separate these events: the adoration of the Magi is used for Epiphany, and the baptism of the Lord is celebrated as a solemnity on the Sunday after January 6. The wedding feast at Cana is used only on the Third Sunday of Ordinary Time, Year A.

Like Easter, Christmas has its preparatory season as well. At the present time it extends four Sundays before Christmas, which means that in some years the fourth week is quite abbreviated. Its character is twofold: "as a season to prepare for Christmas when Christ's first coming to us is remembered; as a season when that remembrance directs the mind and heart to await Christ's Second Coming at the end of time" (*GNLYC*, 39). Such a clear presentation of the timing and theology of Advent belies the complex history of the season and its theologies in the early centuries of the church. Because the date of Christmas was celebrated variously on January 6 or December 25, as we saw above, the preparation period beforehand and its interpretation varied as well.

Not having the space to recount the whole complex history here, nonetheless there are certain contours that can be marked out. First, the very meaning of the word *adventus* gives us a clue to the various theologies connected with the time.[27] The word is by nature ambiguous, and this ambiguity was turned to good effect. It can first be understood, not as a preparation time, but for the actual coming of Christ in the flesh. But there are other *advents,* or comings, of Christ as well: the coming of Christ to us as we celebrate the feast (particularly in Eucharist) and the final coming of Christ in the eschaton. There is another sense of his coming as well in the annunciation to Mary. If we speak of Advent as a period of preparation for the birth, particularly when the birth began to be celebrated on December 25, it has a threefold character. According to Martin Connell, the three traditions are the *scriptural,* based on the infancy narratives of the gospels; the *ascetic,* with its domestic or monastic context; and the *eschatological,* in which the "coming" at the end of time is what the community is waiting for.[28] These three traditions did not emerge chronologically but coexisted at the same time, although not all always in the same place.

To make matters more complicated, the timing of Advent varied from place to place in such liturgical traditions as Northern Italy (Brescia, Milan, and Ravenna), Rome, and Gaul. In Northern Italy there is evidence that there was a preparatory period of Advent before the date of Christmas was fixed on December 25. In this case, the element of fasting in preparation was stressed. In Turin we have evidence that Advent stretched back two Sundays before Christmas; here too the emphasis was on an ascetic preparation of the community for the time when they will celebrate the anamnesis of the Savior's birth. Peter Chrysologus' sermons give evidence of a scriptural emphasis to the preparatory period. The two Sundays preceding Christmas are on the annunciations, first to Zechariah and then to Mary. In addition, because of the christological controversies of the day (second quarter of the fifth century), his sermons are deeply theological regarding the humanity and divinity of the Christ. Other traditions of Northern Italy testify to an Advent season of five Sundays before Christmas, with the first three Sundays having an eschatological character, as evidenced in the scriptural pericopes chosen, and a more historical emphasis on the last two. In Spain we have evidence of a preparatory period from December 17 to January 6, the feast of the Epiphany. The preparation included gathering each day for Eucharist.

There is another tradition of Advent that focuses on its likeness to the paschal preparation time—a forty-day Lent. In the Gallican city of Tours there is evidence that a period of ascetic preparation starting on November 11, the death date of St. Martin of Tours (and thus called St. Martin's Lent). In some councils, such as the sixth-century Council of Macon, we hear of the insistence of fasting and Lenten sacrifice. For some this meant abstaining from meat and fasting from food until three o'clock; for others, fasting from conjugal relations. This connection between Advent and Lent also carried with it a baptismal resonance. This harkened back to the sermons of St. Leo, who tried to persuade his hearers that as they were crucified and raised with Christ in their baptism, so too were they born with him in his nativity.[29] The Roman liturgical books of the sixth century testify to a six-week Lent, but Gregory the Great shortened this to four. With this there was an emphasis on the scriptural and eschatological tradition more than an ascetic one, which might have touched into baptismal preparation. By the beginning of the medieval period, a four-week period of preparation became the norm in the West. As Connell suggests, it carries a threefold tradition of *Scripture, asceticism,* and *eschatology,* but the baptismal resonances that it had in some places seem to have been lost. In present practice, the scriptural tradition remains the same as does the eschatological, but the ascetic has been reduced to using lighter purple or blue for liturgical vesture and design.

A few words need to be spoken about the rest of the Sundays of the year. Thirty-three or thirty-four weeks make up the remaining time outside of Eastertide and its preparation and Christmas and its preparation. The season is called Ordinary Time, not because it is "ordinary," but because it is numbered. According to the *GNLYC,* these Sundays "are devoted to the mystery of Christ in all its aspects" (43). To better acquaint the Catholic community with more of the Scriptures, the year is extended to a three-year cycle of Sundays and a two-year cycle for weekdays. Because the gospels unfold the life of Christ somewhat chronologically, the proclamation of his life and work begins with his birth (or baptism); it gives the impression that historicism rules the day, but that is not necessarily true. The remembrance of Christ week by week is meant to celebrate the whole mystery, even if we look at it one aspect at a time.

It should be apparent to the reader by now that there is a tension between the historical and the anamnetic. By this I mean that the liturgical year has a clear historical consciousness about it, trying to celebrate the death and resurrection of Christ on the anniversary of the actual days as well as a certain historicity regarding his birth. On the other hand, celebrating the entire life of Christ within a single year's time suggests that something else is operative as well. This other emphasis is that of anamnesis. As described in an earlier chapter, anamnesis is the community's act of remembrance of the saving works of Christ in such a way as we become participants in that salvation story. The celebration of the Pasch through the symbol of time is one form of recalling that mystery. The celebration of the Pasch at Easter is marked by a stronger sense of anamnesis than is the celebration of the Incarnation. This was true even in history. Augustine himself regarded Christmas as only an anniversary celebration in distinction with Easter, while Leo stressed the paschal character of both feasts.[30] In our own day it must be acknowledged that, at least on the popular level, Christmas is seen more as a historical celebration than an act of anamnesis of the paschal mystery. The opening prayer for Christmas Mass during the day tries to keep the anamnetic quality to the forefront. "Lord God, we praise you for creating man, and still more for restoring him in Christ. Your Son shared our weakness: may we share his glory." However, the proper prayers of the Christmas Masses are not enough to challenge the cultural emphasis on the birth of the infant Jesus, to say nothing of the challenge to the conspicuous consumption that has come to mark the holiday, at least in this country.

Finally, we need to say something about the sanctoral calendar. The Christian community has a tradition of honoring martyrs and saints—people it judges have personified the way of discipleship—by feasting and dedicating a day to their remembrance. Once again the historical and the anamnetic come together. When possible, we celebrate on the death days of the saints, thus keeping a certain historicity, but there is an anamnetic quality to the sanctoral calendar as well. As John Baldovin says so clearly, "They [the saints] approximate the Christian mystery in a specific way which relates to a local community and so are aids in inserting that community into the mystery of Christ."[31] As the development of a sanctoral calendar is dependent upon the needs of a local community, the list of feasts has a tendency of growing and even overwhelming the seasons of the year. This was the situation addressed by the Vatican II reform of the calendar, and a better balance was created between feasts of the Lord and feasts of the saints. The purpose of feasting the saints is always to point the community to the God of whom the saints were disciples.

Conclusions

We began by stating that the liturgy celebrated in time is a repeatable opportunity for believers to enter into the once-and-for-all event of Christ's saving victory over sin and death. As we have sacraments to celebrate the paschal mystery, so too have we used time as a symbol of that mystery. Honoring the rhythm of the day, Christians have gathered at various Hours to recall the death and resurrection of Christ and to follow his command to "pray always." Likewise, we have established Sunday and the week as another rhythm for gathering and joining in communal praise. Finally, we have used the natural rhythm of the year, marking out seasons and feasts. In all these ways we have tried to keep memory of the Christ mystery and of the saints so as to enter into this saving mystery. There is not a division of sacred and secular time in Christian practice, because we believe that Christ has redeemed all time. Christ has transformed even the past, present, and the future. For believers, the future already impinges upon us; we taste the firstfruits of the fulfillment of all days.

If the Christian community lived by this calendar alone, we would find keeping memory of Christ quite easy. However, we live by many calendars and they have conflicting values among them. We live by a school calendar, a fiscal calendar, a civic calendar, an agricultural or fishing calendar, and more besides. In some cases, the culture has co-opted our feasts, turning Christmas into a celebration of family cheer and extravagant gift giving, and Easter into a time of egg hunts and bunnies. While it is obviously possible to live by several calendars at once, it remains to be seen which calendar takes priority of time and commitment. For the Christian community, there is a call to order our days, weeks, and years according to the Christ mystery. This remains an unmet expectation and a challenge.

CHAPTER SEVEN

Symbolic Nature of
Liturgy and Sacrament

Nowhere do we find such richness and such complexity in the study of liturgy than when we are dealing with symbol. We can begin with the relatively simple distinction between sign and symbol, but from there we are quickly cast into multiple worlds of philosophy, theology, linguistics, psychology, anthropology, and more besides. If any generalization can be made of all these fields regarding symbol, it is that we are at a moment where the symbolic structure of reality is being explored in every single field because of its perceived importance. Already in 1966, Karl Rahner was able to say the "concept of symbol . . . is an essential key-concept in all theological treatises, without which it is impossible to have a correct understanding of the subject-matter of the various treatises in themselves and in relation to other treatises."[1] Writing more recently, Louis-Marie Chauvet is proposing a whole new schema for conceiving reality as distinct from the metaphysical approach that has characterized the West for over two millennia. In his magisterial work, *Symbol and Sacrament: A Sacramental Reinterpretation of Christian Existence*, Chauvet suggests that "the act of symbolization . . . carries out the essential vocation of language: to bring about an alliance where subjects may come into being and recognize themselves as such within their world."[2] Such broad claims for symbol and symbolization suggest that we are far away from the popular understanding of "mere symbols," placeholders for a reality somewhere else.

In this chapter I will explore several important theories of symbols from various fields that have been or are presently important in liturgical discussions.[3] It is unthinkable to consider sacraments without dealing with Rahner's theory of a "real symbol," and it would be irresponsible not to consider Chauvet's major contribution in *Symbol and Sacrament*. French philosopher Paul Ricoeur has likewise made important contributions regarding the interpretation of symbols. The fields of social and cultural anthropology have also been very important in recent liturgical theology, and it will be helpful to consider some general themes on ritual and symbol as well as to take a closer look at Victor Turner's work. My hope is that the reader will develop a taste for the importance of symbol in current theology, and that she or he will likewise have a greater appreciation of what we might call the Catholic sacramental imagination, i.e., the ability to see God in all things, events, and persons, or to put it another way, God's gracious decision to be mediated through earthly and cosmic realities. No more should the reader be embarrassed to speak of the sacraments as symbols of faith or to speak about the symbolic presence of the Eucharist. Rather, as we will see, to speak of something/ someone as symbolic is to posit their deepest reality.

Philosophical and Theological Approaches

Karl Rahner

We might begin by asking whether a symbol is a mere pointer to an absent reality, or whether there is real identity between the symbol and the signified. Another way of posing this question is to ask whether the reality is "present" in the symbol or "behind" the symbol. The answer to this question is important because it determines whether one is seeking the power of the sacraments "behind" the sacraments or through the actual mediation of the symbol itself. In other words, are sacraments efficacious because of a power (God's intention) working through the symbol as through an instrument, or is the efficaciousness of a sacrament due to its very nature as a symbol? We are asking how seriously we should take sacraments' symbolic nature.

Aquinas suggested that sacraments could be understood under the category of instrumental causality (*ST*, 3a. 62, 1, in the Reply). That is, the principal efficient cause of the sacraments is the passion of Christ working through the sacraments as through an instrument. It is the power flowing through the sacraments (*virtus fluens*) that is efficacious. Thus he can say that they effect what they signify. As well as being causes, Aquinas also considered sacraments as being in the "genre of signs" (*ST* 3a, 60, 1 in the Reply). He argued that sacraments are signs or signifiers in that they are signs of a hidden effect. What is unclear in Aquinas is the relationship between signification and causality. Sacraments are efficacious because of the principal agent, but do they cause grace because of their own form as well? Aquinas seems to allow for both interpretations, but he does not develop symbolic causality to the degree that he develops instrumental causality. Consequently, sacramental theology since Aquinas dealt primarily with sacraments as instrumental causes that put the emphasis on God's intention, the priest's intention, and the recipient's intention not to put an obstacle in the way. What Karl Rahner did was to expand Aquinas' thought particularly in the area of symbolic causality, bringing the focus on the actual symbolic forms of the sacraments. How did Rahner accomplish this?

In 1966 Rahner published a very important article, "The Theology of the Symbol," collected in his *Theological Investigations IV*. In it he begins by explaining that his investigation will be to probe what it exactly means to speak of the symbol in the theology of devotion to the Sacred Heart. This seemingly straightforward task moves Rahner to distinguish between signs and symbols and to search for the "highest and most primordial manner in which one reality can represent another—considering the matter primarily from the formal ontological point of view."[4] In other words, Rahner is first stating that from all the myriad ways symbols have been described historically he is trying to get to the most foundational questions; second, he is admitting right from the beginning that he is using metaphysical categories to explore his subject. This is important to note because more recent postmodern writers have gone beyond metaphysics to discuss the questions of symbol. Since Aristotle, metaphysics has been caught up in causality, most especially instrumental causality, and Christian theologians have made use of this schema as a way to delve into such questions as the efficacy of sacraments and sacramental grace. Even Aquinas, who tried to keep sacraments under the "genre of signs," in the end dealt with them more under the rubric of instrumental causality.

Rahner begins with his conclusion that "all beings are by their nature symbolic, because they necessarily 'express' themselves in order to attain their own nature."[5] While he has yet to prove this thesis, he posits that at their deepest reality, all beings (including God) are intrinsically symbolic because of an inner dynamism of expression. This "expression" is a way of representation; it is not a physical but a metaphysical differentiation that allows one reality to render itself present. Once he has made these claims, Rahner goes on to use his metaphysics (Aristotle as read through Aquinas) to explore each section of his assertion.

First he needs to provide an ontology of the finite. Using the meta-physical principles of existence (that you exist [existence], and how you exist [essence]), he suggests that every finite being bears the stigma of finiteness by virtue of the fact that it is not completely simple—there is a real multiplicity in its being. As he says, this multiplicity is usually connected with finite beings, but as we have revelation in our repertoire of tools, we can also posit that the mystery of the Trinity is a prime example of a being whose unity in multiplicity is not a sign of imperfection. Having made this theological leap, Rahner goes on to say that we should not think of the multiplicity of finite beings as a purely negative thing, but that it might be a reflection of the Trinity and that all "being is plural in itself."[6] He then goes on to explain that there is in all beings an original unity that expresses itself in multiplicity, and second, there must be some inner agreement between origin and expression on account of the unity of the being. In Rahner's inimical style, he states that

> a plurality in an original and an originally superior unity can only be understood as follows: the "one" develops, the plural stems from an original "one," in a relationship of origin and consequence; the original unity, which also forms the unity which unites the plural, maintains itself while resolving itself and "disclosing" itself into a plurality in order to find itself precisely there.[7]

One needs to emphasize that we are speaking here of metaphysical principles, not physical properties. So in translation, we might say that all being starts as an original unity; in a distinct metaphysical moment, that original unity expresses its very self, which yields a plurality. But the internal other that is expressed is like the one, corresponds to the one by virtue of its origin. Rahner then moves to another assertion, stating that being expresses itself for the fulfillment of its own being and its unity. Here Rahner suggests that the Trinity is the supreme mode. All being therefore forms something distinct from itself and yet one with itself, for its own fulfillment.

At this point Rahner introduces the term *symbol*. He is suggesting that every being "possesses a plurality as intrinsic element of its significant unity; this plurality constitutes itself, by virtue of its origin from an original unity, as a way to fulfil the unity."[8] At the heart of his argument Rahner can then say this means that this "other" expression is a *symbol* of the original unity. Thus Rahner can say that every being is symbolic because it necessarily goes out of itself into something distinct from itself, but one with itself by virtue of its origin. He claims that this metaphysical symbolizing is the precondition of the ability of the being to know itself and to love itself. The expression, the symbol, "is the way of knowledge of self, possession of self, in general."[9] In other words, a being is symbolic both in itself and for itself. The expression of a being in a symbol of itself is so important that Rahner claims that "the being is known in this symbol, without which it cannot be known at all."[10] Rahner then makes a leap over the history of philosophy to reach a conclusion about the visibility of a being. He suggests that the being constitutes and perfects itself by projecting its visible figure outside itself as its symbol, its appearance. "The essence is there for itself and for others precisely through its appearance . . . according to is own measure of being."[11]

Moving out of a strictly philosophical mode into a theological one, Rahner then suggests that the theology of the Logos is strictly a theology of the symbol, indeed the supreme form of it. Thus he can say that "the Logos is the 'symbol' of the Father . . . the inward symbol which remains distinct from what is symbolized, which is constituted by what is symbolized, where what is symbolized expresses itself and possesses itself."[12] Further, Rahner speaks of the incarnate Word as the absolute symbol of God in the world. He is the expressive presence of what God wishes to be to the world. The truth of the Logos informs created reality and becomes the humanity of the Christ, "really the 'appearance' of the Logos itself, its symbolic reality in the pre-eminent sense."[13] Moving from Christ to the church, Rahner can say that the church continues the symbolic function of the Logos in the world, of course, according to its own human nature. This does not make it a "sign," a simple pointer to another reality, but it remains a symbol in the primordial way in which Rahner has explored the term. Because this is the case, he can speak of the church as the primary sacrament of Christ; it is a "real" symbol of Christ.[14] Bringing the discussion to the human person, Rahner speaks about the Thomistic doctrine that the soul is the substantial form of the body. Here too we find a theology of the symbol.

> It follows at once that what we call body is nothing else than the actuality of the soul itself in the "other" of *materia prima*, the "otherness" produced by the soul itself, and hence its expression and symbol in the very sense which we have given to the term symbolic reality.[15]

In conclusion we can say that Rahner has produced a theology of symbol that suggests that the reality is really present in its symbol, its expression. Symbols are not empty realities pointing to something some-where else, but symbols are full of the reality they symbolize. This leaves us with a very strong sense of symbol and so a distinction between a sign and a symbol. A sign is indeed a pointer to another reality, but a symbol is the presence of the reality in question. This has proven to be extremely helpful in sacramental theology, where the sacramental sym-bols are now seen as being "full" of the reality they signify. Its application to eucharistic presence can easily be traced. The sacramental gifts of bread and wine, after being eucharitized, are symbols of the self-giving of Christ to the church community. There is "real" presencing here; Christ is really present in a sacramental, symbolic form. To put it in Rahner's formula, we could say that Christ goes out of himself into a reality dis-tinct from himself, but one with himself by virtue of its origin, in order to be there for himself and for others. This reality is a real symbol of Christ; the sacrament is the reality of Christ's self-gift actualized in sym-bolic form.

Louis-Marie Chauvet

We now turn to philosopher/theologian Louis-Marie Chauvet and his sacramental theology. Chauvet is interested in the relationship be-tween sacraments and the whole of Christian life and the place of sacra-ments in the relationship between God and humanity. In other words, he is interested in developing a *"foundational theology of sacramentality."* [16] Unlike Rahner, Chauvet has concluded that metaphysics and the con-sideration of sacraments under the rubric of instrumental causality have reached their limit. Like other postmodern scholars, Chauvet argues that metaphysics has a fundamental flaw that requires a completely new approach. While we cannot pursue the failure of metaphysics here, we can follow his alternative approach to the sacramentality of Christian life.

Right from the beginning Chauvet insists that the change he proposes is not a merely cosmetic one but a *"fundamental revision of the terms with which we approach the problem*: those of language and symbol, and no longer those of cause and instrument."* [17] Cause and instrument are code words for metaphysics. Chauvet does not want to amend slight issues within this schema; rather, he wants to propose an entirely new schema, a new way to approach those fundamental questions of sacramentality and Christian identity. Chauvet wants to address issues such as "lan-guage acts, expression, symbol, otherness, corporality, presence and absence," and these do not belong to the realm of metaphysics but, rather, to the symbolic.[18]

Chauvet begins by wondering why Scholasticism chose causality with its implied notion of productivity to speak of the relationship between God and humanity in the sacraments. For him, it was a mistake, but it was also almost inevitable that they could not think otherwise because of the presuppositions undergirding their entire culture. But that culture has changed, and we can take as our point of departure language and the symbolic as a distinct new methodology. Previously in Western thought, language has been considered as an attribute solely belonging to humans. We "use" language as a tool to move from our mental representations to speech, a kind of translation. In the metaphysical tradition, language is a result of the Fall and poses an obstacle to the transparency of the self to the self, to others, and to God. Contemporary philosophy has rejected this understanding in favor of considering humans as possessed and constituted by language. In other words, according to Chauvet, humans never start from a neutral height and then use language to express some uncontextualized reality. Rather, they "start with a concrete language in which a universe is already structured into a 'world,' that is, from a place that is socially arranged and culturally organized."[19]

Pursuing this project a little further, Chauvet suggests that we need to embrace "the symbolic scheme of language, culture, and of desire, we [need to] set up a *discourse from which the believing subject is inseparable—* just as language is inseparable from being or *Dasein* from *Sein*."[20] In place of the schema of causality with its emphasis on utility, we need to have a point of departure that allows us to be *subjects* in communication with God. For Chauvet, symbol is that point of departure. It takes seriously our embodiment and stresses the mediation of all knowledge and relationships. For how else could we understand the coming of God in flesh or in sacrament? "The sacraments," in Chauvet's analysis, "force us to confront *mediation—*mediation, *by way of the senses.* . . . And so, we find ourselves in the end sent back to the *body* as the point where God writes God's self in us."[21]

We need to say something more of mediation. Chauvet speaks of the contemporary belief that "reality is never present to us except in a mediated way, which is to say, *constructed* out of the symbolic network of the culture which fashions us. This *symbolic order* designates the system of connections between the different elements and levels of a culture."[22] It allows individuals to situate themselves within the complex world of the economic, social, political, ethical, etc. This is an important insight because it is a direct rejection of the isolated, self-constituting individual who is present to her/himself in immediacy. The symbolic order necessarily places her/him within a context already there and provides the means through which the individual becomes a self. In other words, we do not use the symbolic order (language) as an instrument but as a mediation of the subject. It is through the mediation of language that we come to be. Through language the world comes to be for us, speaks us and speaks to us. According to Chauvet, *"there is no human reality, however interior or intimate, except through the mediation of language or quasi-language that gives it a body by expressing it."*[23] Sounding much like Rahner, he goes on to say that whatever the form of the expression, it "indicates an act of presence which acts itself out for itself, as a walking-in-place from the interior into exteriority and from the exterior into interiority."[24] This is not to say that the exteriority/expression is a second moment of an interiority acquired somewhere else. Rather, *"to exteriorize oneself consists precisely in differentiating oneself interiorly."*[25]

This can be translated into a discussion of sacraments. Sacraments effect what they symbolize, not because of instrumental causality, but because they are the expression of the intent to be present as one subject to another. They are manifestations of God's intent to be present to us. Chauvet wants to keep the notion that sacraments are still efficacious, but not through instrumental causality. Rather, he suggests that "the expression, insofar as it is manifestation, effects what it signifies: love invents its expression and the expression creates the love."[26] In a new way Chauvet has succeeded in honoring sacrament's identity as being in the "genre of signs." It is through symbolic mediation that they have their efficacy, not through causality.

Expression in language or quasi-linguistic form is also the way that subjects come to presence and come into relationship. Here Chauvet explores modes of exchange between persons as a way of speaking about how a subject comes to be in relationship with other subjects. He argues that exchange is still a fruitful way to explore relationship, but that we need to move out of exchange understood as value. The alternative is to replace it with notions of exchange that are symbols of abundance of the self. In other words, through gift, one does not give an object to another, one gives one's very self to another through the mediation of gift. *"It is subjects who exchange themselves* through the object, who exchange, *under the agency of the Other*, their *lack-in-being* and thus come before each other in the middle of their absence deepened by their exchange, in the middle of their difference experienced radically as otherness because of their exchange."[27] This is what constitutes every human relationship. Through symbolic exchange we constitute ourselves as subjects and create or re-create our relationships with others. Exchange is mutually binding on all parties; we belong to each other because of the exchange.

This has direct implications for an understanding of sacramental grace. Grace is beyond value; it is in the realm of the superabundant and the personal. God graciously gives Godself and gives gratuitously, yet it demands a response, not of value, but of self. The response is not made in immediacy, however, but through the mediation of symbols, of language of one kind or another. Grace then is not an object so much as it is communication between subjects. It is communication of subject to subject through mediation. Through their giving they constitute themselves as subjects; through their giving they create or re-create their relationships. The Christian constitutes herself or himself as a believer in her or his response to the offer of God given through the mediation of sacraments. The Christian grows in relationship with God in their mutual exchange of self in sacrament.

In Chauvet's analysis, two things are clarified: "first, the truth of the believing subject in its relationship with God can come about . . . only through *mediation*"; "second, because it is contemporary with mediation and not anterior to or dissociable from it as an instrument, the subject is *always giving birth* to its truth as a believer, which is the truth of its relationship with God."[28] This truth is effected not by the gift but by the symbolic exchange that is the communication between subjects.

After consideration of these issues, Chauvet suggests that there are three major traits of symbols. First, "the primary function of the symbol is to *join* the persons who produce or receive it with their cultural world . . . and so to identify them as subjects in their relations with other subjects." Second, like language, the symbol provides witness of the subject, not information about the real but the real in expression, a coming to presence. Third, there are differences between sign and symbol. The symbol is not derivative of the sign, nor is the symbol like the sign, a secondary expression of the real or even opposed to the real. "*The symbol touches the most real aspect of ourselves and our world.*" The difference between sign and symbol is as real as the difference between sign as an object of value and symbol as the mediation of communication between subjects.[29]

It is also possible to speak of symbolization as a verb or as an action. Here the etymology of the word "symbol" is helpful. Symbol comes from the Greek word *symbollein*. It means to throw together, to relate two things that are distinct but belong together as in a contract. Put simply, a symbol could be a dollar bill distinctively cut into parts and given to the two parties of a contract. The parts have no value in themselves but only in relation to the other half. The purpose of bringing the two halves together (i.e., the purpose of symbolizing) is for the two parties to recognize one another as holders of a contract. The split dollar bill has no monetary value; its only value is the exchange it permits between the two subjects.

Chauvet suggests that the act of symbolization is to be a revealer and an agent. The first is clear from what we said above; the act of symbolization serves to identify the two subjects as partners. In the second sense "the symbol is an agent of alliance *through* being a revealer of identity."[30] The symbol binds the subjects together in a common project. In this twofold sense we can speak of the efficacy of symbols. Another way to speak of symbol's character as an action is to attend to its performance dimension. Working with performative language theory, Chauvet agrees with J. L. Austin: to say something is at the same time to do something. Applied to symbol, to symbolize is to reveal and create alliances. Chauvet then applies this theory of symbolization to his understanding of grace. Again Chauvet rejects the metaphysical scheme of cause and effect and uses the symbolic scheme of communication through symbol/language. Grace is not so much an object we receive as it is a symbolic work of receiving oneself as a daughter or son of God. Like language, symbol constitutes the subject within a world already there, in this case, a world of relationship with God established in Christ.[31]

Finally, for our purposes, Chauvet returns to the body as the primary place where symbolization happens. As he says, "the sacraments accordingly teach us that *the truest things in our faith occur in no other way than through the concreteness of the 'body.'*"[32] We must resist at all costs a desire for unmediated immediacy either with ourselves, with one another, or with God. The body is inescapable because it is given to us as a means of being there and as a form of communication. It obeys the same laws that govern language—it is contextualized in history, culture, and desire. "Corporality," says Chauvet, "is the body's very speech."[33] And it is the particular way in which humans are in the world. "The body is *the primordial place of every symbolic joining of the 'inside' and the 'outside.'*"[34] I do not so much have a body as I am a body, and that body is enculturated in tradition and nature. I am unavoidably caught up in a symbolic network that constitutes my social and cultural body, that gives me a historic tradition, and that locates me in relation to the cosmos. The body is the symbol where all this comes together in a unique way for every person.

"Any word which seeks to be expressed in a kind of transparent purity is an illusion; no word escapes the necessity of a laborious inscription in a body, a history, a language, a system of signs, a discursive network. Such is the law. The law of mediation. The law of the body."[35]

The implications of this for sacrament are significant. There is a corporality to our faith. It is only in our bodies that the sacraments do their work. It is also our personal body that is the place of convergence of the *social* body, which is the church, the *traditional* body, which the church maintains, and the *cosmic* body of a universe received from God and from which symbolic elements (bread and wine, water, oil, etc.) are recognized as a mediation of God by the Spirit.[36] Thus Chauvet can conclude that sacraments are made of significant materiality. They serve as a reminder that there is no direct connection with Christ. Sacraments tell us that faith has a body and "that to *become a believer is to learn to consent, without resentment, to the corporality of the faith.*"[37] We are a body, and there is no faith unless inscribed on a body. That is our condition and our place of redemption.

Paul Ricoeur

The French philosopher Paul Ricoeur has been extremely influential in the developing area of hermeneutics or interpretation theory. In his work he has taken on religion and religious manifestations in myth and symbol as worthy material to explore, making his work very attractive to theologians. His conversation partners are not just the philosophers but also the phenomenologist Gerardus Van der Leeuw, the historian of religions Mircea Eliade, and the psychologists Sigmund Freud and Carl Jung. His overall project is discourse on the self; but departing from René Descartes' belief that there is a direct route to the self, Ricoeur argues strongly that there is no direct access to the self, only access to the self that is mediated by projections into the world. This brings him to an extensive exploration of myth, symbols, and poetic speech. It is his particular interest in symbols and their interpretation that is of interest to us here.

Symbols are extremely important to Ricoeur, and an explication of them finds a place in many of his works, particularly in the early ones. Ricoeur begins by saying that in a general sense symbols are signs: they stand for something beyond themselves, but the differences between sign and symbol are at least as great as the similarities. Although in a sign there is already a duality, it is not the duality of a symbol. A sign has a "structural duality of a sensory sign and the signification it carries" (in other words, it is both sensory and meaningful); and there is also the duality of the sign and the thing signified. Ricoeur holds these two levels (or expressions of signification and of designation) together by the term "to signify."[38] Importantly, a sign only signifies a single object; a symbol, on the other hand, has a duality "of a higher degree." It presupposes the duality of a sign and adds another duality—that of meaning to meaning.[39] In other words, symbols have a double or even a multiple intentionality (or levels of meaning).

What becomes very important for Ricoeur regarding the relationship of sign and symbol is that the second intentionality of the symbol is available only through the first. One meaning, a literal or conventional meaning, leads us to another to which we would not have access without the first. Ricoeur's example in the *Symbolism of Evil* helps to clarify his point. The word "stain" is itself a sensory sign that signifies a physical spot or blemish. Stain becomes a symbol when upon this first literal meaning is built a second intentionality, which

> points to a certain situation in man in the sacred which is precisely that of being defiled, impure. . . . Thus, contrary to perfectly transparent technical signs, which say only what they want to say . . . symbolic signs are opaque, because the first, literal, obvious meaning itself points analogically to a second meaning which is not given otherwise than in it.[40]

I want to stress here that the meaning of a symbol is not imposed from the outside but arises from within the symbol itself. There is a dynamism in the symbol; it "gives," it "provides," it moves us from the first to the second meaning from within. Because of the "donative" aspect of the first, literal meaning to the second meaning, the first can never be discarded. We are not looking for the idea behind the symbol, but we are trying to interpret the symbol through the symbol. The implications of this for liturgical practice and theology are obvious and significant. Liturgical symbols need to be fulsome not paltry. Bread must look like bread; water needs to be abundant. Second, sacramental theology must use the concrete celebration as its point of departure. In other words, sacramental theology must become liturgical theology.

One might ask where symbols originate. Ricoeur's response would be in the cosmic dimension, in dreams (the oneiric), and in the poetic realm. Ricoeur's entry into the world of cosmic symbols is through the work of phenomenologists of religion such as Van der Leeuw, Maurice Leenhardt, and Eliade, the latter seeming to be the most influential. Recognizing the relationship between myths, rites, and symbols, Ricoeur suggests that these symbols "constitute the language of the sacred, the *verbum* of the 'hierophanies.'"[41] Manifestation is central here. These "words" are the cosmic elements themselves: sky, mountains, water, earth, fire, etc. They provide an inexhaustible source of symbolization. The literal meaning of the mountain gives to a second meaning possibilities such as power, height, awesomeness, immutability, etc. The elements of the universe carry, as it were, the symbol. As Ricoeur remarks, these meanings are not fanciful human projections but are initiated by the symbols themselves.[42] We stand then as receivers and hearers of these words of manifestation. We are carried by the inner dynamics of the symbols themselves, from the first, literal meaning to the second.

Like the cosmos, dreams are another zone for the emergence of symbolism. They too have the double signification as part of their nature. As we have implied above, symbols—be they cosmic, oneiric, or poetic—both conceal and reveal. There is always something more than what first appears. "In dreams," Ricoeur says, "the manifest meaning endlessly refers to hidden meaning."[43] Through the influence of Jung, Ricoeur points out that oneiric representations go beyond individual histories and place one in touch with imagery common to every culture. Of particular importance to Ricoeur is Jung's insight that dreams can point to future possibility. This concern with the creative dimension of human expression is a recurrent theme in Ricoeur's work.

The third zone of emergence of symbols is that of the poetic imagination. Here it must be remembered that Ricoeur never intends a pejorative or narrow understanding of image or imagination but a positive and fulsome one. There is a creative power in the poetic image; it opens up a world of possibility for human being and action.[44] For Ricoeur this was a developing understanding. In his earlier work, Ricoeur understood imagination as a residue of perception—a saying that follows seeing; then he modifies his position to suggest that imagination is a mediation between seeing and saying. Finally, he moves from a view of the imagination as reproduction to that of production or creativity—there is a seeing that follows saying.

It is important to say a word here about the relationship between symbol and speech. With Ricoeur, we might ask if symbols "are anterior to language, or even foreign to it."[45] His response is an emphatic "no." Cosmic symbols, for example, take on their symbolic dimension

> only in the universe of discourse. . . . Even when the elements
> of the universe are what carry the symbol . . . it is a word—the
> word of consecration, of invocation, the mythic commentary—that
> *declares* the cosmic expressiveness. . . . The world's expressive-
> ness achieves language through symbol as double meaning.[46]

In other words, symbols exist in the human world, which is a world of meaning achieved through speech. But the contribution is not just from speech to symbol; it is a mutual exchange. Symbols contribute to speech; they can be understood, as indeed Ricoeur understands them, as the birthplace of speech. We also must add that symbols are for humankind, and their meaning, even if it is cosmic expressiveness, comes to us through our bringing that expressiveness to speech.

The connection between language and symbol is perhaps the easiest to see in Ricoeur's third zone, that of the poetic imagination. Here Ricoeur understands the symbol as a word-image, not as representation but as creative power, a moment of semantic innovation. This creative innova-tion applies in two distinct ways: first, in the internal sense of language itself, what he calls the semantic innovation; and second, in the world that is opened up by the text, what Ricoeur calls its heuristic power. This zone is truly a place where symbols emerge, where language emerges, and where possible ways of being-in-the world are also opened up. What is different between cosmic symbols, for instance, and poetic symbolism (with metaphor serving as the model) is the *bounded* character of cosmic symbols and the *freedom* of metaphor as a free invention of discourse.[47]

In sum, the relationship of speech to the cosmic, oneiric, and the poetic is one of mutual dependence, understood in such a way as not to reduce one to the other. Speech finds its deep roots in the cosmic, oneiric, and poetic, which are birthplaces of language; and they, in turn, are depen-dent on the verbal because they become symbolic for us only as they come to speech. There is no symbolism prior to the human person who brings the cosmic, the oneiric, and the poetic image to speech. The moun-tains and hills need a word to make them hierophanies. Dreams need to be told before their power can be released. The poet needs to bring her images to light in discourse.

It becomes obvious here that we must say something of the relation-ship between symbols and interpretation. It is in the very nature of sym-bols to have a double meaning or a multiple intentionality, to have a depth or a thickness to them. Their opaqueness, as Ricoeur calls it, is their richness. Yet we can also see that this richness is problematic. How do we plumb the richness of symbol's opaqueness? Ricoeur's response is to turn to interpretation as the necessary corollary to symbol. In *Freud and Philosophy* he goes so far as to define one by the other. "Thus a symbol is a double-meaning linguistic expression that requires an interpretation, and interpretation is a work of understanding that aims at deciphering symbols."[48] The task of hermeneutics is understood as discerning the meaning of equivocal expressions.

We need also to say something about symbols, their interpretation, and the development of the self. First of all, according to Ricoeur, all symbols have a social and cultural context and they are part of systems. This means that their interpretation needs to take into account the particular social/cultural worldview of which they are a part. Symbols play both an expressive and a formative function in the society of which they are a part. Ricoeur suggests that there is a constant dialogue with and transformation of the society out of which they arise. There is also a dialogue and transformation of the one who interprets the symbols. The interpreter is invited to engage the symbol in such a way that the self one begins from is put into question by the symbol. For Ricoeur this means that a hermeneutic of symbol requires a personal involvement with the life of the symbol. You must make a wager of belief: "You must understand in order to believe, but you must believe in order to understand."[49]

All this work on symbols and their interpretation has significant importance for liturgical studies. First, it brings a richer understanding of what a symbol is, and second, what is involved in its interpretation. Symbols are the "stuff" of liturgical celebrations, whether they are words, images, objects, persons, or actions. We need to be aware of their rich and complex meanings; we need to respect their first literal meaning before moving on to their second, third, or fourth meaning without ever leaving behind the first level. Interpretation of symbols is necessary. Symbols are always contextualized, and they are part of systems. Accurate interpretation involves being attentive to their context and the relationship among symbols. Interpretation also comes at a personal cost. We risk our very selves by entering into the world of symbols, for they interpret us as much as we interpret them. Concretely we can say that we risk transformation, even conversion, in liturgical participation if we give ourselves over to the symbols of the liturgy. The world they project of a redemptive community can become our world if we give ourselves over to the cleansing waters, the shared table, and the Cross. For Ricoeur, all this work on symbols is in the service of getting access to the self. Within our religious context, Ricoeur would suggest that we need to "lose" ourselves in the symbols of the liturgy, for it is only by doing so that we will "find" ourselves—as believers, as people of faith.

Anthropological Approaches to Symbol and Ritual

Having reviewed three key approaches to symbol that are heavily based in philosophy, it is now appropriate to turn to the social sciences, in particular social and cultural anthropology, for an exploration of symbols and ritual systems. This use of social scientific material is part of the "turn to the subject" that has characterized Catholic theology since shortly before the time of Vatican II. Accordingly, whatever fields give insight into humanity can be appropriated with due caution by theology for its distinct purposes. This appreciation of the social sciences became very important for liturgical theologians since the 1980s, when it was realized that Christian ritual behavior is a species of human ritual behavior. Scholars took what anthropology was learning about society and its ritual processes and applied it to the understanding of Christian ritual. As philosophy does not take over the proper theological task, neither do the social sciences replace liturgical theology; when used with caution, both become helpful tools in the hands of the theologian.

General Contours of the Field

Before turning to individual theorists, it may be helpful to take a general tour of the field of anthropology regarding symbol and ritual and their relationship with society. I am leaving out much detail but intend only to indicate trends within the field that may be applicable to liturgical theology. The reader is invited to read Catherine Bell's longer analysis of the field in her *Ritual: Perspectives and Dimensions*, from which my own summary is taken.[50] We may begin by saying that nineteenth-century anthropology was generally marked by a static view of society and culture. Symbols and rituals were understood at this time as revealing social structures, and there was a bias toward social stability. Symbols and rituals reflected social structures, and reestablished social structures when crisis threatened to upset the stability of the social system. More recent studies presume a much more dynamic view of society and culture, and take a more empirical approach to the study of symbol and ritual.

The so-called social functionalist school of anthropology (Émile Durkheim, Marcel Mauss, A. R. Radcliffe-Brown, and Bronislaw

Malinowski) was particularly interested in the social dimensions of ritual activity, especially how it affects the organization and workings of the social group. Theorists noted how ritual action facilitated social life, how it formed and maintained social bonds, how it socialized individuals through the unconscious appropriation of common values and categories of knowledge and experience. Because of their bias toward social order, their reading of the data suggested that ritual was a means to regulate and stabilize life of social systems, adjust its internal interactions, maintain its group's ethos, and restore harmony after conflict. They sought to find a more or less direct relationship between the forms of social organization and the basic elements of its ritual and belief system. Their limitation is that they posited too direct a relationship between social structure and ritual. That view has been challenged in recent years, but few would deny today that there is a relationship of some kind between the two.

Structuralism, that is, an appreciation of social structure as a system of relationships connecting people or their social roles, was another approach taken, sometimes by functionalists (Arnold van Gennep, for example), and sometimes by others (Max Gluckman and Victor Turner). A key interest of van Gennep was in the actual structure of rituals, and he made a significant contribution in laying out the structure of life-crisis rituals (separation/transition/incorporation). In his reading of the data, rituals ordered chaotic social change. "Rituals are the means for changing and reconstituting groups in an orderly and sanctioned manner."[51] He was also responsible for insisting upon analyzing rituals and symbols within their social settings as well as in the context of larger ritual structures. This countered an approach that suggested there were universal meanings of symbols and ritual actions. Gluckman was more interested in the ritualization of social conflict. In his analysis rituals were the expression of "complex social tensions rather than the affirmation of social unity."[52] Ritual was a major means a community used for working and reworking social relations. Rites of rebellion, for instance, channeled structural conflicts, but they were cathartic and deflected the threat of real social change. Turner combined the functionalist's interest in ritual as a mechanism for maintaining social equilibrium with a more structural perspective on the organization of symbols. He was also responsible for noting the creative contribution of ritual to social dynamics. We will explore his work in this area in more depth below.

Symbolic culturalists (Claude Lévi-Strauss, Edmund Leach, Clifford Geertz) suggested that there was a much weaker link between symbols and social organization than the functionalists who preceded them. Their emphasis was more on symbols as a means of communication and on meaning. Their approach suggested that symbol systems could be analyzed independently of social structure and considered on their own terms. Yet, they maintained that ritual as a cultural artifact was part of the social structure as a whole. More than their predecessors, the contribution of symbolic culturalists was the insight they provided on ritual, culture, and social change. Leach, for example, pointed out that while ritual could reinforce the status quo, it was also a means of modifying the social order. He also suggested that ritual is a medium for the expression of cultural ideals and models that orient other forms of social behavior. In addition, he noted that "we engage in rituals in order to transmit collective messages to ourselves."[53]

Much more could be said of all these categories and approaches, but I will comment on just two areas that are currently being explored by anthropologists. The first is ritual understood as performance, and the second is ritual as praxis. Regarding the former, recent theorists (Turner, Erving Goffman, Maurice Bloch) are stressing ritual as an event, not just an expression of cultural values. In other words, as Bell notes, "performance metaphors and analogies allow [anthropologists] to focus, they say, on what ritual actually *does*, rather than on what it is supposed to mean."[54] Ritual has a power to effect changes in people's perceptions and interpretations. Ritual also acts as a framing mechanism (Gregory Bateson), an interpretive framework within which to understand other acts or messages. Finally, they would suggest that ritual as a cultural artifact is not something that happens to a passive and static social entity. Rather, they suggest that participants actively generate and modify symbol systems and use them to produce culture.

Praxis approaches are not unlike performance approaches (Marshall Sahlins, Pierre Bourdieu, Talal Asad). These theorists argue that ritual is a human strategy by which human beings continually reproduce and reshape their social and cultural environments. Ritual, for example, can bring traditional structures to bear on new situations, enabling them to embrace the new. In this approach, ritual is seen as "strategic practices for transgressing and reshuffling cultural categories in order to meet the needs of real situations."[55] What rituals create are ritualized agents who have the competencies to use ritual in situational and strategic ways.

All these theories have found application in understanding what Christian ritual practice does. With functionalists we can see the relationship of ritual and social structure. Corporate ecclesial rituals clearly reflect social structures and help communities to face conflict and change. More recent studies suggest that rituals are related to social structures, but they are not identical to them. Rituals are systems of cultural meaning. Anthropological studies verify the formative nature of Christian rituals. They express the values and beliefs of a community, and they transmit these beliefs mostly unconsciously to participants. Our interpretation of our rituals needs to be contextualized on several levels if we are to have a comprehensive knowledge of our activity. We need to be attentive to the structure of rituals as systems of meaning and as located within the larger cultural and social context.

While functionalist, structuralist, and culturalist views have been easily applied to Catholic ritual, the more recent theories of ritual as performance and praxis have not yet been well pursued. Their application is very suggestive, however. First of all, a performance approach suggests that liturgical theology must be more empirical in its approach. It must be attentive not just to ancient rituals and their texts but to whole performances of contemporary communities. It also suggests that we attend to what our Christian rituals do rather than just what they mean. A praxis approach suggests that liturgical inculturation is necessary from a number of points of view, not least of which is the fact that liturgical performances equip participants with strategies to confront the challenges of the day. Not only do so-called ritual experts have authority to create and change rituals, but ritual participants are in their own way "adept" at ritual and desire to take more leadership in shaping traditional practices than we have seen to date. We may need to consider the appropriate balance between decision making at the level of the Congregation of Worship and Sacraments and decision making at the "localest" level. Lack of attention to the actual dynamics of ritual can and has led to conflict and misunderstanding.

Much more could be said in this regard, but at the moment we have to be suggestive rather than comprehensive. We turn now to one anthropologist who has been extremely influential in liturgical studies since the 1980s. Because of his influence, it is appropriate to take a more in-depth view of his work.

Victor Turner

Victor Turner did his fieldwork with the Ndembu tribe of Zambia and found that he could not account for what was going on in the society without attending to its rituals.[56] Accordingly, he found himself needing to explore the social process itself, ritual's role in the social process, and the component parts of ritual, their characteristics and interpretation. It is parts two and three of his agenda that have been particularly interesting to liturgical theologians, but a word needs to be said about all three aspects of his work.

Turner reacted negatively to the structuralist approach to society of his teachers and other anthropologists.[57] In his perception structural analysis did not take enough account of the dynamism that marked societies. In his view society was in process, constantly moving between what he called structure and anti-structure.[58] What he means here is that society is on the one hand "structured" in institutional organizations and positions: "the patterned arrangements of role-sets, status-sets, and status-sequences on the whole consciously recognized and regularly operative in a given society."[59] But this does not do justice to the complexity or dynamism of society. He suggests that there is another dimension to society that is less structured (hence he calls it anti-structure), more spontaneous, that momentarily releases people from their structured patterns and positions. Turner refers to this second dimension as "communitas."[60] It was an important time of creativity and reconfiguration of the status quo, yet the appeal of communitas led societies to "institutionalize" these more free-flowing moments into structure. Human social life, in Turner's view, was a dialectical, dynamic process involving successive experiences of communitas and structure.[61]

The processual nature of society led Turner to reflect upon the rituals that the society celebrated. From his study he concluded that ritual also bore this characteristic of process; it arose within the social process and it participated in the social process. In his view rituals often arose in the period of communitas or from persons on the margins of society.[62] However, rituals born in this state can and do move into structure as a result of the routinization of spontaneous communitas. This leads us to the question of the role of ritual in the social process.

What rituals did in the social process of the Ndembu was to help the community deal with life-crisis events, like initiation, and experiences of affliction, such as reproductive problems or illness. Rituals allowed the society to confront the crisis, reconsider their social norms in light of the crisis, and possibly reconfigure their society as a result or reestablish the status quo. For Turner, ritual itself was a process, and it played an important part in the social process.

The context of ritual was an important consideration in interpreting its meaning and significance. For Turner, this meant attending to ritual within the social process and considering individual elements of rituals within the whole field. Turner understands ritual to be a "system of meanings" and these meanings appear within a complex social system of meanings.[63] This has implications for the proper interpretation of ritual. As he says, "I found that I could not analyze ritual symbols without studying them in a time series in relation to other 'events,' for symbols are essentially involved in social process."[64] Ritual is also a system of symbols in Turner's view. He suggests that rituals should be studied as "a sequence and field of symbol-vehicles and their signification."[65] In other words, one gains nothing by isolating a symbol from the rest of its ritual context; rather, symbols must be considered in relationship to one another.

Turner, like Ricoeur, also draws a distinction between sign and symbols based on the nature of their signification and the multiplicity of their intentionality (which Turner calls their "signifieds").[66] A sign carries a meaning that is arbitrarily assigned; this is different from a symbol that has a natural association between the signifier and the signified. Another distinction that Turner makes is that "signs are usually organized in 'closed systems,' with the signifier generally carrying only one meaning, whereas symbols tend to be 'semantically open,' and are capable of carrying multiple meanings."[67] It is helpful to consider Turner's definition of ritual symbols. He calls them "the smallest units of ritual behavior, whether object, activity, relationship, word, gesture or spatial arrangement in a ritual situation."[68] These ritual symbols, in Turner's view, can be considered either instrumental or dominant. Instrumental symbols are exactly that. They serve to support dominant symbols and contribute to the accomplishment of the goals of the ritual. A dominant symbol is also as it sounds, a central or master symbol, and it has three properties: it condenses meanings, it unifies disparate meanings, and it polarizes meanings.[69] Each of these is important to consider. Parts one and two reveal symbols' ability to carry multiple meanings (akin to Ricoeur's understanding of the multiple referents of symbols). The polarization of meaning is less obvious. In Turner's view symbols have the capacity to collect meanings on the "sensory pole," which he expects would arouse desires and feelings. The other pole he considers the "normative" or "ideological pole." This signifies ethical values and principles, religious doctrines, political ideals and moral views, etc.[70] This duality can account for a symbol's ability to affect so deeply the human person in both conscious and unconscious ways. What a dominant symbol does is to affect us on every level of our personhood, from our intellectual and cognitive capacities to our emotional and physical ones.

A few further words must be said here about the interpretation of symbols and rituals. As already mentioned, symbols arise from a society and must be considered in relationship to that society and its contexts. There are no universal meanings of symbols in Turner's view. Symbols also make up a semantic field.[71] This means that symbols must be interpreted within the ritual context. Because of the multivocality of symbols, their context will determine which meaning/s apply in a particular situation. A further influence on the interpretation of symbols is the role of the interpreter. This means that the place of the participant in the ritual action also will determine to a degree what a ritual symbol or a whole ritual unit will mean. Who you ask about a ritual matters. Finally, symbols have the capacity to gain and lose meaning over time and from one context to another. Once again, interpretation will depend upon a careful consideration of context.

The observant reader will realize many of the implications of this work for a consideration of Christian ritual and symbol. The community is in process, and ritual plays a part in the continual evolution of the community. This work presses us to consider how ritual expresses not only who we are but who we might become. Ritual can present codified meanings for its participant, but it also can be a dynamic tool in the hands of a community to address current situations and needs. Ritual can have a creative function in the social process. This, of course, raises questions about who has the authority to change rituals in whole or in part and who benefits from such changes. Understanding the context of symbols either within the social process or within the semantic field is also important for the understanding of Christian ritual. Once again, the quality of ritual symbols becomes important in the expression and interpretation of meaning. As we saw with Paul Ricoeur, the contextual nature of ritual and symbol implies that liturgical studies needs to be much more empirical and comprehensive in its approach than it has been to date. Not only do "institutional meanings" need to be considered, but the actual meanings that emerge from liturgical performance need to be taken into account as well. Liturgical theology can no longer appeal to an interpretation of texts as sufficient data upon which to make its judgments on the meaning of ritual units. Neither can it isolate individual symbols from their social context and from the relationship of one symbol to another. In sum, the turn to the social sciences has widened the field of liturgical theology considerably. The challenge remains to keep abreast of the field as theories continue to be modified and expanded.

Conclusions

Having made this brief foray into the vast world of symbolic studies, we may draw some conclusions regarding their importance for liturgy and sacrament. Working within traditional metaphysics, Rahner sought to lay the foundation for understanding symbol, or more correctly, for understanding all of being as symbolic. His theory of a "real symbol" raised the importance of symbol in sacramental discussion and extended Aquinas' work on sacraments being in the "genre of signs." In Rahner's view there is "real presencing" going on in sacramental celebration. Chauvet concluded that metaphysics had reached its limit and that another way had to be found to explore questions of sacraments in the relationship between God and humanity. For him the way was symbolic mediation of subject to subject. Chauvet's approach takes seriously the body in sacramental theology and insists that there is no other route to the divine/human relationship other than through the mediation of the body that is enculturated and historically determined. Our faith is rooted in corporeality, and we must learn to accept this and work with this reality without resentment. Embodiment is not a problem for Chauvet as much as an opportunity, indeed, the only opportunity for relationship. Ricoeur is also interested in the reality of the true self, but his point of departure is a rejection of Descartes' theory of direct access to the self. For Ricoeur there is only access to the self through reflection on those symbols of the self that we project into the world. Interpretation of symbols is an important focus of Ricoeur's work, and it is extremely helpful in liturgical practice and theology. Symbols "give" themselves to us and we "give" ourselves to the world of the symbol. Taking the risk of engaging with the symbol is necessary for us to understand, but in the process, we are transformed, even converted, by entering the world of the symbol. This is extremely helpful in enabling us to understand the formative nature of the liturgy and what is entailed in "full, conscious, and active participation" in the liturgy.

Anthropology has opened a whole new way for liturgical theologians to approach their work. It challenges us to look at symbols and rituals in relation to social structure, social process, culture, and symbolic systems. Performance and praxis approaches suggest that ritual is an activity of a "ritualized subject" who has learned through ritual participation to use ritual as a strategy. Turner deals with the empirical study of symbols and suggests that they are dynamic and have a dynamic function in the social process. Once again, this suggests to us that rituals as systems of symbols are meaningful in the context of the community and also contribute to the social process. Turner helps us understand the characteristics of symbols and their interpretation in context. He enlarges the field of liturgical theology particularly by pressing it to become more empirical in its methodology.

There is an enormous bibliography on symbol and ritual, but these few selections are enough to indicate the importance of symbol and ritual in sacramental and liturgical celebration and reflection on those experiences. As I said in the beginning, this work leaves us with a strong sense of symbolic realities and discourages us from considering sacraments as mere symbols of an absent reality or as mere pointers to the really real. In symbols there is real presencing; in symbols we are made present to ourselves, to one another, and to God. Respecting what God has made, God relates to us also by mediation through the body and all created reality.

CHAPTER EIGHT

Symbol and Liturgical Celebration

Having discussed the nature of symbol as it applies to liturgy and sacrament, it is now time to discuss the actual use of symbols in liturgical celebration. As we have indicated in the previous chapter, ritual is comprised of a complex semantic field. That is, liturgy is made up of a whole world of symbolic utterances, all of which work together to accomplish the ends of the particular liturgical celebration in question. This complex semantic field is made up of a combination of different symbolic vehicles. They include the linguistic, the aural, the visual, the kinesthetic, and the bodily. Spoken of in another way, the symbols of the liturgy are language, space, music, silence, color, the various arts, the use of bodies, actions, interactions, and transactions. Each of these has its distinctive symbolic character that when brought together make up a full celebration. All symbols, individually and together, need to be attended to for the proper interpretation of the liturgy.

The purpose of this chapter is to explore the different symbolic languages, if you will, that make up our liturgical celebrations. These languages are used to a greater or lesser extent in the liturgies we create for special occasions, such as an Advent prayer service, or for the official liturgies of church, whether the Liturgy of the Hours, the sacraments, or sacramental services. The Constitution on the Sacred Liturgy of Vatican II teaches us that "In the liturgy, by means of signs perceptible to the senses, human sanctification is signified and brought about in ways proper to each of these signs" (*CSL* 7). This suggests to us two things: first, that we are embodied subjects, as Chauvet persuasively argues; and second, that the liturgy does its work through signs/symbols perceptible to the senses. In other words, human sanctification happens to us only through the mediation of the body and through the mediation of symbols. Embodiment and symbols are the key factors in Christian liturgical life. The effectiveness of the liturgy will depend to a significant degree upon the authenticity and quality of the symbols used and, as Ricoeur suggests, the willingness of the participants to enter into the world of the symbols.

Liturgy and the Body

As we indicated above, our theological anthropology teaches us that we are our bodies. We have no other way of being in the world for ourselves or for others than through the mediation of the body. It follows that the human person has no other choice but to participate in the liturgy through the body and its senses. Here I am talking about not just the materiality of the body but the whole complex that makes up human persons: intellect, will, emotions, and bodily capacities. For the liturgy to be effective, it needs to attend to every one of these dimensions, at least across the whole semantic field. Individual symbols may affect the person more strongly in the intellect or in the emotions, but the whole liturgy together ought to address the whole person. Those responsible for the creation of liturgical rites or for their celebration are well advised to take account of the whole body-self in the formulation of liturgical language, the creation of worship spaces, and the use of liturgical actions, sounds, or silence.

Here, Turner's insights into the dynamics of dominant symbols are helpful. If you recall, a dominant symbol is a major symbol in a ritual unit whose meanings are polarized around both the orectic pole (oriented to the emotions and physiology) and the ideological pole (oriented to the intellect). Within Christian ritual, water, bread, wine, the cross, and oil could all be considered dominant symbols. Take water as an example. The meanings of water are polarized around a physiological pole of body fluids and the emotional spheres of delight in refreshment or fear of death; on the ideological pole, we have the ideas of cleansing, sustenance, and satisfaction. It is obvious that the water symbol affects the whole person, from the physiological to the ideological. Simply through the natural properties of water we are caught up into the possibilities of life and death. When the water symbol is joined to the biblical story, as it is in baptism, its meanings expand to include the passage through the waters of the Red Sea, the waters of refreshment in the desert, and the saving waters of the Jordan. But as Ricoeur reminds us, we enter into those secondary meanings by way of the first literal meanings that can never be left behind. For the water symbol to do its work it must be fulsome; it needs to be abundant; it needs to be seen, heard, and felt. Thus our current emphasis on baptismal fonts that have enough water that one could even drown in them. Saint Benedict the African Church in Chicago takes this to the extreme in its baptismal pool that contains some 10,000 gallons. Most other recently built fonts are more modest in size, but they still convey the sense of abundance that is required for the meanings of life and death to be evoked.

Bodies have a whole range of senses that good liturgy should address. Scientists tell us that one of the most powerful senses of the body is the sense of smell. Not only is there the immediate sensation of odor, but our olfactory senses seem to be connected to memory and emotions. It takes only the briefest whiff of home-baked bread or pies to bring us back to our own homes of origin and memories of family and security. Of course, some smells can have equally powerful references to bad memories as well. Christian ritual takes advantage of the human capacity to smell by its use of aromatic oils, candles, and incense. Chrism oil is imbued with balsam that makes it distinctive from the oil of the sick and the oil of catechumens. Its rich odor connects us with celebrations of baptism, confirmation, and ordination. Its meanings are rooted in the natural properties of oil and the additional meanings given to it from the biblical accounts of anointing of priests and prophets and of the woman who anointed Jesus' feet with rich, aromatic oil. Importantly, it connects our stories of initiation or ordination with the story of salvation history.

Incense too addresses us in our body selves. There was a time when distinctive scents were used at Easter or at Christmas, helping to make the connection with these liturgical seasons and the mysteries they celebrate through the memory of the body. Today we are usually not as attentive to this. However, we are attentive to incensing the book of the gospels, the presider, the community, and the bodies of our beloved dead. Our prayers rise like incense in Evening Prayer, and incense leads the way for the Eucharist as it is brought to the altar of repose on Holy Thursday's Mass of the Lord's Supper.

Perhaps it is in regard to smells that we are apt to ask not so much what they "mean" as what they "do." As we indicated in the last chapter, performance approaches to the liturgy suggest that we may have overemphasized the meaningfulness of symbols and rituals and not attended sufficiently to what they do or accomplish. With incense we reverence persons and objects like the gospel book and the reserved sacrament. We connect the olfactory with the visual when we use incense in Evening Prayer and pray Psalm 141 as the smoke wafts over the assembly. With repeated uses of oil we bring back memories of our own faith journeys as we celebrate those of others in initiation and orders. We connect our personal experience with that of the paschal mystery, the story of our salvation. All these things that address the olfactory senses are done through the mediation of symbols.

The visual is not so different from the olfactory. By way of our eyes we bring the whole world into our orbit. With the current emphasis on the quality of symbols, we are much more conscious of the impact of the visual. The cross, a dominant symbol in our tradition, solemnly leads processions. Gestures of reverence are deliberate and visually arresting. Bread looks more like bread, and wine is carried up in glass decanters so that it might be seen. Ritual gestures are understood as revelatory rather than as utilitarian and so are done with care rather than out of obedience to rubrics—because of the impact of the visual. Think of the signing of the catechumens at their rite of acceptance into the catechumenate. We scatter the catechumens through the church, and make these signings large enough for all to see. Think too of the importance of color in the more liturgical churches. It is impossible to think of Lent without the dark violets of altar falls and vestments, just as we cannot fail to see the brightness of white and gold without thinking of the mysteries of Easter and Incarnation.

The sense of touch also allows for a distinct symbolic vehicle. Think of the impositions of hands on persons at confirmation, ordination, or during the catechumenate. The church's care of the individual is made clear through ritual touching that is both free and bounded. By that I mean that we allow ministers to touch us in ways that go beyond casual social interaction, but which are bounded by rules of propriety and custom within the context of the ritual. Liturgical signings put flesh to flesh as do rituals of anointing and blessing. As they are contextualized by word and intention, they both do things and mean things. Those individuals seeking to join our faith community are made members by the ritual signing of the cross on their foreheads and senses; the gesture speaks of following Christ crucified. Ritual anointing of the sick touches those whom illness has made "untouchable"; it speaks of the church's care of persons in all states on the path between birth and death.

The power of speech and the sense of hearing together allow the church to proclaim her beliefs to the gathered assembly and allow the assembly to appropriate those meanings through speaking and hearing.

Philosopher Suzanne Langer suggests that in ritual we rehearse "right attitudes." This is particularly true in the area of liturgical speech. The official liturgies of the church put words of praise, thanksgiving, and petition into our mouths week after week until they become our words. Through our physical speaking, we come to appropriate the tradition that comes to us at first from without, but in time we come to literally embody that tradition.

Liturgical prayer of all kinds fills the ear with word and image, with metaphor and simile. The story of God's care for the earth and for a chosen people comes to us through our sense of hearing. In particular, our hearing allows all other symbols to become focused and meaningful in specific ways. The prayer during the imposition of hands calls the Spirit to come and transform the eucharistic gifts in one instance, while the prayer with the imposition of hands on confirmation candidates calls the Spirit to come, strengthen, and send the gifts of the Spirit in another context. The multivalency of symbols or their ability to carry multiple meanings is both their richness and their problem. On the one hand, the multiple levels of meaning allow the same symbol to address people in multiple life situations. On the other hand, the multiplicity of meanings can be disconcerting and even confusing. Linking language to gesture, object, or person focuses the meaning in one direction rather than another, while allowing a richness and an ambiguity to remain.

Our hearing not only puts us in touch with "meaningful" speech, it also puts us in touch with all manner of acoustic symbols, from the sound of the human voice, to the ringing of bells, to the sounds of silence. We will address it more below, but for the moment we can suggest that music, distinct from any verbal language connected with it, both does something and means something. It creates moods in the assembly by its use of timbre, rhythm, tempo, melody, and harmony. It allows us to create the mood of solemn processions, the somberness of Lent, the delight and joy of Easter. Music is expressive of human emotions in a unique manner. Music can express grief in a way no words can match, just as it can relay exuberance as nothing else can. Music, like smells, is also tied to human memory and contexts, and it can carry the meaningfulness of liturgical seasons and celebrations from year to year. Sound is a carrier of culture, urging assemblies to address the contemporary world with one musical form (e.g., praise music) while carrying the tradition of the church with another (e.g., Gregorian chant). Our sense of hearing provides an opening into our bodies that touches all dimensions of our persons. What we hear addresses our intellect as much as our emotions. Sound expresses our triumphs as much as our failures, our memories as much as our desires.

To speak of sound is also to speak of silence. On the micro level silence is what separates one word from another, one note from another. On a larger scale, silence can allow other symbols to sink into our bodies and our psyches. It provides periods of rest to dwell in the Word, to reverberate with the sound of chant or song, to give our desires the space to emerge. Silence too can have its moods. There is the silence of expectation, the silence of contentment, and the silence of negative emotions. Proper liturgical planning needs to attend both to sound and to silence, and the appropriate balance of both together. We can become overwhelmed with sound of whatever kind, and we need silence to find our place amid the myriad meanings that come to us through liturgical rituals and symbols. There is also the silence that speaks of the Unspeakable, and we do well to remember that we cannot adequately address God.

A final word needs to be said of liturgy and the body, and that is the use of the body in liturgical action. We have already looked at some of the uses of the body as we reviewed the senses, but more needs to be said of bodily posture and action. As we have seen in our discussion of Chauvet, we are our bodies, and those bodies are enculturated and historicized. There are ways in which our bodies and what we can do with them are a given. We cannot turn our heads almost all the way around as can a duck; neither can we see infrared signals as can an eagle or hawk. But beyond the physiological givens, we learn to use our bodies and conceive of our bodies from our family and culture. It is clear that Scandinavian reserve and Brazilian exuberance lead to a very different way of being in the world and of celebrating the liturgy. Culture and history of a people determine either how freely or how stiffly one carries one's body. They determine too whether the primary form of expression is dance, language, or song. A puritan ethic that fears the body will use the body in worship in a very different way than a culture that delights in the body and bodily means of expression.

As Edmund Bishop said at the turn of the twentieth century in his lecture "The Genius of the Roman Rite," the Roman liturgy is marked by a certain sobriety and reserve. That restraint affects all its symbolic expressions. This is as true for its euchology (prayer tradition) as for its bodily gestures. The rubrics for the official liturgies of the Roman Church speak of standing, sitting, and kneeling, of profound bows and quiet genuflections. These are clearly one culture's perception of what is acceptable ritual behavior. We have seen in the video work of Thomas Kane that communities in Africa and Oceania have a very different approach to bodily participation in the liturgy.[1] For these communities, as Kane says, "to dance is to breathe." Dance is not an incidental symbol one adds to the preparation of gifts; dance is a primary means for expression and ritual action. It is used throughout the liturgy: it gathers the community; it celebrates the gospel; it expresses the *Magnificat* in Evening Prayer, etc. As we said above, it is more appropriate to be attentive to what some liturgical symbols "do" than what they "mean." Dance, like music, is one of those symbols. In some communities the liturgy cannot be celebrated without dance. In these instances there is not dancing at the liturgy; the liturgy is literally danced.

In sum, the body has its own ways of knowledge, remembrance, and expression, and various symbolic vehicles inscribe the faith on our bodies through the five senses. While some cultures literally carve their central beliefs into the flesh of initiands, Christian ritual, though less dramatic, can be equally as powerful. We employ all our senses in Christian ritual, although some traditions may emphasize one more than another at a given period of time. Physiology, culture, and tradition all play a role regarding the use of the body. We can speak of the meaningfulness of the body and its symbols, but sometimes we must more accurately attend to what symbols "do" rather than what they "mean." This is particularly true of bodily symbols. We do a disservice to our people if we do not attend with care to all the distinct symbolic languages in our liturgical repertoire and their effects on the embodied person.

Up to this point we have been speaking about liturgical symbols in reference to the body and its senses. It is also possible to speak more directly of liturgical symbols, looking at them in their own characteristics, and we will do that now.

The Various Symbolic Vehicles

The Verbal

When we consider the verbal, we are addressing one of the principal symbolic vehicles in liturgy. In the previous chapter we spoke about the "turn to the subject," or the anthropocentric turn. More recent studies have moved beyond this understanding with its implied sense of immediate self-presencing to what may be called the "turn to language" or hermeneutics. We attended to this in the treatment of Ricoeur and his theories of interpretation of symbol. In the linguistic turn thinkers have attempted to consider how language is not so much an instrument we use but a way of being. As David Power has shown in his recent approach to sacrament:

> The use of language shows how understanding and existence, perspective on life and living, go hand in hand. It reveals how people are, how what they are and what they think or feel belong together. The language traditions in which people belong show how life addresses them, how they address it, and how its possibilities, comedies, and tragedies are projected into some kind of living venture.[2]

It is not so much a matter of human experience moving to language but a simultaneity of language and life, even if we allow for the "unsaid," the more that never comes to speech.[3] It is important to be aware that contemporary language theorists consider language to be not only verbal but, rather, to include all forms of human expressiveness. For our purposes here, however, we will be attending to the verbal.

Language is particularly important for those who value the self-giving and self-expression of God in cosmos and history. Sacramental language, as Power says,

> allows us to see God's action in the past and in the present, without having to relate them by an unbroken sequence of events. . . . A ritual or sacramental event relates to an event within time past through the capacities and power of language to carry it forward and to allow it to enter afresh into lives.[4]

Language allows a movement of past to present and even into the future. What we do with language in Christian liturgy is to recount the paschal mystery in such a way that it impinges on our present and determines the shape of our future, if we open ourselves to the sacramental event. Sacramental language in the largest sense is not explanation but power; it configures our world. Further, when the church proclaims the redemptive story, it does so not just through the power of language but also in the power of the Spirit. Our remembrance of these saving mysteries through the mediation of story, blessing, praise, and thanksgiving, and in the power of the Spirit constitutes the sacramental event. It is through ritual remembrance expressed in language that we are brought into relationship with the God who is committed to our salvation, and we reciprocate God's self-giving with actions of our own. This mutual exchange of "selves" is what constitutes the sacramental event, and it occurs through the mediation of language.

While much more could be said regarding sacrament as a language event,[5] let us now turn to particular genres of language that are used in our sacramental rites.

LITERARY GENRES

The content of linguistic expression communicates meaning, but the forms of our speech do so as well. The Christian tradition, borrowing many of its forms from Judaism, makes particular use of narrative, foundational story, parable, prophecy, wisdom literature, and hagiography as well as the various genres of prayer—blessing, praise, thanksgiving, intercession, exorcism, repentance, offering, and lament.[6] The particular form of speech chosen provides the starting place for interpretation and appropriation. Historical narratives give insight into God's self-giving very differently than do parables or blessings. It is attention to the genre that gives entrée into further levels of meaning, much like attention to the actual shape of symbolic objects gives entrée to second and third levels of meaning.

Whatever genres are chosen for our liturgical celebration, be they historical or poetic, they are always contemporaneous proclamations to the believing community that hears the texts within its own life situation, desires, and sorrows. A story is never heard exactly the same in two different cultures or in two different eras. The Christian community believes that its narratives in Scripture or in the prayers of the Eucharist are Spirit-filled events, addressed by the living God to a historically and culturally defined community. The particular assembly in which these texts are proclaimed is invited to let these stories be the ones that define its identity and hopes. Appropriation happens when the community makes its wager of faith to let these stories become its stories with all the ethical implications that flow from them.

David Power suggests that the genre *narrative* is basic to keeping memorial of past events, and that it comes in four distinct forms: institution narrative, foundational story, foundational myth, and parable.[7] *Institution narratives* often set out the foundational events that formed the people and many times include a direct command to continue a given practice. Examples from the Jewish tradition include the story of the paschal lamb and the command to gather each year and tell the story of God's saving works for the people. In Christian practice we have such explicit commands as "do this in remembrance of me" regarding the

Eucharist, and other commands such as "go, preach and baptize" for initiation. Mandates for other sacraments are not as direct as for Eucharist and baptism, but we still depend upon Jesus' teachings and example to root Christian sacrament. Looking at the institution narrative of the Eucharist, it is not enough to say that in the West it is considered the consecratory moment. To properly interpret this text, we must look at the function of institution narratives in the tradition. For example, by including both the general narrative of Jesus' ministry and the command to remember in the great prayer of eucharistic blessing, we give warrant for doing what we do. The ancient eucharistic prayer of Sarapion, bishop of Thmuis, is extremely explicit about the relationship between what Jesus did at the Last Supper and what the Christian community does in its ritual meal. It states that "For the Lord Jesus Christ, in the night when he was betrayed, took bread, broke it. . . . Therefore we also offered the bread, making the likeness of the death."[8] And the same is said for the wine. To faithfully fulfill the command of Jesus is to accomplish what Jesus desired by doing what he did: to offer his presence in the symbols of eucharatized bread and wine, that is, bread and wine over which thanksgiving was offered and then shared.

Foundational stories or *narratives* of a people are often the contexts for institution narratives. This is true of the Paschal Seder where "the ritual mandate to eat the Paschal Lamb as an act of remembrance is set within the commemoration of the larger story of the liberation from Egypt."[9] The foundation story that roots the eucharistic mandate is the passion narrative inclusive of the accounts of the resurrection, but at times we include foundational stories beginning with creation. In the fourth eucharistic prayer of the present Roman Rite, we have an extended narrative beginning with God, and extending through creation, the flood, the covenants and the prophets, until this climaxes with the narrative of Jesus' life and example, especially what he did "on the night before he died"—the so-called institution narrative. When we baptize at the Paschal Vigil, we baptize within the foundational stories of the creation, the historical narratives of the chosen people, and the Christ event. Each year, by repeating these narratives in ever-new contexts, our identity is affirmed and, we may even say, re-created. We self-identify with the Christ story in this place and this time and renew a commitment to live according to the mandates of the Gospel.

Foundational myths are also within the genre of narrative. Rather than being historical records of the beginnings of the cosmos and human life, they are poetic accounts that place the human person within the context of God's graciousness and the fact of evil. Demythologization of the myths is necessary, not so that we can dismiss them as feeble attempts to trace the origins of the cosmos, but so that we can take up the stories as poetic narratives that can continue to address human complicity with evil while maintaining faith in a good God. Recognition of the genre of myth allows for a second naiveté that releases us from a literalizing of the text and allows entrance into a second and third level of meaning, all by way of attention to the primary meaning of the myth.

In recent years, biblical research on the *parables* of Jesus has cast new light on this genre in the Scriptures.[10] The genre itself suggests that traditional wisdom may need to be rethought. Jesus' parables indicate that God's ways of justice may not coincide with our concept of a living wage, true neighborliness, or divine generosity. Power suggests that parables reflect a standard of moral wisdom that can deeply influence the way of living one's life in the shadow of the Cross. He states that the importance of parable to sacrament "is that it is the kind of story, and teaching through story, which reaches people in their daily lives and challenges the ethical perspectives which they bring to these."[11] Attention to parable and its particular characteristics remind us of the kind of irruption that the reign of God makes in our very ordered lives. In a sense, parable prepares us to hear what the kingdom may be like inclusive even of suffering unto death for love of others.

Prophecy is also a genre that challenges believers. In the first place, prophecy highlights God's initiative with the chosen people and provides the context of love to hear God's offer of relationship. But prophecy does more, and it is why the prophets were often subject to persecution. The prophet spoke in God's name and called the people to account for their covenant responsibilities. Many times prophets challenged the status quo of both the priestly and kingdom institutions of Israel. Power suggests there is a subversive nature to prophecy that ought to be part of sacrament and that we ignore only to our peril.[12] It is the kind of narrative that calls for repeated acts of conversion and rededication. There is a need for prophecy to call even treasured church structures to account about how they do or do not reflect the Gospel.

PRAYER GENRES

Having established the dialogical nature of the liturgy in an earlier chapter, it is appropriate to speak about the various genres of prayer that make up Christian celebration. Of particular importance are those of praise, thanksgiving, blessing, and intercession. It is sometimes difficult to distinguish between *praise* and *thanksgiving,* but one clarification that has been given is that praise "gives voice to admiration at God's name and eternal, ineffable mystery," while thanksgiving "is an articulation of gratitude that emerges from the recall of God's salvific deeds or actions."[13] *Intercession* places the Christian community in an expectant position before the God of creation and redemption. We invoke God, describe our needs, and offer intercession. Intercessory prayers range from asking favors of God to asking God's favor. New attention in intercessory prayer is being placed on our role in effecting what God desires.

The genre of *blessing* prayers has received enormous attention in recent years, yielding significant insights into the structure and meaning of the eucharistic prayer. In general we can say that blessings are Spirit-led prayers of sacramental rites that bring together praise of God, commemoration of God's work in human history, invocation of God's power over the elements in question, and intercession for the church—its desire for the effect of God's power in its life. Blessings recall God's being as creator, redeemer, and sanctifier, remembrance of the covenants, and invocation of God as Father of Jesus Christ whose life of self-emptying love for humanity is shown through the Cross. They often also include a confession of sin. It must be remembered that blessing prayers are said over concrete elements such as bread and wine, oil and water, which bind the human person to the earth and relate God to us through these symbols. In Christian prayers of blessing there is almost always a trinitarian structure and an eschatological thrust. In sum, blessing is a complex prayer that unites many facets of the community's belief system. In summarizing blessings' characteristics, Power suggests that blessings relate "God's action through Word and Spirit to creation, to covenant, and to redemption"; it is symbolic, prophetic, creedal, narrative, doxological, and grounded in God's own mandates.[14]

It is possible to have prayers that are primarily one form or another, but it is often the case that the genres are combined in a single prayer. This is particularly true for the great eucharistic prayers but also for less complex forms such as the opening collects of the Mass. The alternative opening prayer or collect for the Christmas Mass at dawn reads as follows:

> Almighty God and Father of light,
> a child is born for us and a son is given to us.
> Your eternal Word leaped down from heaven
> in the silent watches of the night,
> and now your Church is filled with wonder
> at the nearness of her God.

> Open our hearts to receive his life
> and increase our vision with the rising of dawn,
> that our lives may be filled with his glory and his peace,
> who lives and reigns for ever and ever.

Without articulating it in so many words, this collect is clearly a prayer of gratitude or thanksgiving for God's saving deed of sending the Son to be with us. Within that context it is commemorative. The prayer moves from thanksgiving and gratitude to intercession as the church pleads that our lives be changed because of the Son's coming.

In summary, verbal symbolism plays a very important part in Christian ritual. In some cases verbal prayer such as a collect is the ritual action itself. At other times verbal prayers are joined to ritual actions in such a way that they focus the meaning of the community's activities or interactions with one another. This would be true of blessings, consecrations, or exorcisms. As a symbol, the verbal has its distinct presentation through various literary genres. Attention to the genres of institution narrative, parable, or blessing is essential for understanding the meaning and purpose of the verbal symbolism. Like all symbols, the verbal makes demands on the community. It asks for participation, for commitment to the world proposed by the text. Above all these things is the conviction that God works through created realities, in this case the created reality of language in its many forms.

Bodily Gestures

In speaking of the body, we related some information on the use of the body in liturgy through liturgical gestures. Here we want to attend a bit more thoroughly to the nonverbal expression of the body in posture and gesture. Robert Ver Eecke speaks about the categories of liturgical gesture as "those actions of the body which a) express or embody an interior attitude (e.g., folding or opening and lifting hands); b) serve a symbolic purpose (e.g., imposition of hands as a symbol of empowerment); c) express the relationship between persons in the assembly (e.g., joining hands for the Our Father) or between the assembly and the transcendent (e.g., genuflection and kneeling); and d) serve a functional purpose (e.g., movement of a person from one place to another in order to perform an action)."[15]

Bodily movement normally falls within one of three categories: posture, actions, and gestures. Posture is both cultural and traditional. We have a range of postures that are physiologically possible, and the Christian community has made choices from among these according to culture and context. Some postures, like standing, have remained constant over time, while others, such as kneeling, have varied in use and meaning. Standing usually denotes an attitude of reverence, and so standing has traditionally been connected with hearing the Scriptures, especially the gospel, and as the preferred posture during Sundays and seasons of rejoicing. Sitting became more possible after chairs or pews were introduced into the church for the assembly; it is a posture most conducive to listening. In Asia, sitting on the ground is the preferred mode of bodily attitude, and it is often viewed as a gesture of respect. Kneeling often indicates a position of supplication or adoration; in some cases, it denotes an attitude of sorrow for sin. Accordingly the Council of Nicea forbade kneeling on Sundays and during the Easter season. During the medieval period, however, kneeling became more accepted as the normal posture for prayer, and it carried the meaning of adoration. Kneeling throughout most of the Mass became common, particularly as the assembly's active participation in the Mass decreased dramatically. As Ver Eecke states, "private prayer, penance and distant adoration became the dominant mode of eucharistic worship which continued to the 20th century."[16] At the present time, kneeling is recommended during most of the eucharistic prayer, although some communities, despite regulations to the contrary, continue to prefer the practice of standing.

Liturgical actions include bowing, genuflection, and processions. Bowing ranges from a small bow of the head to a profound bow from the waist. The extreme form of bowing is complete prostration. This is usually reserved for gestures of total self-giving at religious professions and ordinations. Genuflection is an abbreviated version of kneeling, revealing an attitude of adoration and reverence. It is most commonly associated with respect toward the Blessed Sacrament, either during the eucharistic celebration or before the reserved sacrament. Processions involve the community or members thereof in a formal movement from place to place. The moods of processions range from the joy of the wedding procession and the journey to the baptismal font to the reserved and somber mood of the procession with the body during the funeral Mass. Processions can either be toward a revered object, such as the procession to reverence the cross on Good Friday, or may be with an object, such as the procession with palms on Palm Sunday. Processions involving just the liturgical ministers happen with regularity during the entrance rites of the Mass, Solemn Evening Prayer, and other services, and they too sometimes involve the carrying of sacred objects, such as the holy oils during the Chrism Mass or with the reserved sacrament to the altar of repose on Holy Thursday.

Liturgical actions involve liturgical ministers to a great extent and the whole assembly to a lesser extent. Ministers elevate arms and hands during presidential prayers, and the assembly is beginning to do this as well in some instances. Ministers also kiss sacred objects such as the altar, the gospel books and the cross, although the whole assembly generally venerates the cross on Good Friday with a kiss. The kiss of peace has been restored to everyone in the assembly in the contemporary eucharistic celebration. Perhaps one of the most often used liturgical actions is that of making the sign of the cross. This action is done as a private devotion and it begins and ends every official liturgy (except Good Friday and the Easter Vigil when a single signing on Holy Thursday begins the Triduum liturgies). We sign catechumens, those anointed with the oil of the sick, and those to be confirmed with chrism. The extension of the hands in blessing is another important liturgical action once mainly performed by presiding celebrants but more recently by members of the assembly as well, such as during the scrutiny Masses and for those about to receive the sacrament of the sick.

In sum, the body with its postures and actions is one of the primary liturgical symbols we have to work with. We engage in actions that simply involve ourselves, like genuflections, but we also join actions with objects and we act upon other persons. With more attention to the right of people to their own culture, we are seeing greater diversity in liturgical body movements than the current Roman Rite generally allows. As we indicated above, dancing is a major form of liturgical participation in some cultures. The body is perhaps one of the most eloquent nonverbal symbols in our repertoire. It has the ability to express mood, intensity, reverence, awe, joy, sorrow, etc., without necessarily needing other symbols to help focus its meaning or its "action." Like many other symbolic vehicles, we join bodily movement with music and with text that help to amplify its meaning even further.

Symbolic Space and Objects

We have spoken of the cosmos as a place of emergence of symbols, but we must also attend to those dedicated spaces that the Christian community constructs for its individual and communal worship. Architecture is one of the principal symbolic vehicles that humans use to express their self-understanding and desires. Christian church architecture is a symbol that likewise expresses Christian identity, faith, and hope. Since the earliest days of the church, Christians have found the need to create spaces that shelter the assembly and allow the liturgies of the community to unfold. They have also used architecture to express what is difficult to express through other symbolic vehicles. Christian life is a faith journey, and so church buildings have allowed for processional spaces that follow the pattern of entrance into the church from the doors to the inner sanctum. Christianity holds that its life on earth is only a temporary dwelling place and that its future is in the heavenly Jerusalem, and so Byzantine churches associate the lower levels of the church building with the earth and the upper levels with heaven. Christian life is essentially communal, and so church spaces have tried with varying degrees of success to hold the community together as it celebrates its communal rites. Early church basilicas and more contemporary churches are shaped more consciously for the full participation of the whole assembly than were medieval models. The church community itself is a dwelling place for God; likewise its gathering spaces have been understood to be particular dwelling places of holy mystery. Hagia Sophia in Istanbul is probably the quintessential example of architecture attempting to capture a sense of the magnitude and presence of God through use of grandiose space and light.

Liturgical artist Marchita Mauck speaks of the vocabulary of space, namely, its shape, proportion, perspective, or orientation and the effects on it of lighting, color, and textures.[17] The shape of early Christian basilicas convey a very different understanding of community and its relationship with God than do the soaring Gothic spaces of the late medieval period. The proportion and scale of the great Cluniac monastery churches speak a very different language and theology than do Cistercian spaces that were deliberately created to human scale with attention to acoustics rather than to the visual. The perspective of chapels that open to sky, forest, or city also convey a different theology of relationship to the earth and culture than does the cave-like church at Ronchamp designed by Le Corbusier. Lighting, color, and texture also make a difference to the assembly and its worship. Consider the dark interiors of Romanesque churches or the light, open spaces of much contemporary architecture awash in the rich colors of stained glass.

Liturgical objects are important to consider when seeking to understand Christian liturgy. There are several main objects in worship spaces that orient the worship to the central meaning of the faith. In contemporary church designs, the major liturgical objects are the altar, the ambo, the chair, and the baptismal font. Attention to the Liturgy of the Word and the Liturgy of the Eucharist has led to a decision to design worship spaces such that the ambo and table are related to each other and in proportion to one another, often made of similar design and materials. One can see here the liturgy constitution's insistence on the presence of God in word as much as in sacrament (*CSL* 7). The placement of such objects also matters in that the council's mandate for full, conscious, and active participation suggests that the assembly be actually gathered around the ambo and altar to better allow its participation. The presider's chair, according to the new *GIRM* (310), should not look like a throne but should be placed in such a way as to signify the priest's role of presiding over the assembly and its prayer. Placement of objects in liturgical space—whether the chair for the presider or the chairs (or spaces) reserved for the assembly—reveals an ecclesiology. Ritual space and placement of members can signify communion and equality in baptism or it can stress the distinctiveness of our order and roles within the church.

Recent concern about the placement of the tabernacle reveals a renewed emphasis on the reserved sacrament and in piety pertaining to it. The spatial relationship between tabernacle and altar speaks of the relationship between the celebration of the Eucharist and the reservation of the sacrament. The repeated reverences to the reserved sacrament on the altar itself in the Tridentine Mass revealed a certain priority of the reserved sacrament over the actual celebration of the Eucharist. Placement of the tabernacle in its own separate but related space assures a more balanced view of the appropriate priority of the celebration of the Eucharist over eucharistic devotion.

The baptismal font has been given a much more prominent place in contemporary churches than in the immediate past period. According to *Built of Living Stones*, the 2000 document of the Bishops' Committee on the Liturgy of the USCC/NCCB on art, architecture, and worship, "because the rites of initiation of the Church begin with baptism and are completed by the reception of the Eucharist, the baptismal font and its location reflect the Christian's journey *through* the waters of baptism *to* the altar" (66). As I mentioned earlier, the size of baptismal fonts is a necessary condition for their complex meanings to emerge.

Other ritual furnishings, such as the cross, candles, and the paschal candle, are ritual symbols that express central beliefs of the church and order the journey of faith. It is not only the cross that is important; but what we do with the cross expands its meaning and function. We often process with a cross to the altar at the beginning of Mass, and we lead the baptized to the font with the cross. At the Easter Vigil we illumine the church with the new fire, proclaiming as the paschal candle is carried in procession through the church, "Light of Christ." Likewise we incense the paschal candle and proclaim the *Exsultet* immediately after, recounting our foundational story in song by the light of the new fire.

The ritual oils we use (oil of catechumens, oils of the sick, and chrism) have been given a new prominence by being housed in an ambry visible for all to see. Not only are the oils seen, but also a more fulsome use of the oils touches the olfactory as much as the visual. Water has been brought out of private baptisteries and into the assembly space, often placed at the very entrance and on axis with the altar. Baptismal consciousness is reinforced by several symbolic vehicles: through the symbol of water, the placement of the font, and through liturgical actions such as renewal of baptismal promises.

In summary, all these symbolic vehicles enable the community to express itself, to remind itself of its identity and beliefs, and to act out its fundamental covenant with God in the paschal mystery. As we discussed in the previous chapter, symbols are dense with meaning. They have the capacity to gain and lose meaning over time and in changed circumstances. They address the whole person in all of her capacities, and draw participants into their world. Because of the multivalence of symbols, the juxtaposition of objects with verbal symbols helps focus the meaning of these rich signifiers. Symbols not only "mean" but are also performative, i.e., they "do" something. Ritual space orders the assembly, white garments wrap the initiands and deceased in Christ, and the cross leads to the font and to the table of the Lord. As with verbal symbols, attention to the particular genre of liturgical objects enables more faithful interpretation of their meaning and actions.

Symbol of Music

Sound also functions as a symbol within the human repertoire of expression. Since time immemorial human communities have raised their voices in song and filled their ritual events with the sounds of rhythmic drumming and melodies of horn, flute, and stringed instruments. Christian worship has likewise used both vocal and instrumental music in a variety of ways in its ritual life. Since Vatican II there has been significant interest in exploring the symbolic nature of music as well as the ritual function of music within Christian worship.

The Milwaukee Symposia for Church Composers: A Ten-Year Report (MR), written in 1992 by a group of liturgists, text writers, musicians, composers, and pastoral practitioners under the auspices of Archbishop Rembert Weakland, is one such document that offers a summary of contemporary thought on the symbolic nature of sacred music.[18] Depending heavily upon the authors reviewed in the last chapter, this document speaks of the symbolic nature of sound itself. Beginning with its inherent nature, sound allows for other levels of meaning to emerge within the ritual context, in particular, the self-revelation of God. It is helpful to quote this document at length on this subject.

> Sound itself is our starting point for understanding music and its capacity to serve as a vehicle for God's self-revelation. Sound's temporality, for example, symbolizes a God active in creation and history; its seemingly insubstantial nature symbolizes a God who is both present and hidden; its dynamism symbolizes a God who calls us into dialogue; its ability to unify symbolizes our union with God and others; its evocation of personal presence symbolizes a God whom we perceive as personal. (*MR* 13)

If sound, in general, is symbolic, it follows then that music as a particular manifestation of sound is likewise symbolic. Not only does it serve as a vehicle for God's self-expression, it also serves the human community in its encounter with the divine.

> [R]hythmic elements underscore the temporality of human existence into which God has intervened, and a familiar melody can contribute to a heightened experience of unity with each other and God. . . . Because sound and, by extension, music are natural vehicles for the self-revelation of the God of Judaeo-Christian revelation, and because liturgy is the locus for encounter with and the revelation of such a God, it is understandable why music unites itself so intimately to Christian liturgy. (*MR* 14)

Consideration of the use of music in the liturgy has led to a gradual distinction of the kinds of sacred music and their characteristics. Joseph Gelineau, writing in 1964, made the distinction, within the general category of "sacred music," between liturgical music and religious music.[19] Liturgical music is "that which the Church admits, both in law and in practice, to the celebration of her official and public worship."[20] Religious music, on the other hand, is music that expresses religious sentiment but is not used in the liturgy.[21] In his description of liturgical music, Gelineau refines the definition further to include: (a) strictly liturgical chant, (b) chant and music that accompany the liturgy, and (c) song and music of ceremonies that are not strictly liturgical.[22] Helmut Hucke and Bernard Huijbers, writing a few years after Gelineau's publication, made a clarification that has been very useful in subsequent years. Hucke distinguished between (a) singing in the liturgy, (b) song accompanying the ritual, and (c) music "which is itself a rite."[23] The first would include a Communion reflection hymn; the second, a litany accompanying a procession to the baptismal font; and the third, the singing of the *Exsultet* or the *Gloria*.

It is possible to speak of the characteristics of liturgical music. Pius X, publishing an instruction in 1903 on sacred music, *Tra le sollecitudini*, spoke of a threefold quality: holiness, beauty, and universality (*TLS* 2). In addition, the document stated in its opening paragraph that sacred music "being an integral part of the liturgy, is directed to the general object of this liturgy, namely, the glory of God and the sanctification and edification of the faithful" (*TLS* 1). The Constitution on the Sacred Liturgy of 1964 affirmed these characteristics and stressed the "ministerial function supplied by sacred music in the service of the Lord" (*CSL* 112). Later documents, such as *Musicam Sacram* (*MS*), a 1967 instruction on sacred music by the Sacred Congregation for Divine Worship, also included the three characteristics of *TLS* but offered more functional qualities as well. Music, it said, does not have to be of any special sort (e.g., chant), as long as it "matches the spirit of the service itself and the character of the individual parts and is not a hindrance to the required active participation of the people" (*MS* 9). In addition, it must suit the solemnity of the day while respecting the integrity of the rites (*MS* 10, 11). *MS* spoke of music's role in giving the liturgy a nobler aspect, providing a more graceful expression to prayer, bringing out the distinctly hierarchic character of the liturgy, achieving union of hearts, raising the mind to heavenly realities, and making the liturgy a symbol of the heavenly Jerusalem (*MS* 5).

Music in Catholic Worship (*MCW*), a 1972 document from the U.S. Episcopal Conference, also stressed the ministerial function of music. It must assist the assembly to express and share the faith as well as strengthen it. It should heighten the texts so that they speak more fully and more effectively. Finally, it should unify the congregation while also expressing meaning and feeling that only music can express (*MCW* 23 and 24). Perhaps the most important contribution of this document was to suggest that a threefold judgment must be made to test the suitability of a particular piece of music for the liturgy: musical, liturgical, and pastoral (*MCW* 25). Written ten years later as a follow-up document to *MCW*, *Liturgical Music Today* (*LMT*) stresses the functional quality of music. Reminiscent of the categories of Hucke, *LMT* suggests that sometimes song is meant to accompany the ritual actions; at other times, it constitutes the rite itself (*LMT* 9, 10). The *Milwaukee Report* of 1992 speaks explicitly of the symbolic function of music: its ability to express what we believe and to shape that belief (*MR* 12). In addition, it comments on the threefold judgment on liturgical music of *MCW* that had suffered some criticism. It suggests that these three elements (liturgical, musical, pastoral judgments) not be considered separately or as hierarchically ordered to the pastoral, but that there be "a balancing of the various facets of this single judgment and not the opposition of one element to another. The process of the judgment, therefore, is not chronological but dynamic and interactive" (*MR* 82).

In sum, we have come to recognize the symbolic nature of sound in general and ritual music in particular. We have likewise come to distinguish ritual music as comprising that which is done in the liturgy, which accompanies ritual action, or which constitutes the ritual action itself. In addition, we have come to understand ritual music as having the same purposes as the liturgy in general—the glorification of God and the sanctification of the human person. The characteristics can be as generic as holiness, beauty, and universality, and as specific as the ministerial function of expressing and sharing the faith, highlighting the meaning of texts, and uniquely expressing human meanings and emotion.

Conclusions

Having reviewed the body in Christian liturgy and the various symbolic vehicles used, it is obvious that the symbolic nature of the liturgy is at once complex, meaningful, and performative. The entire body is involved in Christian worship, and the symbolic vehicles of the liturgy are addressed to the mind, the will, the psyche, and the emotions through the five senses. Culture and context have often determined the preferred bodily attitudes and involvement, ranging from restraint to exuberance. Sensitivity to culture and history reminds us that we do not have first an idea of "reverence," for example, and then find a bodily attitude to express it. Rather, different cultures use their bodies differently and the meaning of reverence changes according to the bodily expression. Such awareness suggests that regulations regarding universal postures may need to be rethought.

Attention to the particular genres of symbolic vehicles is extremely important for proper understanding and appropriation. This is true for verbal symbolism as much as for space, objects, and music. Theologians have been interested not only in the meaning of these symbolic vehicles but also in their ability to express the self-revelation of God and the divine/human relationship. Attention to symbols' role in the glorification of God and the sanctification of human persons continues to be of central importance. In short, it is only through the body and symbols that this divine/human relationship is expressed, developed, and celebrated. Attention to the liturgy and its symbols is all about mediation.

CHAPTER NINE

Liturgy and Culture

Culture and the Social Sciences

Developments in the social sciences have brought new attention to the variety of cultures and to the role of culture in human affairs, and this has subsequently influenced all branches of theology. It is not that culture has gone unnoticed in past history; rather, it was presumed that there was one, universal culture applicable to all persons in all places. Bernard Lonergan refers to this as a "classicist view" of culture.[1] In the North Atlantic, Western world, to be cultured was to be schooled in the cumulative values and arts of the Greco-Roman world as passed down through a curriculum in the liberal arts. To be cultured was the opposite of barbarism. As Lonergan notes, it was a normative notion of culture that stressed values not facts, was universal, and was a set of ideals to be imitated, of eternal truths and universally valid laws. From the classicist point of view, particular circumstances are incidental; normative values and truths hold for all people in all situations. Other cultures were not valued; all others were expected to give up their own culture in favor of the more advanced and universally applicable culture of the West. Of course, the persons who judged all others as deficient were the persons formed in this Western, classicist culture. The effects of this classicist view can easily be seen in the colonialism of the fifteenth to twentieth centuries. Countless cultures were dismantled; peoples were deprived of their languages, customs, and ideas, all in the name of so-called progress.

The classicist approach to culture affected Christian evangelization as well. Not only was the faith spread throughout the world, but so too was Western culture. For much of the church's more recent history, the evangelizing dynamic was a one-way street; new cultures were on the receiving end of evangelization and had nothing to add to the Christian practice of older churches. Theologically this meant that the diversity of peoples added nothing essential to the faith, only a superficial difference in dress, so to speak. The liturgy continued to be celebrated according to the Roman Rite and in Latin without any modifications, despite the community's inability to understand or relate to those ritual patterns.

The empirical social sciences challenged this classicist view at its roots. In 1973 Clifford Geertz spoke about culture as "an historically transmitted pattern of meanings embodied in symbols, a system of inherited conceptions expressed in symbolic forms by means of which [men] communicate, perpetuate, and develop their knowledge about and attitudes toward life."[2] Numerous cultural theorists followed along these lines, developing what would become viewed as an "empiricist notion of culture." This position posits that there are as many cultures as there are distinct sets of meanings and values. Culture is what is learned in human societies, what societies share in common. History and context play a decisive role in the development of culture, and principles are explored as they operate in changing circumstances. There is a sense that the particular is more important than the universal. Importantly, no one culture is given superior status over others. This understanding of culture suggests a dynamic and open-ended view of culture. It is always changing as individuals and groups constantly interact with their environment and circumstances, leading to modification of their worldview and its mediation through symbol systems.

Louis Luzbetak suggests this new understanding of culture has significant implications for Christian mission and liturgical life. He views culture as a design or plan for living. It is a set of norms, standards, notions, and beliefs that enables a community to adapt itself to its physical, social, and ideational environment.[3] Very importantly, it *intends* to be a successful negotiation of life, but it does not have to be successful. Its concept of the world could be true or not, but it intends to be true. It could be functional, but it might be dysfunctional. It aims at the well-being of society, but it might not serve all members of the society equally well. In sum, culture is only a partial achievement of human community and meaning.[4] This is exceedingly important from a missiological standpoint in that it suggests that all cultures are fallible; all cultures are in need of redemption. Thus Christianity always has something to offer a culture.

Christianity and Culture

This brings us to views of culture within church practice. The history is quite mixed. In fact, from its earliest years, the church had to deal with issues of culture and diversity. Christianity took shape within a diverse Jewish practice—a more conservative Hebrew- and Aramaic-speaking Judaism and a more liberal Hellenized Judaism. Almost immediately Christians had to deal with whether or not to continue participation in the Temple cult, a practice that was contested within Judaism itself. The First Council of Jerusalem, then, had to deal with the issue of how to initiate Gentiles into Christianity and whether or not Christianity would continue its Jewish ritual practices. As we know from the Acts of the Apostles, the nascent church decided that one did not have to continue all Jewish practices to become a Christian.

The issue of language was an important one. As Christianity spread throughout the Mediterranean basin, it took on the language of *koinē* Greek, but that lasted only for about two and a half centuries until Latin became the common language. While this change from Greek to Latin did not seem to cause significant upheaval at the time, it subsequently became an issue in the church's missionary efforts. People began to ask whether there was something essential about teaching Christianity and celebrating Christian rituals in Latin. In the ninth century, missionaries St. Cyril and St. Methodius, apostles to the Slavs, recognized the significance of vernacular worship and they translated liturgical books and biblical texts into Old Slavonic. This allowed Christianity to take on a new "inculturated" form, different from what was developing in the West. In spite of some opposition from those who argued for a Latin Christianity, it took hold in Slavic lands within their own culture.

The acceptance of different cultural practices within Latin Christianity was not always a problem. There were times when cultural diversity was welcomed or at least tolerated. This was true during the medieval period of Western Christianity. The history of Roman liturgical books is a history of their modification by the cultures of northern Europe as missionaries brought the Christian Gospel to the peoples of the British Isles, the Franks, the Gauls, and the Germans. Roman books were imported to these countries but were modified according to their needs and their cultures. While remaining in Latin, the liturgical prayers were modified according to the genius of these peoples, often rejecting the sobriety of Roman euchology in favor of more fulsome expression. Dramatic rituals of light and darkness and various processions were incorporated into the Roman books and then sent back to Rome to be subsequently distributed throughout the world. The history of European Christianity is a history of the transformation of culture by the faith and the transformation of the faith by culture.

The history of Christianity in China is not so happy. Jesuit Matteo Ricci and colleagues dedicated themselves to evangelization of the Chinese by incorporating elements from their native culture. While this practice was carried out with some opposition on and off for some 150 years, it was finally condemned in 1742, with the result that China was basically lost to Christianity.[5] In spite of this huge failure, the church continued to follow a classicist view of culture even as missionaries continued to plead for some allowances for cultural differences.

The Second Vatican Council exhibited a much different attitude toward culture than had previous generations. Using the theological category of the Incarnation, the council suggested that the church must implant itself in new cultures as Jesus did in his own time. *Ad Gentes*, the council's document on missionary activity, states that "if the church is to be in a position to offer all women and men the mystery of salvation and the life brought by God, then it must implant itself among all these groups in the same way that Christ by his incarnation committed himself to the particular social cultural circumstances of the women and men among whom he lived" (*AG* 10). And later,

> just as happened in the economy of the incarnation, the young churches, which are rooted in Christ and built on the foundations of the apostles, take over all the riches of the nations which have been given to Christ as an inheritance (cf. Ps 2:8). They borrow from the customs, traditions, wisdom, teaching, arts and sciences of their people everything which could be used to praise the glory of the Creator. (*AG* 22)

Gaudium et Spes, the conciliar document on the church in the modern world, states that

> the Church has been sent to all ages and nations and, therefore, is not tied exclusively and indissolubly to any race or nation, to any one particular way of life, or to any set of customs, ancient or modern. The Church is faithful to its traditions and is at the same time conscious of its universal mission; it can, then, enter into communion with different forms of culture, thereby enriching both itself and the cultures themselves. (*GS* 58)

This more open-ended approach to culture, indeed this genuine appreciation of culture, has wide implications for the shape of Christianity to come, and we are just beginning to see the fruits of this process.

The Constitution on the Sacred Liturgy was the first document approved by the council fathers, and, since it was discussed at the very beginning of the conciliar process, it did not reflect the explicit openness to other cultures that the later documents exhibit. However, there were some important principles articulated in paragraphs 37 to 40 regarding liturgy and culture. First, the Constitution insisted that it did not want to "impose a rigid uniformity" but that the church "respects and fosters the genius and talents of the various races and people" (*CSL* 37). It further argued that whatever is not explicitly tied to superstition and error is to be regarded with sympathy, and the church would admit such elements into the liturgy. In paragraph 38 the document provided for "legitimate variations and adaptations to different groups, regions, and peoples, especially in mission lands" in the revision of liturgical books, "provided the substantial unity of the Roman Rite is preserved." Three things are of utmost importance in these texts. First, that simple fact of allowing diversity in practice was a significant departure from immediate past practice. Second, there is no indication that older churches need also to address issues of culture, although this would change in time. Third, in these paragraphs the term *adaptation* is used to speak of the changes that the council foresaw, especially in mission lands. Later commentators would speak about the tentative nature of the term *adaptation* and its tendency to reflect more of a superficial modification of the Roman Rite. However, paragraph 40 goes further by stating that "in some places and circumstances, however, an even more radical adaptation of the liturgy is needed." This was an extraordinary breakthrough regarding change and the Roman Rite. It would remain to future decades to explore exactly what this meant and what processes would be put into place to carry out these more radical reforms.

It is important to take a moment here and speak about terminology. I have already referred to the word *adaptation*, but I have also spoken about its limitations. Different terminology was required to speak of a more profound transformation of cultures and the transformation of the faith. Theologians turned to the human sciences for some help in this regard. Since culture is that which is learned in a society, it stands to reason that we can speak of the process whereby individuals consciously and unconsciously take on the values, ideas, and expressions of their own culture. Anthropologists refer to this as the process of enculturation. While some would identify this process with socialization, they are closely allied but not identical. Luzbetak himself prefers to regard enculturation as the "lifelong process of mastering an adaptive system."[6] *Acculturation* is another term borrowed from anthropology that speaks about the relationship of one society to another and the effects of this relationship on their respective cultures. In the 1970s theorists defined the term as "those phenomena which result when groups of individuals having different cultures come into continuous firsthand contact, with subsequent change in the original culture patterns of either or both groups."[7] More recently the term has come to mean the contact between a weaker and more powerful society, where the weaker society adapts itself to the stronger society. One layer is placed on top of another, so to speak; true mutual transformation does not take place.

This notion of cultural meeting and exchange clearly relates to Christianity's contact with new and different cultures. It had been established that Christianity does not come "naked" into a culture, but that it is already clothed in a culture as Christ himself had taken on a distinctive culture and history. What has received more attention in recent years is the phenomenon of Christianity clothed in one culture coming into contact with another culture. While in the classicist view of culture, the dominant culture won out; in an empiricist view there is more room for reciprocity and exchange between cultures and therefore of true transformation. There are really two issues at stake here. First, the process by which Christianity becomes embodied in a new culture; second, the effect on the universal church as a new expression of Christianity is offered back to the evangelizing culture. Theologians needed a new term to speak about this phenomenon of the faith taking root in a new culture and the exchange that then follows. The term chosen for this was the neologism *inculturation*. It was first used as early as 1962 by Joseph Masson, SJ, in an article in *Nouvelle Revue Théologique* 84, but was picked up by a Protestant missionary and professor, George Barney, in 1973 in a book entitled *The Gospel and Frontier Peoples*. Later the term was discussed at the Jesuits' 32nd General Congregation in 1975, and it was taken up more generally by theologians after that time. The first time it came into papal use was in 1979 when Pope John Paul II used it in his Address to the Pontifical Biblical Commission.[8]

While the origin of the term may be interesting, the meaning of the term is far more important. Inculturation refers to that process when Christianity, coming from another culture, begins to take root in a new culture. It is a dialogue between faith and culture that transforms and enriches the culture in which the faith is proclaimed. Based on the definition of culture as a partial achievement of human meaning, the Gospel comes with something to offer the target culture. Those hearing the Gospel proclaimed accept the Gospel, but on their own terms and from within the view of their own culture. While the missionary may make a noble effort to evangelize within the culture of a people, it is only the receivers of the Gospel message who are truly able to "inculturate" the Gospel in the new culture. In this way, inculturation is not an imposition from the outside but a transformation from within. John Paul II had spoken often of the relationship between faith and culture, stressing the importance of an in-depth transformation of the culture. In his opening address to the Pontifical Council for Culture in 1982, John Paul II said, "The synthesis between culture and faith is not just a demand of culture, but also of faith. A faith which does not become culture is a faith which has not been fully received, not thoroughly thought through, not fully lived out."[9] It is this reciprocal dynamism between faith and culture that is the earmark of inculturation.

This first part of the inculturation process has perhaps received the most attention from theologians, pastors, and the magisterium. In 1994, the Sacred Congregation of Worship and the Discipline of the Sacraments published the Fourth Instruction on the Right Application of the Conciliar Constitution on the Liturgy (Nos. 37–40) entitled "The Roman Liturgy and Inculturation" (*Varietates Legitimae*).[10] This document is really in two distinct parts. Part one sets out a theology of inculturation as it has developed from 1962 to 1994. Quoting John Paul II frequently, it speaks of inculturation as signifying "an intimate transformation of the authentic cultural values by their integration into Christianity and the implantation of Christianity into different human cultures" (*VL* 4). But it goes further by stating that inculturation involves a double movement of making "the Gospel incarnate in different cultures and at the same time introduces peoples, together with their cultures, into her own community" (*VL* 4). The assimilation of these new cultural values is credited as "deepen[ing] understanding of Christ's message and giv[ing] it more effective expression in the liturgy and in the many different aspects of the life of the community of believers." The document stresses the necessity of the Christian message finding a permanent place in a culture and that the inculturation of the faith in Christian life and liturgy is the fruit of a progressive maturity in faith (*VL* 5). In addition, it speaks of the need for all churches to address the question of culture, new and old, and that none are required to renounce their own culture. The document speaks of the delicate balance that must be achieved in the liturgy being fully traditional and yet expressing itself in every human culture (*VL* 18).

Based on the limited nature of any culture, the liturgy helps to purify and sanctify the culture (*VL* 19).

The second part of the document takes a completely different tack. First, it acknowledges that despite what it says about inculturation, it is interested only in addressing issues of adaptation (*VL* 3). In addition, its main concern is procedural, that is, how the process of adaptation is to be regulated by the Holy See. Interestingly, despite the reciprocity that is at the very heart of the definition of inculturation, the document is concerned only with regulating the incarnation of the Gospel in a culture. The process of integrating that newly inculturated faith within the universal church is simply left out of the conversation. There is also a sense that step one of inculturation, the inculcation of the faith in a new culture, is seen as necessary yet difficult and problem wrought. Care must be taken at every step to make sure nothing of the Gospel is lost in translation. The second half of inculturation, the mutual exchange of gifts between the newly inculturated faith and the evangelizing culture, seems to be a step that the official church is not yet ready to address. This double movement involves an ecclesiology of respect between local churches, local churches and Rome, and trust that the Holy Spirit will guide the process. It requires humility on the part of older churches in that they must open themselves to the new insights of young churches as authentic interpretations of the Gospel. It means putting aside once and for all a classicist view of culture that still is suspicious of cultures outside the Western, North Atlantic ambit. Inculturation suggests that both the new culture and the church have something to learn from one another. Mark Francis suggests that "true inculturation entails conversion, a purification of those attitudes and practices in a given culture that do not conform to the gospel of Jesus. Inculturation also involves the humble assessment on the part of the church of the limited way it has sometimes proclaimed the gospel."[11] One can only hope that the next document on inculturation will deal just as rigorously with the second part of inculturation as *Varietates Legitimae* dealt with the first.

Liturgy: Adaptation and Inculturation

Up until this point, I have been speaking in broad terms of a theology of inculturation. In other words, I have addressed the larger issue of inculturating the Christian faith in general in new or changing cultural contexts. Now it is appropriate to address the more specific case of liturgical inculturation. Many of the same concerns apply to liturgical inculturation as to the broader inculturation of the faith: proclamation of the Gospel, reception of the Gospel from within a new culture, mutual exchange between local churches and local churches and Rome. However, there are specific issues that affect the adaptation and inculturation of the liturgy.

Perhaps the largest issue of inculturation is that it would lead to the creation of new Rites within the Catholic Church. At this time the church has rejected any such moves (*VL* 33, 36). Perhaps the most radical adaptation of the Mass approved by Rome has been the 1988 Mass of Zaire. However, it does not constitute a new rite but is carefully called "The Roman Missal for the Dioceses of Zaire." Since a more radical inculturation of the gospel and the liturgy was not imagined at the time of the council, and since *Varietates Legitimae* restricted itself to issues of adaptation, we are left to deal with less momentous—though still important— issues. What remains problematic, and will be obvious below, is that the theological and pastoral conversation has moved to issues of inculturation, while the legislation still remains with adaptation.

To begin, we must recognize that the liturgical renewal has resulted in the publication of *editiones typicae*, or typical editions, of the liturgical books that are meant to be used for all churches of the Latin Roman Rite. This means that the liturgy has a specific point of departure from which it must work. The mandate of the council was that these Latin editions were to be translated and adapted to the culture of particular churches. Translation of Latin texts has become a neuralgic issue in recent years. There has been a significant shift between the norms for translation in the 1969 document *Comme le prévoit* and the 2001 document *Liturgiam Authenticam* (On the Use of Vernacular Languages in the Publication of the Books of the Roman Liturgy). In the former, the particular character of the target language shapes the translation, while in the latter, the language of origin (Latin) determines the translation. Adaptation also raises the question of not only what can be changed but who has the authority to make such changes and for what purpose. What has come up repeatedly since the time of the council is the authority of episcopal conferences, the authority of the Congregation for Worship, and the relationship between the two. The current struggle over the translation of the third edition of the Roman Missal for the United States church is a case in point. The Congregation for Worship rejected the proposed translation by the U.S. bishops and demanded that a new translation be undertaken. As of this writing, the new translation process is still incomplete and is receiving considerable criticism for its stilted language.

As indicated above, it is clear that the Liturgy Constitution envisioned only an adaptation of the *editiones typicae*, not a more radical inculturation of the faith and then the expression of that faith in liturgy. Nonetheless, we are dealing with the issue of changes resulting in the appropriation of the faith and changes in the appropriation of the liturgical tradition. We are forced to raise the question of where we begin—with the faith or the liturgy. Sri Lankan theologian Aloysius Pieris argues persuasively that one begins not with inculturating the Eucharist but with inculturating the faith. In his understanding, Eucharist is a sign of the inculturation the church already accomplished.[12] While one might argue that the process of inculturation does not happen in such clearly delineated steps and does not take into account the role of ritual to negotiate change, there is something insightful about his comments. However, because of the intent of the conciliar constitution, we are forced to ask about changes to the liturgy even if there are larger issues at stake.

When we speak of adapting the liturgy, we are clearly talking about change in content and form. The council document on the liturgy noted that "the liturgy is made up of immutable elements, divinely instituted, and of elements subject to change. These not only may but ought to be changed . . ." (*CSL* 21). Just a few paragraphs later it also stated that "there must be no innovations unless the good of the Church genuinely and certainly requires them; care must be taken that any new forms adopted should in some way grow organically from forms already existing" (*CSL* 23). While these norms are helpful guidelines, the specific ways that they are to be applied has proven to be more difficult than first imagined. There are three issues of particular interest. First, *CSL* says that that there are things that are unchanging and things that can/ought to be changed. While at first glance this may be obvious, what is less obvious is exactly what falls into each column. Taking Eucharist as an example, clearly the memorial of Jesus Christ is of divine origin and cannot be changed, but what of the eucharistic elements? Is the use of bread and wine absolutely required for ritual memorial of Christ's paschal mystery or may the meal be of corn bread and beer? Many churches do not have wheat bread and wine in their culture and have petitioned for alternative foods. At this point, such permission has not been granted, but the issue remains. Another example is more poignant. Should baptism be done by the pouring of water over the head in a society like the Maasai of East Africa when to do that is to curse a woman with infertility?

Examples like these could be multiplied, but these are enough to suggest the depth of the problem.[13]

CSL states that any changes made must be for the good of the church. Using the same example as above, several mission churches have requested the change of the eucharistic matter for the good of their churches and the integrity of their culture. What remains contested is a process that allows more freedom for episcopal conferences to make significant changes within their own regions even while remaining in dialogue with the Congregation for Worship. In other words, does a local church have the authority to inculturate the faith, come up with culturally appropriate expressions of that faith in liturgical matters, and will the Roman See honor those choices? At the moment, according to *Varietates Legitimae* the balance of authority is clearly tilted toward the Congregation.

The third issue is that of organic growth. This norm clearly has as its concern the continuity of the tradition, but one might wonder if the Christian community has expressed in its liturgical rites every essential element of the gospel at this time. Could it not be that once the gospel is inculturated into a new culture some new insights and expressions could emerge? The question of whether such innovation would be permissible under current norms is left unaddressed at this time.

Having reviewed some of the issues that attend to the adaptation and inculturation of the liturgy, it is appropriate now to turn to the work of some liturgical theologians who have been working in the area. Anscar Chupungco, a Benedictine priest from the Philippines, has been working on these issues perhaps longer than anyone and has developed some clear methodologies.[14] First, Chupungco defines liturgical inculturation and it is helpful to quote him at length.

> Liturgical inculturation . . . may be defined as the process of inserting the texts and rites of the liturgy into the framework of the local culture. As a result, the texts and rites assimilate the people's thought, language, value, ritual, symbolic, and artistic pattern. . . . It means that liturgy and culture share the same pattern of thinking, speaking, and expressing themselves through rites, symbols, and artistic forms. In short, the liturgy is inserted into the culture, history, and tradition of the people among whom the Church dwells.[15]

He then suggests that two things are necessary: first, in-depth consideration of the *editiones typicae* from the historical, theological, and pastoral perspectives; second, clear recognition of the cultural pattern of the local church. In his view, "a liturgy whose cultural pattern differs radically from that of the local Church has to adapt or be pushed to irrelevance."[16] This brings us to the question of methods of liturgical inculturation. Chupungco names three: dynamic equivalence, creative assimilation, and organic progression.

"Dynamic equivalence consists in replacing an element of the Roman liturgy with something in the local culture that has an equal meaning or value."[17] This means that "linguistic, ritual, and symbolic elements of the Roman liturgy are reexpressed" in the new culture according to their own cultural patterns.[18] There are two different possibilities for translating text and ritual from one culture to another: a more literal translation where one seeks a one-to-one correspondence between one and the other culture, and a more dynamic translation that seeks to capture the essence of what is said in a new cultural pattern. Chupungco gives several examples from Latin to English of more static equivalents: "mystery" for *mysterion*, "sacrament" for *sacramentum*, "dignity" for *dignitas*. Dynamic equivalence includes "celebrate the memory," "in memory of," "call to mind," for the Latin term *memores* and *memoriale celebrantes*.[19] Examples of dynamic equivalents are more striking when we take examples from other cultures. As we indicated above, "dignity" is a static equivalent to the Latin *dignitas*. In Igbo, the native language of Nigeria, a proposed dynamic equivalent for *dignitas* is "to wear an eagle's feather," a sign of the dignity and position a person holds in society.[20] Ritual actions can also be "translated" in a dynamic way. For example, "in the Zairean order of Mass the sign of peace takes place after the penitential rite, which concludes the Liturgy of the Word." A simple handshake is offered as the typical gesture, but an alternative form is also offered. It consists of washing hands in the same bowl of water.[21] In both these examples, native cultural forms are used to express the theological content of the Latin original.

The second method Chupungco suggests is that of creative assimilation. By that he means the process whereby elements from the culture are added to the churches' own rites. In the history of the Roman liturgy we can see this process in the addition of a cup of milk and honey in the baptismal liturgy of Hippolytus and the washing of the feet in Milan. *CSL* makes several allowances for such cultural borrowing, for example, in the rite of marriage. *CSL* 77 allows the conferences of bishops "to draw up, in accord with art. 63, its own rite [of marriage], suited to the usages of place and peoples." In other words, creative assimilation is not the equivalent of what is already in the *editiones typicae* but the addition of something from within a local church.

The method of organic progression is perhaps Chupungco's most noted methodology. "It is the work of supplementing and completing the shape of the liturgy established by the Constitution on the Liturgy and by the Holy See after the council."[22] Organic progression moves on from where the framers of the typical editions left off. In the liturgical books there are lacunae or gaps that need to be filled by local churches. For example, in the *Rite of Christian Initiation for Adults*, the text provided an outline for the preparation of uncatechized adults for confirmation and Eucharist, but it provided no ritual content for this. In the 1988 United States edition of this Order, these rites are filled out. In this local church, pastoral need called for more than the typical edition provided. This process speaks of the contribution that local churches can make to the liturgical reform.

Peter Phan, a Vietnamese American priest, is a theologian who has addressed the issue of inculturation in general and liturgical inculturation in particular on several occasions.[23] Writing from an Asian perspective, he is particularly interested in the issues of interreligious dialogue and the transformation of unjust structures. He outlines six theological issues that are at stake in the inculturation process in general. He suggests that: (a) inculturation is impossible unless the negative view of non-Christian religions is abandoned; (b) liturgical and theological inculturation is made possible by a new pneumatology that sees the divine Spirit present and active in collective realties such as cultures and religions; (c) in recognizing the role of Christ as the unique and universal savior, other religious founders may need to be considered as mediators of salvation and other religions as ways to God; (d) we need an ecclesiology that is truly a communion ecclesiology recognizing a certain autonomy of local churches; (e) ancestor worship may be a practice that could expand our theology of the communion of saints; (f) we need a renewed theology of popular devotion or popular religiosity.[24] Applying these principles to liturgical inculturation, Phan argues that it is never a simple matter of appropriating rituals, sacred texts, and religious symbols of non-Christian religions for Christian use. Liturgical inculturation must be predicated upon a positive regard for and acceptance of this non-Christian worldview. Second, effective liturgical inculturation presupposes a particular brand of a theology of religions, of the Holy Spirit, christology, church, communion of the saints, and popular religiosity. Third, like Pieris, he suggests that liturgical inculturation must not be carried out apart from interreligious dialogue and the work of integral liberation. Last, liturgical inculturation needs close collaboration between local churches and the Congregation for Divine Worship that is truly a dialogue of mutuality.

Conclusions

I began by speaking of the nature of culture in human affairs and suggested that the social sciences have had a significant effect on our consciousness of the variety and legitimacy of human culture. While a prevailing view of culture in the West has been that of a classicist view, valuing its own culture at the expense of any other, more recently an empiricist view has made us reconsider our presuppositions of superiority. The church has had a mixed history of attention to culture and subsequent variety in Christian practice. Certainly the differences between the Eastern and Western branches of Christianity have long been noted and are increasingly being valued. However, in the development of Christianity in the West, there has also been significant variety. I noted the effects of the Gallican, Frankish, and Germanic influence on the development of so-called Roman liturgical books and suggested that what we now know as the Roman liturgy is actually a synthesis of several cultural adaptations/inculturations of the faith. Such a welcoming of difference, however, was usually limited only to the European continent. As European Christianity sent out its missionaries to the Americas, to Africa, and to Asia a classicist view of culture dominated. While there were significant efforts in China to allow for native cultural elements to affect the celebration of the Christian liturgy, this process was in the end rejected.

The Second Vatican Council brought a fresh approach to the question of culture and Christian faith. Especially in its later documents, the council expressed a decidedly open approach to diversity. Using the theological category of the Incarnation, the church proposed that the faith must take root in culture and that such a process enriches the universal church. The interest in cultural diversity was addressed in the Liturgy Constitution, but in a slightly more limited way. Using the term *adaptation*, the Constitution called for changes in the liturgy, particularly in mission lands, in a way that was organic and that maintained the integrity of the Roman Rite. It gave authority to episcopal conferences in dialogue with the Holy See to adapt the liturgy to their needs.

In the ensuing years, however, adaptation was seen as a superficial adjustment in the faith and in the liturgy that did not go far enough in the kind of thoroughgoing transformation that John Paul II often spoke about in his journeys around the globe. Theologians and missiologists gradually developed a more inclusive term, inculturation, to include both the transformation of the target culture by the Gospel and the reciprocal transformation of the Gospel by the new culture. The 1994 document *Inculturation and the Liturgy* took these developments into account on the theoretical level but chose only to develop legislative norms for adaptation.

Liturgical theologians such as Anscar Chupungco and others developed methods of adaptation and inculturation regarding liturgical matters. Asian theologians particularly have raised questions of interreligious dialogue and attention to the overwhelming poverty of Asia as integral to any efforts of inculturation, liturgical or otherwise. What appears clear at this point is that the inculturation of the faith and the inculturation of the liturgy are currently the most challenging issues we are facing. There is a theoretical openness to the new but a real reserve in the practical implications of inculturation. Not only are issues of liturgical change at stake, but issues of authority, ecclesial issues of local church, and the relationship of local churches to the church universal are also being negotiated. Likewise issues of christology, soteriology, pneumatology, and grace are all involved, as we see the expansion of Christianity in the East and in the Southern Hemisphere. We can only conclude that we are at the beginning of a very long and important process. As Karl Rahner reminded us, we are only now becoming truly a world church.[25] It remains to be seen if his predictions of the liturgy will come to fruition.

> But, as a result of the diversity of liturgical languages, there will be a necessary and irreversible process of development of a variety of liturgies, even though it is impossible to predict with certainty and accuracy the relationship between similarity and diversity of the regional liturgies. In the long run the liturgy of the Church as a whole will not simply be the liturgy of the Roman church in translation, but a unity in the variety of regional liturgies, each of which will have its own peculiar character which will not consist merely in its language.[26]

Epilogue

The field of liturgical theology is rich and complex. It involves not only theological questions and methods, but it increasingly has become multidisciplinary as well. I have, of necessity, been able to touch only a few of the most basic issues of Christian worship. My hope is that the reader has come to a deeper appreciation of the content of Christian worship and to a greater appreciation of the theological reflection being done on the church's worship. Ultimately, my hope is that the reader's participation in liturgy will become more profound as a result of this study. In conclusion, it might be helpful to review in broad strokes what I have covered.

I began this text with a general introduction to the twentieth-century liturgical reform movement and with the Liturgy Constitution of the Second Vatican Council. It is clear that the effort to reform the church's liturgy was the fruit of a long process that involved the magisterium, liturgical scholars, pastors, and the laity themselves. While some changes in practice and understanding had developed in select local churches and in particular areas of liturgical practice prior to the council, Vatican II initiated a thoroughgoing process of liturgical reform for the universal church. That process involved a rethinking of ecclesiology, the relationship between clergy and laity, and the implications of these changes in liturgical practice. It also involved a historical, theological, and pastoral study of every official rite of the church before they were revised.

Of major importance was a retrieval of a theology of the liturgical assembly, including its biblical roots and its fate throughout the history of Christian worship. This attention to the assembly resulted in a rediscovery of the corporate nature of liturgical prayer and a consequent rethinking of the forms of liturgical participation. Liturgy, it was argued, is the work of the whole people of God; clergy and laity alike participating according to their distinct orders and roles. No longer is the liturgy to be done by the clergy for the benefit of the community; the whole community together is the subject of liturgical action.

This momentous shift, changing hundreds of years of ecclesial practice, has taken enormous energy in the years since the council. Only gradually has the laity assumed its active role in the celebration of the rites of the church. Some have argued that this stress on the action of the assembly has taken away from the understanding of the liturgy as the work of God. I have argued that an adequate understanding of the liturgy must hold these two poles in dynamic tension. The liturgy in whole and in part is an exercise of the divine/human dialogue that God has initiated for our benefit. In the Catholic tradition, it cannot be attention to *either* the work of the assembly *or* the work of God; it must be *both/and*. The initiative is always from God, but even God awaits our response in freedom and love. Perhaps what still demands our attention is the two-fold purpose of the liturgy as articulated in the conciliar constitution—the worship of God and the sanctification of the human person. In my own pastoral work, I have come to wonder whether the church community has a clear sense of the purposefulness and intentionality of its worship.

What the liturgy celebrates above all is the paschal mystery of Jesus Christ and our participation in that mystery for our salvation and the salvation of the world. The last half of the twentieth century saw a new attention to the theological meaning of anamnesis or memorial. Being outside of scholastic categories, this term has enabled significant agreement to emerge in ecumenical dialogue, and it has given new insight into what the community is doing when it celebrates the sacraments and liturgies of the church. Part and parcel of this discovery have been a new emphasis on the role of blessing and, in particular, a new understanding of the structure and meaning of the great eucharistic prayer. In the discussion of memorial I have drawn attention to the question of how well we have remembered the church and all its members, suggesting that more adequate memorial of the women of the church is a question of justice. Theological reflection in this area is challenging pastoral practice.

It is impossible to reflect upon the liturgy without reflecting upon how we name God. It may have become a neuralgic issue only recently, but naming God has always been an important theological issue. Because of God's utter incomprehensibility, I have argued that we can only name "toward" God and that it is an important and justifiable human task. Our own spirit reaches out to the infinite, and the Holy Spirit assists us in our search for the truth. I have outlined the theological reasons for care in God-language and have suggested that it is important for God's sake as well as our own. Like Elizabeth Johnson, I have argued that God-language functions in human communities. We need to be aware of how it functions and make changes accordingly. Once again, I have argued that issues of inclusion are issues of justice.

To be human is to be in the flow of time. God acts in history, and for us history is past, present, and future. Our vocation to remember God is a call to acknowledge what God has done in the past, what God is doing now, and what God holds out to us in the future. We have come to understand that participation in the liturgy is participation in the salvation offered by God. And so Christians have chosen to gather daily, weekly, and yearly to celebrate in memorial of the One who saves. Our practices have drawn heavily on Jewish traditions, but the Christ Mystery has caused us to order time differently and with a different theological thrust. Christ is the meaning of time, and the symbols of light and darkness, morning and night, Sunday and the year are all ordered to Christ.

To speak of liturgy and sacrament is to engage in an extensive discussion of symbol. I have chosen to discuss this complex idea from two different perspectives. First, I have dealt with more philosophical/theological approaches to symbol and their implications in sacrament. Several key thinkers such as Karl Rahner, Louis-Marie Chauvet, and Paul Ricoeur have had and continue to have enormous impact on sacramental theology. Through their work we have come to understand the distinction between a "mere symbol" and a "real symbol." Rahner laid the foundation for understanding the symbolic nature of all reality but from within a metaphysical perspective. Chauvet has gone beyond metaphysics but has still argued that symbol must be at the center of our discourse. For him all knowledge and relationships are mediated by symbol, and by the body in particular. Sacraments continue to be understood as efficacious, not through the modality of causality, but through the mediation of symbol. Ricoeur has been exceedingly instrumental in helping us understand the process of interpretation and appropriation, especially of symbols. The current stress we place on the quality of symbols in our liturgies is important in Ricoeur's view because it is only by going through the first, literal meaning of the symbol that we can arrive at second and third levels of meaning.

Not only has philosophy contributed a great deal to our understanding of symbols but so too have the social sciences, in particular cultural anthropology. Through anthropological work we have come to a greater appreciation of the role and dynamics of symbol and ritual in human life. Anthropologists have stressed the relationship between symbol and ritual systems and social structures and processes, but they have also stressed the meaningfulness of symbols. Symbols and rituals express community meaning; they also shape community identity and beliefs. Victor Turner has been very influential in recent years in helping us to understand the dynamics of symbols and their ability to affect the whole human person and the social process. More recent theorists have addressed performance and praxis approaches to ritual and symbol. Importantly, some theorists suggest that ritual creates persons with a competency to use ritual as a strategy in human affairs. This instrumental understanding of ritual is very suggestive in the area of liturgical studies, but it has not yet been pursued that much.

Symbols and rituals can not only be approached from a philosophical, theological, and anthropological view; they also can be addressed in a very concrete way and in the way they affect the embodied person. The liturgy is made up of a whole field of symbolic utterances that include the linguistic, the aural, the visual, the kinesthetic, and the bodily. We use space, sound, and movement to carry out the intent of our liturgies. I explored the body's capacity to engage symbols and looked at the different symbolic vehicles that make up our liturgical celebrations. I noted that symbols and rituals mediate the self-revelation of God and the divine/human relationship. Our bodies have distinctive capacities for posture, movement, and action, but those physical possibilities are tied to history and culture. Not everyone stands to show respect, nor do we all dance to express ourselves and our beliefs.

Finally, I looked at the issues of liturgy and culture. The social sciences have been very instrumental in helping us to understand the differences and the dignity of world cultures. We have moved from a classicist understanding of culture, where one culture dominated over all others, to a more empirical approach to culture that admits of the variety of cultures and the right of all people to a culture. From the perspective of the church and culture, we have seen that diverse cultural realities have always been an issue in the church. What has varied has been the openness to allow cultural differences to affect the faith in general and the liturgy in particular. At times, the church has incorporated the genius of diverse peoples into her expression; at other times, she has directly rejected the inclusion of so-called foreign cultures into her practice. In the time since Vatican II, we have moved from a preliminary approach of adaptation of the Roman Rite to a much more dynamic understanding of the relationship of the faith and the culture known as inculturation. Inculturation involves the double movement of the transformation of the faith to culture and culture to the faith. Second, it involves the dialogue of local churches with the wider church in an exchange of mutual respect and recognition. The implications of inculturation are profound, and at this point the church is taking very cautious steps in this regard. At the level of official teaching on liturgical inculturation, the church has chosen to develop norms only about adaptation.

It is my hope that this text has equipped the reader with the concepts and vocabulary to continue studies in the area and provided a greater appreciation of the church's actual worship practices. In the introduction I noted that this text is meant as a first course in liturgical theology with the expectation that other readings would accompany this text. At this point I would also like to acknowledge that a second course on the history of the liturgy is just as important to trace the ways in which the church, East and West, has shaped its liturgies.

Notes

Chapter One, pages 1–18

1. Prosper Guéranger, *Institutions liturgique*, vol. 3 (Paris: Julien, Lanier et Ce, Editeurs, 1851), 170–71, quoted in Robert L. Tuzik, *How Firm a Foundation: Leaders of the Liturgical Movement* (Chicago: Liturgy Training Publications, 1990), 17.

2. Louis Bouyer, *Liturgical Piety* (Notre Dame, IN: University of Notre Dame Press, 1970), 64.

3. Nov. 22, 1903: *AAS* 36 (1903): 329–39. See the translation in Kevin Seasoltz, *The New Liturgy: A Documentation, 1903–1965* (New York: Herder and Herder, 1966), 3–10.

4. Dec. 22, 1905: *AAS* 38 (1905): 400-406; Seasoltz, 11–15.

5. Dec. 20, 1928: *AAS* 21 (1928): 33–41; Seasoltz, 58–63.

6. Nov. 20, 1947: *AAS* 39 (1947): 521–95; Seasoltz, 107–59.

7. Frederick McManus, *The Rites of Holy Week* (Paterson, NJ: Saint Anthony Guild Press, 1956; 2nd ed., 1957), vi–vii.

8. Sept. 3, 1958: *AAS* 50 (1958): 630–63.

9. Unless otherwise noted, conciliar, papal, and curial texts are from *Documents on the Liturgy: 1963–1979 Conciliar, Papal, and Curial Texts* (Collegeville, MN: Liturgical Press, 1982).

10. Kathleen Hughes, "Overview of the Constitution on the Sacred Liturgy," in *The Liturgy Documents: a Parish Resource*, 3rd ed. (Chicago: Liturgy Training Publications, 1991), 3.

Chapter Two, pages 19–50

1. Henri Chirat, *L'Assemblée chrétienne à l'âge apostolique* (Paris: Éditions du Cerf, 1949). This work is available only in French. Any quotations are the author's translation.

2. There are four principal articles by Martimort in the decade before the council that served as the foundation for the development of a theology of assembly at this time: "L'Assemblée liturgique," *La Maison Dieu* 20 (1949): 135–75; "L'Assemblée liturgique, mystère du Christ," *LMD* 40 (1954): 5–29; "Dimanche, assemblée et

paroisse," *LMD* 57 (1959): 55–84; "Précisions sur l'assemblée," *LMD* 60 (1959): 7–34. These articles are available only in French. Any quotations are the author's translation.

3. Chirat, *L'Assemblée chrétienne*, 21, 10.

4. The rite of *fermentum* was the practice of sending a small bit of the Eucharist from the bishop's celebration to other gatherings of the faithful where a presbyter was presiding. Stational liturgies were liturgies where the bishop moved from parish to parish so that he could be personally present for Eucharist to all areas of his diocese over time.

5. Martimort, "Dimanche," 561–64, 75–76.

6. Ibid., 76–80.

7. Ibid., 81. See Session 22 of the Council of Trent, *Decretum de observandis et evitandis in celebratione missae.*

8. Martimort, "L'Assemblée liturgique," 156; "Précisions," 8–10.

9. Martimort, "Précisions," 8–10.

10. Ibid., 10–11.

11. Ibid., 8–9; "L'Assemblée liturgique," 155. R. Gantoy "L'assemblée dans l'économie salut," *Assemblées du Seigneur* 1 (Bruges: Biblica, 1962): 57.

12. Martimort, "Précisions," 29–30.

13. Gantoy, "L'assemblée dans l'économie salut," 72.

14. Afanassieff, "Le sacrement de l'assemblée," *Internationale Kirchliche Zeitschrift* 46 (1956): 206; Thierry Maertens "L'Assemblée festive du dimanche," *L'Assemblée du Seigneur* 1 (1962): 39–40.

15. Louis Bouyer, "From the Jewish Qahal to the Christian Ecclesia," in *Liturgical Piety* (Notre Dame: University of Notre Dame Press, 1955), 23–37.

16. Pagination is from the English translation, *Assembly for Christ* (London: Darton, Longman & Todd, Ltd., 1970), 1–36.

17. Maertens, *Assembly for Christ*, 37–59.

18. Chirat, *L'Assemblée chrétienne*, 87, 46.

19. J. Dupont, "Le première Pentecote chrétienne," *Assemblée du Seigneur* 51 (Bruges: Biblica, 1963), 42; Martimort, "Précisions," 20–21, and "Dimanche," 56–58.

20. Maertens, *Assembly for Christ*, 71–77, 86–88, 90.

21. Ibid., 88–90. See also Chirat, *L'Assemblée chrétienne*, 239–42.

22. Martimort, "Précisions," 34–35, and "Mystère du Christ," 15–16.

23. Martimort, "L'Assemblée liturgique," 154, 155, 163; "Dimanche," 59–62.

24. Martimort, "Dimanche," 59, 63; Chirat, *L'Assemblée chrétienne*, 246.

25. Martimort, "Dimanche," 68; "L'Assemblée liturgique," 154–55.

26. Martimort, "Dimanche," 64; Rouillard, "Signification du Dimanche," *Assemblée de Seigneur* 1 (1962): 43.

27. Robeyns, "Les droits des baptizes," 124, quoted in Martimort, "Mystère du Christ," 10; Jean Hild, "Le mystère du célébration," *LMD* 20 (1949): 83–113.

28. Martimort, "Mystère du Christ," 9–10; I. H. Dalmais, "La liturgie, acte de l'Église," *LMD* 19 (1949): 15.

29. Martimort, "L'Assemblée liturgique," 174; "Précisions," 21–22; Hild, "Le mystère du célébration," 102; Gantoy, "L'Assemblée dans l'économie salut," 62.

30. Martimort, "Mystère du Christ," 9–10. See also Hild, "Le mystère du célébration," 101.

31. Martimort, "L'Assemblée liturgique," 174–75; "Mystère du Christ," 8–10; "Précisions," passim. See also Roguet, "The Theology of the Liturgical Assembly," 130–31.

32. Martimort, "L'Assemblée liturgique," 159–61; "Mystère du Christ," 20.

33. Martimort, "L'Assemblée liturgique," 174. It is important to note that while Martimort included the Holy Spirit in his initial definition, his attention subsequently focused almost exclusively on the presence of Christ.

34. Martimort, "L'Assemblée liturgique," 139.

35. Martimort, "Précisions," 31.

36. Paul Ricoeur, "The Symbol . . . Food for Thought," *Philosophy Today* 4 (1960): 199–200; *The Conflict of Interpretations: Essays in Hermeneutics*, ed. Don Ihde (Evanston, IL.: Northwestern Press 1974), 298.

37. Martimort, "L'Assemblée liturgique," 163, 168; "Précisions," 15.

38. Martimort, "L'Assemblée liturgique," 99–100.

39. This role of commentator, or *meneur de jeu*, was incorporated into the French diocesan directory of 1956 and became general law through its inclusion in the 1958 *Instruction on Sacred Music*.

40. Martimort, "L'Assemblée liturgique," 100; 1958 *Instruction* 96, a and b. If the commentator was a cleric, he could stand within the sanctuary; if a layman, only outside.

41. Martimort, "L'Assemblée liturgique," 97.

42. Ibid., 103.

43. Roguet, "The Theology of the Liturgical Assembly," 135; Maertens, "L'Assemblée festive du Dimanche," 40.

44. Gantoy, "L'Assemblée dans l'économie salut," 75.

45. Martimort, "Mystère du Christ," 13.

46. Sacred Congregation of Divine Worship, Third Instruction on the orderly carrying out of the Constitution on the Liturgy, 5 September 1970: *AAS* 62 (1970): 692–704, *DOL* 52.

47. *DOL* 52 no. 531.

48. There have been five editions of the *General Instruction of the Roman Missal* (hereafter, *GIRM*) since its first publication in 1969. The most recent revision was published in 2002. All translations and numbering are from the edition published by the International Committee on English in the Liturgy.

49. *GIRM* 5.

50. "The Assembly in Christian Worship," in *Newsletter* of the Bishops' Committee on the Liturgy, September 1977, 82.

51. Paul VI, *Mysterium Fidei*, September 3, 1965: *AAS* 57 (1965): 35–38; *DOL* 176 nos. 1179–82.

52. Sacred Congregation of Rites, *Eucharisticum Mysterium*, *AAS* 59 (1967): 9; *DOL* 179 no. 1238.

53. *DOL* 179 no. 1284.

54. See the *Relatio* of Bishop Zauner, bishop of Linz, regarding the emendations made to the schema on the liturgical year in *Acta Synodalia*, II/III (Typis Polyglotis Vaticanis, 1970), 273–74.

55. See Bishop H. Jenny's commentary on this point. He notes that "the Christians, not taken individually but gathered together, proclaim their testimony to the Resurrection, and come together to form the people of God." "The Proper of the Time," in

The Commentary on the Constitution and on the Instruction of the Sacred Liturgy, eds. A. Bugnini and C. Braga (New York: Benzinger Brothers, 1965), 234.

56. See Martimort's analysis of Sunday in the Liturgy Constitution, where he both expands on the history and incorporates his own research on the assembly. "Quelques aspects doctrinaux de la constitution *Sacrosanctum Concilium*," in *Teologia liturgia storia: Miscellanae in onre di Carlo Manziana*, ed. Carlo Ghidelli (Morcelliana: La Scuola, 1977), 179–96.

57. Sacred Congregation of Rites, *General Norms for the Liturgical Year and the Calendar*, March 21, 1969, in *DOL* 442.

58. Paul VI, Epistle, *Piscariensium Civitas*. August 4, 1977: *AAS* 69 (1977): 565–67, in *DOL* 450 no. 3843.

59. *DOL* 450 no. 3844.

60. Cardinal J. Villot, Letter on the occasion of the 28th National Liturgical Week of Italy, on the theme: "The Lord's Day is the Lord of Days" (Pescara, August 29–September 2). *DOL* 451 no. 3846.

61. Congregation for Divine Worship, *Directory for Sunday Celebrations in the Absence of a Priest*, May 21, 1988. In *Origins*, 18, no. 19 (October 20, 1988): 302–7.

62. John Paul II, Apostolic Letter, May 1998, *Dies Domini*: "On Keeping the Lord's Day Holy," in *The Liturgy Documents: Volume Two* (Chicago: Liturgy Training Publications, 1999), 9–49.

63. Reflections of the American Bishops Commemorating the Fifteenth Anniversary of the Issuance of the *Decree on the Apostolate of the Laity*, Nov. 13, 1980 (Washington, DC: USCC).

64. Joseph Cardinal Bernardin, Pastoral Letter on the Liturgy, *Our Communion, Our Peace, Our Promise* (Chicago: Liturgy Training Publications, 1984), 2.

65. *DOL* 179 nos. 1240 and 1241.

66. *GIRM* uses the language of "Particular Ministries" (*ministeria peculiaria*) to describe the roles of acolyte, reader, cantor, ministers of Communion, commentator, and other lesser ministries, such as bearing ritual objects or the ministry of hospitality.

67. Sacred Congregation of Bishops, Directory on the Pastoral Ministry of Bishops, *Ecclesiae Imago*, February 22, 1973; *DOL* 329.

68. *EI* 15, 75, 59; *DOL* 329 nos. 2640, 2643, and 2645.

69. *EI* 76; *DOL* 329 no. 2646.

70. At the time of the council, tonsure was still considered as entrance into the clerical state. This was changed in 1972 by Paul VI in *Ministeria Quaedam, DOL* 340 no. 2926. Entrance into the clerical state is now joined to the diaconate.

71. *DOL* 340 no. 2923.

72. *MQ* VII; *DOL* 340 no. 2932.

73. *DOL* 208 no. 1456 n.e.

74. *LI* 7; *DOL* 52 no. 525.

75. *DOL* 208 no. 1450 and note h.

76. Bishops' Committee on the Liturgy, February 14, 1971, "Place of Women in the Liturgy." In *Thirty Years of Liturgical Renewal*, ed. Frederick McManus (Washington, DC: USCC, 1987), 137.

77. *LI* 7; *DOL* 52 no. 525.

78. See the letter to presidents of episcopal conferences in *Notitiae* 30 (1994): 333–35.

79. Sacred Congregation for the Discipline of the Sacraments, *Fidei Custos*, March 10, 1966; *DOL* 259.

80. *DOL* 259 no. 2046.

81. *DOL* 259 no. 2048.

82. Sacred Congregation on the Discipline of the Sacraments, *Immensae Caritatis*, January 29, 1973: *AAS* 65 (1973): 264–271; *DOL* 264.

83. *DOL* 264 no. 2078.

84. See, for instance, *Holy Communion and Worship of the Eucharist* (1973); *Inaestimabile donum* (1980); and the *Norms for the Distribution and Reception of Holy Communion Under Both Kinds in the Dioceses of the United States of America* (2002).

Chapter Three, pages 51–63

1. Augustine Bea, "The Pastoral Value of the Word of God in the Sacred Liturgy," in *The Assisi Papers* (Collegeville, MN: Liturgical Press, 1957), 74–90.

2. Ibid., 81; original emphasis.

3. Ibid., 86–87.

4. Ibid., 87.

5. David Power, *Sacrament: The Language of God's Giving* (New York: Herder and Herder, 1999), 276.

6. Ibid., 277.

7. This is why we must leave room for some dimension of the "new" in the inculturation of the liturgy. The church has not yet fully given form to the reality of God's self-giving in Christ and the Spirit. Nor has it yet fully given form to its own response in mutuality and love. More remains to be said.

8. Ibid., 282. See also Jean-Luc Marion, *God Without Being*, trans. Thomas A. Carlson (Chicago: University of Chicago Press, 1991).

9. Power, *Sacrament*, 283.

10. Ibid.

11. Ibid.

12. Ibid., 286.

Chapter Four, pages 64–80

1. Some of this material is taken from my article "A History of Holy Week," in *Liturgical Ministry* 13 (Summer 2004): 105–18.

2. Thomas Talley, *The Origins of the Liturgical Year*, 2nd ed. (Collegeville, MN: Pueblo/Liturgical Press, 1986), 1.

3. Justin Martyr, *Dialogue with Trypho* 40.1-3, as reproduced in Raniero Cantalamessa's collection of texts, *Easter in the Early Church* (Collegeville, MN: Liturgical Press, 1993), text no. 18.

4. Melito of Sardis, *On the Pascha*, in Lucien Deiss, *Springtime of the Liturgy: Liturgical Texts of the First Four Centuries*, trans. Matthew J. O'Connell (Collegeville, MN: Liturgical Press, 1979), 100.

5. Melito of Sardis, *On the Pascha* 100–103, in Cantalamessa, *Easter*, no 24.

6. Pseudo-Chrysostom, *Homilies on the Holy Pascha* 7, 39, in Cantalamessa, *Easter*, no. 77.

7. Melito of Sardis, *On the Pascha*, 46, in Cantalamessa, *Easter*, no. 21.

8. Those who chose to celebrate the Pascha on the fourteenth of Nisan.

9. Pseudo-Tertullian, *Against the Jews* 10, 18, in Cantalamessa, *Easter*, no. 98.

10. Pseudo-Cyprian, *Computus from the Pascha*, 2, in Cantalamessa, *Easter*, no. 100.

11. Origen, *On the Pascha*, 1, in Cantalamessa, *Easter*, no. 37.

12. Talley, *The Origins of the Liturgical Year*, 26.

13. Cantalamessa, *Easter*, 18.

14. Augustine, *Exposition of Psalm 120*, 6, in Cantalamessa, *Easter*, no. 126.

15. Ibid.

16. James Empereur, "Paschal Mystery, " in *The New Dictionary of Theology*, eds. J. Komonchak, M. Collins, D. Lane (Collegeville, MN: Michael Glazier/Liturgical Press, 1987), 745.

17. Sofia Cavaletti, *The Jewish Roots of Christian Liturgy*, ed. Eugene J. Fisher (New York: Paulist Press, 1990), 19.

18. Patrick McGoldrick, "Memorial," in *The New Dictionary of Theology*, 644.

19. *Dialogue with Trypho*, 41.1. English translation in R.C.D. Jasper and G. J. Cuming, *Prayers of the Eucharist: Early and Reformed*, 3rd ed. (New York: Pueblo Publishing Company, 1987), 27.

20. Justin Martyr, *First Apology*. English translation in Jasper and Cuming, *Prayers of the Eucharist*, 29.

21. Theodore of Mopsuestia, *Baptismal Homily* 3.2. English translation in Thomas Finn, *Early Christian Baptism and the Catechumenate: West and East Syria* (Collegeville, MN: Michael Glazier/Liturgical Press, 1992), 84.

22. Ibid., 3.5, in Finn, 86.

23. Cyril of Jerusalem, *Baptismal Catechesis* 2.5, in Finn, 48.

24. Ambrose, *On the Sacraments* 1.12, in Thomas Finn, *Early Christian Baptism and the Catechumenate: Italy, North Africa, and Egypt* (Collegeville, MN: Michael Glazier/Liturgical Press, 1992), 64.

25. Robert Taft, "Toward a Theology of the Christian Feast," in *Beyond East and West: Problems in Liturgical Understanding* (Washington, DC: Pastoral Press, 1984), 2.

26. Ibid., 4.

27. Ibid., 7.

28. I refer the reader to works by Rosemary Radford Ruether, Elisabeth Schüssler Fiorenza, Elizabeth Johnson, Margaret Farley, Sandra Schneiders, Lisa Sowell Cahill, Mary Collins, and many more, all of whom are credentialed theologians and consider themselves very much in the Catholic community.

29. Phyllis Trible, *God and the Rhetoric of Sexuality* (Philadelphia: Fortress Press, 1978); idem, *Texts of Terror: Literary-Feminist Readings of Biblical Narrative* (Philadelphia: Fortress Press, 1984); Elisabeth Schüssler Fiorenza, *In Memory of Her: A Feminist Theological Reconstruction of Christian Origins* (New York: Crossroad, 1983); idem, *Bread Not Stone: The Challenge of Feminist Biblical Interpretation* (Boston: Beacon Press, 1983); idem, *Searching the Scriptures* (New York: Crossroad, 1993); idem, *Wisdom Ways: Introducing Feminist Biblical Interpretation* (Maryknoll, New York: Orbis Books, 2001).

30. Elizabeth J. Smith, *Bearing Fruit in Due Season: Feminist Hermeneutics and the Bible in Worship* (Collegeville, MN: Pueblo/Liturgical Press, 1999), 81. See the following texts for an in-depth look at the Lectionary from a feminist perspective: Barbara Field, "Positioning Women as Subordinate: The Semiosis of the Weekly Lectionary in the Anglican Church," *St. Mark's Review* 144 (Summer 1991): 16–21; Marie-Louis

Uhr, "The Portrayal of Women in the Lectionary," *St. Mark's Review* 135 (Spring 1988): 22–25; Marjorie Procter-Smith, "Images of Women in the Lectionary," in Elisabeth Schüssler Fiorenza and Mary Collins, eds., *Women—Invisible in Church and Theology*, Concilium 182 (Edinburgh: T&T Clark, 1985), 51–62; idem, "Feminist Interpretation and Liturgical Proclamation," in Elisabeth Schüssler Fiorenza, ed., with the assistance of Shelly Matthews, *Searching the Scriptures, Volume One: A Feminist Introduction* (New York: Crossroad, 1993), 313–25.

31. See the following for further documentation: Regina Boisclair, "Amnesia in the Catholic Sunday Lectionary: Women Silenced from the Memories of Salvation History," in *Women and Theology*, eds. Mary Ann Hinsdale and Phyllis H. Kaminski, 109–135, Annual Publication of the College Theology Society, 1994, vol. 40 (Maryknoll, New York: Orbis Books, 1995); Jean Campbell, "The Feminine as Omitted, Optional, or Alternative Story: A Feminist Review of the Episcopal Eucharistic Lectionary," in *Proceeding of the North American Academy of Liturgy* (1990); Marjorie Proctor-Smith, "Images of Women in the Lectionary," in *Women: Invisible in Church and Theology*, Concilium 182, 53–60 (London: T&T Clark, 1985); idem, "Liturgical Anamnesis and Women's Memory: Something Missing," *Worship* 61 (1987): 406–18; Eileen Schuller, "Women in the Lectionary," *National Liturgy Bulletin* (Canada) 27 (1994): 108.

32. See, for example, Teresa Berger, *Women's Ways of Worship: Gender Analysis and Liturgical History* (Collegeville, MN: Pueblo/Liturgical Press, 1999); *Fragment of Real Presence: Liturgical Traditions in the Hands of Women* (New York: Crossroad, 2005).

Chapter Five, pages 81–100

1. The Hebrew bible has the name in the first person ʿ*ehyeh* while the third person would read Yahweh. YHWH (the tetragrammaton) appears as the designation for God over 6,700 times, more frequently that all other designations combined. There is no certitude regarding how ancient Israel understood this "name" except to say that it related God to creation and the covenant. Late Judaism found this word too sacred to pronounce and so substituted *Adonai*, "my Lord."

2. Elizabeth Johnson, *She Who Is: The Mystery of God in Feminist Theological Discourse* (New York: Crossroad, 1992), 4.

3. Juan Luis Segundo, *Our Idea of God*, trans. John Drury (Maryknoll, New York: Orbis Books, 1974), 7–8, as quoted in ibid., 14.

4. Karl Rahner, *Foundations of Christian Faith* (New York: Seabury Press, 1978), 54.

5. I will address the biblical naming of God further below in this essay.

6. Rahner, *Foundations*, 58.

7. Ibid., chap. 2, "Man in the Presence of Absolute Mystery."

8. Ibid., 46.

9. Ibid., 46–47.

10. Ibid., 50.

11. Johnson, *She Who Is*, 16–22, 42–44, passim.

12. Rosemary Radford Ruether, *Sexism and God-Talk* (Boston: Beacon Press, 1983), 46.

13. Aquinas, *De Divinibus Nominibus*, 1.2, as quoted in Johnson, *She Who Is*, 115.

14. "Joyful is the Dark." Words: Brian Wren. © 1989 Hope Publishing Co., Carol Stream, IL, 60188. All rights reserved. Used by permission.

15. The theological use of analogy is neither simple nor uncontested. See the work of David Tracy on the *Analogical Imagination* (New York: Crossroad, 1981), especially chap. 10 and n. 2.

16. Tracy, *Analogical Imagination*, 408.

17. Johnson, *She Who Is*, 113.

18. Tracy, *The Analogical Imagination*, 413.

19. Johnson, *She Who Is*, 115.

20. Pseudo-Dionysius Areopagite. *Divine Names and Mystical Theology*. John D. Jones, translator. Copyright © 1999. Milwaukee, WI: Marquette University Press. Reprinted by permission of the publisher. All rights reserved. www.marquette.edu/mupress.

21. Aquinas, *Summa Theologiae* I, q. 3, preface as quoted in Johnson, *She Who Is*, 109.

22. R.C.D. Jasper and G. J. Cuming, *Prayers of the Eucharist: Early and Reformed*, 3rd ed. (Collegeville, MN: Liturgical Press, 1992), 76.

23. Ibid., 132.

24. Gail Ramshaw, *Reviving Sacred Speech: The Meaning of Liturgical Language* (Akron, OH: OSL Publications, 2000), 8.

25. Many of these images are collected in Brian Wren, *What Language Shall I Borrow? God-Talk in Worship: A Male Response to Feminist Theology* (New York: Crossroad, 1989).

26. On the inerrancy of the biblical text, the Vatican II fathers wrote that the Scriptures "firmly, faithfully, and without error, teach that truth which God, for the sake of our salvation, wished to see confided to the sacred scriptures" (*Dei Verbum* 11). See also the analysis of this text and debate on it in Alois Grillmeier, *Commentary on the Documents of Vatican II*, ed. Herbert Vorgrimler (New York: Herder & Herder, 1969) 3:199–246.

27. Augustine, *On Christian Doctrine*, as quoted in Ramshaw, *Reviving Sacred Speech*, 30.

28. Meister Eckhart, "Sermon 83," as quoted in Ramshaw, *Reviving Sacred Speech*, 29.

29. Catherine of Siena, *The Dialogue*, trans. and intro. Suzanne Noffke, OP (New York: Paulist Press, 1980), 325.

30. Johnson, *She Who Is*, 118.

31. Joachim Jeremias, "Abba," in *The Central Message of the New Testament* (London: SCM Press, 1965), 9–30; and his *The Prayers of Jesus* (London: SCM Press, 1967), 11–65.

32. James Dunn, *Christology in the Making* (Philadelphia: Westminster, 1980), 30, as quoted in Johnson, *She Who Is*, 81.

33. The *editio typical*, or the official Latin version of the Sacramentary, has 703 collects of which 509, or 72 percent, use *Deus* (God); 22, or 3 percent, use *Domine Deus* (Lord God); 166, or 24 percent, use *Domine* (Lord); and 6, or 0.8 percent, use *Pater* (Father). It remains to be seen how the newest translation of the Sacramentary will translate these titles.

34. Anselm K. Min, "Naming the Unnameable God: Levinas, Derrida, and Marion," *International Journal of Philosophy and Religion* 60 (2006): 99.

35. The revised Order of Roman Catholic rites gives significantly more leeway in addressing the community than the previous Order of Pius V. See such examples as the Introductory rites of the Mass, the various rites of the RCIA, the Order of Christian Funerals, etc.

36. Wren, *What Language*, 5.

37. Vince Ambrosetti, text and music © 1992, 1993, International Liturgy Publications.

38. Delores Dufner, OSB, © 1992, 1993, The Sisters of St. Benedict, published by OCP Publications. Used by permission.

39. "God of Many Names." Words: Brian Wren. © 1986 Hope Publishing Co., Carol Stream, IL, 60188. All rights reserved. Used by permission.

40. "Name Unnamed." Words: Brian Wren. © 1989 Hope Publishing Co., Carol Stream, IL, 60188. All rights reserved. Used by permission.

Chapter Six, pages 101–119

1. Mircea Eliade, *Cosmos and History: The Myth of the Eternal Return* (New York: Harper Torchbooks, 1959), 104.

2. Kevin Irwin, *Liturgy, Prayer and Spirituality* (New York: Paulist Press, 1984), 186.

3. Robert Taft, "Toward a Theology of Christian Feast," in *Beyond East and West: Problems in Liturgical Understanding* (Washington, DC: Pastoral Press, 1984), 2–3.

4. *Didache* 8.2-3, as quoted in I. H. Dalmais, P. Jounel, and A. G. Martimort, *The Church at Prayer*, vol. 4, *The Liturgy and Time* (Collegeville, MN: Liturgical Press, 1986), 163.

5. A. G. Martimort, "The Hours of Prayer," in *The Church at Prayer*, vol. 4, 163.

6. Origen, *De oratione* 12, as quoted in *The Church at Prayer*, vol. 4, 165.

7. Tertullian, *De oratione* 25, in *The Church at Prayer*, vol. 4, 166.

8. Hippolytus, *Apostolic Tradition* 41, as quoted in *The Church at Prayer*, vol. 4, 167.

9. Cyprian, *Di dominica oratione* 35, as quoted in *The Church at Prayer*, vol. 4, 169.

10. John Cassian, *De institutes coenobiorum* III, 3, 9–10, as quoted in *The Church at Prayer*, vol. 4, 263.

11. Paul Bradshaw, *Daily Prayer in the Early Church* (New York: Oxford University Press, 1982), 151–52.

12. Ignatius of Antioch, *Ad Magnesios* 9, as quoted in *The Church at Prayer*, vol. 4, 14.

13. Justin Martyr, *Apologia I* 67, 3 and 7, as quoted in *The Church at Prayer*, vol. 4, 14.

14. Augustine, *Ep.* 55, 17, as quoted in *The Church at Prayer*, vol. 4, 18.

15. Jounel, *The Church at Prayer*, vol. 4, 19.

16. John Paul II, Apostolic Letter *Dies Domini* (1998), in David Lysik, ed., *The Liturgy Documents: Volume Two* (Chicago: Liturgy Training Publications, 1999), 9–49.

17. Origen, *Homilies on Exodus* 5.2, as quoted in Raniero Cantalamessa, *Easter in the Early Church* (Collegeville, MN: Liturgical Press, 1993), no. 39.

18. Patrick Regan, "The Three Days and the Forty Days," in *Between Memory and Hope: Readings on the Liturgical Year,* ed. Maxwell E. Johnson (Collegeville, MN: Liturgical Press, 2000), 134.

19. Thomas Talley, "The Origins of Lent at Alexandria," in *Between Memory and Hope*, 193.

20. Ibid., 205.

21. Socrates, *Historia Ecclesiastica* 5.22, as quoted in Maxwell Johnson, "Preparation for Pascha? Lent in Christian Antiquity," in *Between Memory and Hope*, 210.

22. Ibid., 220.

23. See Susan Roll, "The Origins of Christmas: The State of the Question," in *Between Memory and Hope*, 273–90.

24. Roll, "The Origins of Christmas," 285–86.

25. Jounel, *The Church at Prayer*, vol. 4, 80–81.

26. The Armenian Monophysite Church continues to celebrate January 6 as the three mysteries of the birth, the adoration of the Magi, and the baptism.

27. See Martin J. Connell, "The Origins and Evolution of Advent in the West," in *Beyond Memory and Hope*, 352–53.

28. Ibid., 351.

29. Ibid., 350.

30. Ibid., 349.

31. John Baldovin, "On Feasting the Saints," in *Between Memory and Hope*, 377.

Chapter Seven, pages 120–143

1. Karl Rahner, "Theology of Symbol," in *Theological Investigations IV* (London: Darton, Longman & Todd, 1966; New York: Seabury Press, 1974), 245.

2. Louis-Marie Chauvet, *Symbol and Sacrament: A Sacramental Reinterpretation of Christian Existence* (Collegeville, MN: Liturgical Press, 1995, French in 1987), 130.

3. The author presumes that the reader will go to these primary texts after reading this brief introduction of them.

4. Rahner, "Theology of the Symbol," 225.

5. Ibid., 224.

6. Ibid., 227.

7. Ibid.

8. Ibid., 229.

9. Ibid., 230.

10. Ibid., 231.

11. Ibid.

12. Ibid., 236.

13. Ibid., 238.

14. Ibid., 241.

15. Ibid., 247.

16. Chauvet, *Symbol and Sacrament*, 1.

17. Ibid., 2.

18. Ibid., 3.

19. Ibid., 36.

20. Ibid., 43.

21. Ibid., 83.

22. Ibid., 84.

23. Ibid., 90.

24. E. Ortigues, *Discours et symbole*, quoted in ibid.

25. Ibid.

26. A. Vergote, *Interprétation du langage religieux*, quoted in ibid., 91.

27. Ibid., 107.

28. Ibid., 109.

29. Ibid., 120–23.

30. Ibid., 130.

31. Ibid., 140.

32. Ibid., 140–41.

33. Ibid., 146.

34. Ibid., 147.

35. Ibid., 151.

36. Ibid., 152.

37. Ibid., 153.

38. Paul Ricoeur, *Freud and Philosophy: An Essay on Interpretation,* trans. Denis Savage (New Haven: Yale University Press, 1970), 12.

39. Ibid., 13.

40. Paul Ricoeur, *The Symbolism of Evil* (Boston: Beacon Press, 1967), 15.

41. Ricoeur, *Freud and Philosophy,* 14.

42. Paul Ricoeur, "The Symbol . . . Food for Thought," *Philosophy Today* 4 (1960): 199.

43. Ricoeur, *Freud and Philosophy,* 15–16.

44. Ibid.

45. Ricoeur, *Symbolism of Evil,* 11.

46. Ricoeur, *Freud and Philosophy,* 14–15.

47. Paul Ricoeur, "Manifestation et proclamation" *Archivo di Filosofia* 44 (1974): 62.

48. Ricoeur, *Freud and Philosophy,* 9.

49. Paul Ricoeur, *Conflict of Interpretations: Essays in Hermeneutics,* ed. Don Ihde, (Evanston, IL: Northwestern Press, 1974), 298.

50. Catherine Bell, *Ritual: Perspectives and Dimensions* (Oxford: Oxford University Press, 1997), see especially chaps. 2, 3, and 7.

51. Ibid., 37.

52. Ibid., 38.

53. Ibid., 64.

54. Ibid., 73.

55. Ibid., 78.

56. Victor Turner, *The Ritual Process: Structure and Anti-Structure* (Ithaca, NY: Aldine, 1969), 6–10.

57. For this summary of Turner's work I am largely indebted to Margaret Mary Kelleher and her unpublished dissertation "Liturgy as an Ecclesial Act of Meaning: Foundations and Methodological Consequences for a Liturgical Spirituality" (PhD diss., The Catholic University of America, 1983), 95–165, although I have also done significant work with his material myself.

58. Turner, *The Ritual Process,* vii, 203.

59. Victor Turner, "Variations on a Theme of Liminality," in *Secular Ritual,* ed. Sally F. Moore, and Barbara C. Myerhoff (Assen: Van Gorcum, 1977), 46.

60. Ibid.

61. Turner, *The Ritual Process,* 97.

62. Ibid., 128.

63. Victor Turner, *The Forest of Symbols: Aspects of Ndembu Ritual* (Ithaca, NY: Cornell University Press, 1967), 46.

64. Ibid., 20.

65. Victor Turner, "Encounter with Freud: The Making of a Comparative Symbologist," in *The Making of Psychological Anthropology,* ed. George D. Spindler (Berkeley: University of California Press, 1978), 576.

66. Victor Turner, "Process, System, and Symbol: A New Anthropological Synthesis," *Daedalus* 106 (Summer 1977): 77.

67. Ibid. See Kelleher, note 57 above, 129.

68. Turner, "Process, System, and Symbol," 77.

69. Turner, *The Forest of Symbols*, 30.

70. Victor Turner, "Symbolic Studies," *Annual Review of Anthropology* 4 (1975): 156.

71. Victor Turner, "Liminal to Liminoid, in Play, Flow and Ritual: An Essay in Comparative Symbology," in *The Anthropological Study of Human Play*, ed. Edward Norbeck, Rice University Studies, vol. 60, no. 3 (Summer 1974): 55.

Chapter Eight, pages 144–165

1. See his two videos, *The Dancing Church of Africa* and *The Dancing Church of the South Pacific*.

2. David N. Power, *Sacrament: The Language of God's Giving* (New York: Crossroad, 1999), 63.

3. Power refers to hermeneutics as the "art of discovering the unsaid of discourse, in the recognition of the effort to say which is behind the said and continually transcends it in the quest to communicate and to express meaning." *Sacrament*, 67.

4. Power, *Sacrament*, 75.

5. I urge the reader to read Power's text *Sacrament*, especially chap. 2 where he explicates his understanding of sacrament as a language event.

6. Once again the reader is invited to turn to Power's text, especially chap. 5, where he does an extensive review of this material.

7. Power, *Sacrament*, 152.

8. The Prayer of Sarapion as quoted in R.C.D. Jasper and G. J. Cuming, *Prayers of the Eucharist: Early and Reformed* (Collegeville, MN: Liturgical Press, 1992), 77.

9. Power, *Sacrament*, 155.

10. See, for example, John R. Donahue, *The Gospel in Parable: Metaphor, Narrative, and Theology in the Synoptic Gospels* (Philadelphia: Fortress Press, 1988).

11. Power, *Sacrament*, 158.

12. Ibid., 161.

13. Ibid., 165.

14. Ibid., 80.

15. Robert Ver Eecke, "Gesture," in *The New Dictionary of Sacramental Worship*, ed. Peter Fink (Collegeville, MN: Michael Glazier/Liturgical Press, 1990), 503.

16. Ibid., 507.

17. Marchita Mauck, "Buildings That House the Church," *Liturgy* 5, no. 4 (1986): 28.

18. This document appears as Archdiocese of Milwaukee, *The Milwaukee Symposia for Church Composers: A Ten-Year Report* (Washington, DC/Chicago: Pastoral Press/ Liturgy Training Publications, 1992).

19. Joseph Gelineau, *Voices and Instruments in Christian Worship: Principles, Laws, Applications*, trans. Clifford Howell (Collegeville, MN: Liturgical Press, 1964).

20. Ibid., 60.

21. Ibid., 62.

22. Edward Foley and Mary McGann, *Music and the Eucharistic Prayer* (Washington, DC: Pastoral Press, 1988), 8.

23. Ibid., 9.

Chapter Nine, pages 166–180

1. Bernard Lonergan, *Method in Theology* (New York: Seabury Press, 1972), 301–2.

2. Clifford Geertz, *The Interpretation of Cultures* (New York: Basic Books, 1973), 89.

3. Louis Luzbetak, *The Church and Cultures: New Perspectives in Missiological Anthropology* (Maryknoll, NY: Orbis Books, 1988), 156–57.

4. Ibid., 157–58.

5. For a brief history of the Chinese Rites controversy, see Peter Phan, "Culture and Liturgy: Ancestor Veneration as a Test Case," *Worship* 76, no. 5 (2002): 403–30.

6. Luzbetak, *The Church and Cultures*, 182.

7. Ibid., 308.

8. This history is noted in Keith Pecklers, *Worship: A Primer in Christian Ritual* (Collegeville, MN: Liturgical Press, 2003), 123–25.

9. John Paul II, *The Pope Speaks* 27 (1982), 157.

10. *Varietates Legitimae* in *Origens* 23, no. 43 (April 14, 1994): 746–56.

11. Mark R. Francis, *Shape a Circle Ever Wider: Liturgical Inculturation in the United States* (Chicago: Liturgy Training Publications, 2000), 60.

12. Aloysius Pieris, "Inculturation: Some Critical Reflections," *Vidyajyoti* 57 (1993): 641–51.

13. See, for example, Peter Phan's account of anomalous practices in his native Vietnam. "How Much Uniformity Can We Stand? How Much Do We Want? Church and Worship in the Next Millennium," *Worship* 72 (1998): 194–209.

14. Anscar Chupungco, *Cultural Adaptation of the Liturgy* (New York: Paulist Press, 1982); *Liturgies of the Future* (New York: Paulist Press, 1989); *Liturgical Inculturation: Sacramentals, Religiosity, and Catechesis* (Collegeville, MN: Liturgical Press, 1992); *Worship: Tradition and Progress* (Washington, DC: Pastoral Press, 1993).

15. Chupungco, *Liturgical Inculturation*, 30.

16. Ibid., 36.

17. Ibid., 37.

18. Ibid., 38.

19. Ibid.

20. A. Echiegu, *Translating the Collects of the "Sollemnitates Domini" of the "Missale Romanum" of Paul VI in the Language of the African* (Münster, 1984), 313.

21. Chupungco, *Liturgical Inculturation*, 40–41.

22. Ibid., 47.

23. Peter Phan, "How Much Uniformity Can We Stand?" "Culture and Liturgy: Ancestor Veneration as a Test Case," *Worship* 76, no. 5 (2002): 403–30.

24. Phan, "Culture and Liturgy," 413–21.

25. Karl Rahner, "The Abiding Significance of the Second Vatican Council," in *Concern for the Church*, Theological Investigations XX (New York: Crossroad, 1981), 91.

26. Ibid., 92.

Recommended Readings

Chapter One

Bernstein, Eleanor, and Martin F. Connell, eds. *The Renewal That Awaits Us*. Chicago: Liturgy Training Publications, 1997.

Bernstein, Eleanor, and Martin F. Connell, eds. *Traditions and Transitions*. Chicago: Liturgy Training Publications, 1998.

Botte, Bernard. *From Silence to Participation: An Insider's View of Liturgical Renewal*. Washington, DC: Pastoral Press, 1988.

Hughes, Kathleen. *How Firm a Foundation: Voices of the Early Liturgical Movement*. Chicago: Liturgy Training Publications, 1990.

Palazzo, Eric. *A History of Liturgical Books: From the Beginning to the Thirteenth Century*. Collegeville, MN: Pueblo Book/Liturgical Press, 1998.

Tuzik, Robert L. *How Firm a Foundation: Leaders of the Liturgical Movement*. Chicago: Liturgy Training Publications, 1990.

Weakland, Rembert G. *Themes of Renewal*. Washington, DC: Pastoral Press, 1995.

Chapter Two

Bouyer, Louis. "From the Jewish Qahal to the Christian Ecclesia," in *Liturgical Piety*, 23–37. Notre Dame: University of Notre Dame Press, 1955.

Canadian Conference of Catholic Bishops. "The Assembly." *National Bulletin on Liturgy* 24/127 (Dec. 1991).

Hoffman, Lawrence. "Assembling in Worship." *Worship* 56 (1982): 98–112.

Maertens, Thierry. *Assembly For Christ*. London: Darton, Longman & Todd, 1970.

McManus, Frederick. *Liturgical Participation: An Ongoing Assessment*. Washington, DC: Pastoral Press, 1988.

The Institute for Liturgical Ministry at Maria Stein. "Ministry of the Assembly." *Liturgical Ministry* 3 (Spring 1994).

Worship Office of the Archdiocese of Cincinnati. *We Gather in Christ: Our Identity as Assembly*. Chicago: Liturgy Training Publications, 1996.

Chapter Three

Empereur, James. "Liturgy as Proclamation." In *Worship: Exploring the Sacred*, 119–32. Washington, DC: Pastoral Press, 1987.

Kilmartin, Edward. *Christian Liturgy: Theology and Practice*. Kansas City, MO: Sheed and Ward, 1988. See especially chap. 17.

Notre Dame Pastoral Liturgy Conference. *The Many Presences of Christ*. Edited by T. Fitzgerald and D. Lysik. Chicago: Liturgy Training Publications, 1999.

Power, David. *Sacrament: The Language of God's Giving*. New York: Herder and Herder, 1999. See especially chap. 9.

Chapter Four

Empereur, James. "Paschal Mystery. " In *The New Dictionary of Theology*, 744–47. Edited by J. Komonchak, M. Collins, D. Lane. Collegeville, MN: Michael Glazier/Liturgical Press, 1987.

Procter-Smith, Marjorie. *In Her Own Rite: Constructing Feminist Liturgical Tradition*. Nashville: Abingdon Press, 1990. See especially chap. 2.

Taft, Robert. "Toward a Theology of the Christian Feast." In *Beyond East and West: Problems in Liturgical Understanding*, 1–30. Washington, DC: Pastoral Press, 1984.

Vincie, Catherine. "A History of Holy Week." *Liturgical Ministry* 13 (Summer 2004): 105–18.

Chapter Five

Johnson, Elizabeth. *She Who Is: The Mystery of God in Feminist Theological Discourse*. New York: Crossroad, 1992.

Groome, Thomas. *Language for a "Catholic" Church*. New York: Sheed and Ward, 1991.

Rahner, Karl. *Foundations of Christian Faith*. New York: Seabury Press, 1978. See especially chap. 2.

Ramshaw, Gail. *Reviving Sacred Speech: The Meaning of Liturgical Language*. Akron, OH: OSL Publications, 2000.

Tracy, David. *The Analogical Imagination*. New York: Crossroad, 1981. See especially chap. 10.

Wren, Brian. *What Language Shall I Borrow? God-Talk in Worship: A Male Response to Feminist Theology*. New York: Crossroad, 1993.

Chapter Six

Johnson, Maxwell, ed. *Between Memory and Hope: Readings on the Liturgical Year*. Collegeville, MN: Liturgical Press, 2000.

Kelly, Joseph. *The Origins of Christmas*. Collegeville, MN: Liturgical Press, 2004.

Martimort, A. G., I. H. Dalmais, and P. Jounel. *The Church at Prayer*, vol. 4, *The Liturgy and Time*. Collegeville, MN: Liturgical Press, 1986.

Stevenson, Kenneth. *Jerusalem Revisited: The Liturgical Meaning of Holy Week*. Portland, OR: Pastoral Press, 1988.

Talley, Thomas. *The Origins of the Liturgical Year*. 2nd ed. Collegeville, MN: Pueblo/Liturgical Press, 1986.

Chapter Seven

Bell, Catherine. *Ritual: Perspectives and Dimensions*. Oxford: Oxford University Press, 1997. See especially chaps. 2, 3, and 7.

Chauvet, Louis-Marie. *Symbol and Sacrament: A Sacramental Reinterpretation of Christian Existence*. Collegeville, MN: Liturgical Press, 1995; French in 1987.

———. *The Sacraments: The Word of God at the Mercy of the Body*. Collegeville, MN: Liturgical Press, 2001; French in 1997.

Rahner, Karl. "Theology of Symbol." In *Theological Investigations IV*. London: Darton, Longman & Todd, 1966; New York: Seabury Press, 1974.

Ricoeur, Paul. *Conflict of Interpretations: Essays in Hermeneutics*. Edited by Don Ihde. Evanston, IL: Northwestern Press, 1974.

Chapter Eight

DeSanctis, Michael. *Building from Belief: Advance, Retreat, and Compromise in the Remaking of Catholic Architecture*. Collegeville, MN: Liturgical Press, 2002.

Foley, Edward. *Music in Ritual: A Pre-Theological Investigation*. Washington, DC: Pastoral Press, 1984.

Foley, Edward, and Mary McGann. *Music and the Eucharistic Prayer*. Washington DC: Pastoral Press, 1988.

Joncas, Jan Michael. *From Sacred Song to Ritual Music: Twentieth-Century Understandings of Roman Catholic Worship Music*. Collegeville, MN: Liturgical Press, 1997.

Morrill, Bruce, ed. *Bodies of Worship: Explorations in Theory and Practice*. Collegeville, MN: Liturgical Press, 1999.

Power, David. *Sacrament: The Language of God's Giving*. New York: Crossroad, 1999, especially chaps. 2 and 5.

Ramshaw, Gail. *Reviving Sacred Speech: The Meaning of Liturgical Language*. Akron, OH: OSL Publications, 2000.

Seasoltz, Kevin. *Sense of the Sacred: Theological Foundations of Christian Architecture and Art*. New York: Continuum, 2005.

Uzukwu, Elochukwu. *Worship as Body Language: Introduction to Christian Worship: An African Orientation*. Collegeville, MN: Pueblo/Liturgical Press, 1997.

Chapter Nine

Chupungco, Anscar. *Liturgical Inculturation: Sacramental, Religiosity, and Catechesis.* Collegeville, MN: Pueblo/Liturgical Press, 1992.

———. *Worship: Progress and Tradition.* Beltsville, MD: Pastoral Press, 1995.

Francis, Mark R. *Shape a Circle Ever Wider: Liturgical Inculturation in the United States.* Chicago: Liturgy Training Publications, 2000.

Gallagher, Michael Paul. *Clashing Symbols: An Introduction to Faith and Culture.* London: Darton, Longman & Todd, 1997.

Luzbetak, Louis J. *The Church and Cultures: New Perspectives in Missiological Anthropology.* Maryknoll, NY: Orbis Books, 1988.

Mitchell, Nathan D. *Liturgy and the Social Sciences.* Collegeville, MN: Liturgical Press, 1999.

Schineller, Peter. *A Handbook on Inculturation.* New York: Paulist Press, 1990.

Schreiter, Robert. *Constructing Local Theologies.* Maryknoll, NY: Orbis Books, 1985.

Shorter, Aylward. *Toward a Theology of Inculturation.* Maryknoll, NY: Orbis Books, 1988.

Index

Abba, 94–95
active participation, 4–6, 9, 10, 11–12, 16, 13, 22, 29, 34, 160
Advent, 115–17
Afanassieff, Nicolas, 23
Ambrose, 67, 72
Ambrosetti, Vince, 98
Andrieu, Michel, 4
Aquinas, Thomas, 76, 87, 89–90, 121–22
Aristotle, 122
Asad, Talal, 137
Augustine, 67, 76, 93, 108, 118
Austin, J. L., 129

Baldovin, John, 118
Bateson, Gregory, 137
Bea, Augustine, 56
Beauduin, Lambert, 6
Bell, Catherine, 135, 137
Bernadin, Joseph Cardinal, 42–43
Beuron monastery, 5
Bishop, Edmund, 149
Bloch, Maurice, 137
body, 129–30
Bourdieu, Pierre, 137
Bouyer, Louis, 6

calendar of saints, 77–78
Cassian, John, 105
Catherine of Siena, 77, 93
Centre de Pastorale Liturgique de Paris, 7
Centro di Arione Liturgical, 7
Chauvet, Louis-Marie, 120, 121, 125–30, 142, 149, 183
Chavasse, Antoine, 4
Chirat, Henri, 20, 21
Christmas, 114–15, 116, 117, 118, 119
Chrysologus, Peter, 116
Chupungco, Anscar, 176–78
Clement, 104
Cluny, 106
Connell, Martin, 116
Constantine, 105
Council of Trent, 3, 22
Cyprian, 104
Cyril of Jerusalem, 72

Descartes, René, 130, 142
Deshusses, Jean, 4
dialogue Mass, 6
Diekmann, Godfrey, 8
divinum commercium, 57–59
Duchesne, Louis, 115

Dufner, Delores, 98
Durkheim, Émile, 135
dynamic equivalence, 177

Easter Triduum, 111–12
Ebner, Adalbert, 4
Eckhart, Meister, 93
Egeria, 105
Eliade, Mircea, 101, 130, 132
Ellard, Gerard, 7
Empereur, James, 68
Engberding, Frank, 115

Francis, Mark, 173
Freud, Sigmund, 130

Gamber, Klaus, 4
Gantoy, Robert, 20, 23
Geertz, Clifford, 136, 173
Gelineua, Joseph, 162–63
Gluckman, Max, 136
Goffman, Erving, 137
Gregory the Great, 117
Gregory of Nazianzus, 108
Guéranger, Prosper, 4–5

Hammenstede, Albert, 6
Hellriegal, Martin, 7
Herwegen, Ildefons, 6
Hild, Jean, 27
Hillenbrand, Reynold, 7
Hippolytus, 104
Hucke, Helmut, 163, 164
Huijbers, Bernard, 163

icon, 60–62
Ignatius of Antioch, 107
incomprehensibility of God, 82,
    85–86, 88, 89, 93, 99
instrumental causality, 122, 127
Irwin, Kevin, 102

Jeremias, Joachim, 95
John Cassian, 105

John Chrysostom, 90
John Paul II, 109–11, 171, 172
John XXIII, 12
Johnson, Elizabeth, 83, 87–89, 94–95,
    183
Johnson, Maxwell, 112–13
Jounel, Pierre, 20, 109
Jung, Carl, 130, 132
Jungmann, Josef, 4
Justin Martyr, 70–71, 107, 110

Kane, Thomas, 149–50
Klauser, Theodore, 4

Langer, Suzanne, 96
language, 126–27, 129, 132–33,
    150–52, 168
Leach, Edmund, 136, 137
lectionary, 77, 80
Leenhardt, Maurice, 132
Lent, 112–14
Leo the Great, 112, 117, 118
Leroquais, Victor, 4
Lévi-Strauss, Claude, 136
liturgical adaptation, 170, 173, 175
liturgical anamnesis, 69–80, 118
liturgical assembly, 14–15, 19–50,
    53–55
    as gathered people, 24, 28–29
    as event, 37–41, 54–55
    presence of Christ, 36–37
    roles, 41–49
    subject of celebration, 34–35, 36, 37,
        42, 51
liturgical experiments, 6, 7
liturgical inculturation, 171–79
liturgical movement, 3–12, 20, 51, 52
liturgical reforms of Vatican II, 1–3,
    12–17, 106
liturgical time, 101–19
    daily cycle of prayer, 103–7
    weekly cycle of prayer, 107–11
    yearly cycle of prayer, 111–18
Liturgische Institut, 7

liturgy and culture, 166–80
liturgy and sacrament as God's gift, 58–62
liturgy as dialogue, 51–58
local church, 16–17, 22, 26, 28, 42, 44
Lonergan, Bernard, 97, 166
Luzbetak, Louis, 167, 171

Maertens, Thierry, 20, 23–25, 29, 30, 32, 39
Malinowski, Bronislaw, 135–36
manifestation, 132
Maredsous monastery, 5
Maria-Laach monastery, 5, 6
Marion, Jean-Luc, 60, 97
Martimort, Aimé-George, 20–30, 49, 54
Martin of Tours, 117
Mauck, Marchita, 159
McGoldrick, Patrick, 69
McManus, Frederick, 8–9, 11
mediation, 126–27, 128, 143, 145, 147
Melito of Sardis, 65–66
memorial, 64, 69–75
memory of women, 76–79
Michel, Virgil, 7, 8
Mont Cesar abbey, 5
mysterion, 68, 70

naming God, 81–100
   naming by abundance, 93–94
   naming by analogy, 59–60, 88–89
   naming by metaphor, 90–93
   naming by negation, 89–90
   naming God in liturgy, 95–99

Ordinary Time, 117–18
Origin, 67, 104, 112

Pasch, 65, 67, 111–12, 114, 118
Pascha, 64, 65, 67
Paschal Mystery, 64–80
passio, 67
Passover, 64, 65, 68, 69, 70, 102

patriarchy, 76, 78–79, 92, 93, 95
Paul VI, 39, 41, 46
pesach, 64
Phan, Peter, 178–79
Piana Commission, 11, 12
Pieris, Aloysius, 175
Pius X, 5, 8, 9, 10, 163
Pius XI, 10
Pius XII, 10–12
Power, David, 58–61, 150, 152–55
prayer, 20, 21, 22, 34, 51, 82, 96, 103–7, 109

qahal Yahweh, 24–25, 54

Radcliffe-Brown, A.R., 135
Radford Ruether, Rosemary, 87
Rahner, Karl, 84, 85, 86, 120, 121–25, 127, 142, 183
Ramshaw, Gail, 91
Regan, Patrick, 112
Ricci, Matteo, 169
Ricoeur, Paul, 29, 121, 130–35, 142, 150, 183
ritual, 135–38, 139–41, 143, 156
Robeyne, Anselme, 20
Roguet, A. M., 20, 30
Rouillard, Philippe, 20, 27

Sahlins, Marshall, 137
Saint John's Collegeville, 7
Sarapion of Thmius, 90, 153
Schillebeeckx, Edward, 84
Schüssler Fiorenza, Elisabeth, 76
Segundo, Juan Luis, 83
Smith, Elizabeth, 77
Solemnes, 4, 9
Stevens, Georgia, 8
Sunday, 37–41, 107–11
symbol and the body, 145–50
symbol in anthropology, 138–41
symbol in philosophy and theology, 121–38

symbol, the emergence of, 132
  the interpretation of, 134–35
symbolic vehicles, 150–65
  bodily gestures, 156–58
  literary genres, 152–54
  music, 161–64
  prayer genres, 154–56
  space and objects, 158–61

Taft, Robert, 73, 74, 102–3
Talley, Thomas, 67, 112
Teresa of Avila, 77
Tertullian, 76, 104
Theodore of Mopsuestia, 71–72
Thérèse of Lisieux, 77
Tracy, David, 88
Transitus, 67

Trible, Phyllis, 76
Trinity, 123
Turner, Victor, 121, 136, 138–41, 142, 184

van Caloen, Gerard, 5
Van der Leeuw, Gerardus, 130, 132
van Gennep, Arnold, 136
Vatican II, 1–3, 12–17, 33–34, 37–39, 42, 106
Ver Eecke, Robert, 156, 157
vernacular, 11, 12, 168
Villot, J. Cardinal, 39, 41

Ward, Justine, 8
Wilmart, André, 4
Wren, Brian, 97–99